PROCESS MYSTICISM

Process Mysticism

Daniel A. Dombrowski

Published by State University of New York Press, Albany

© 2023 State University of New York

All rights reserved

Printed in the United States of America

No part of this book may be used or reproduced in any manner whatsoever without written permission. No part of this book may be stored in a retrieval system or transmitted in any form or by any means including electronic, electrostatic, magnetic tape, mechanical, photocopying, recording, or otherwise without the prior permission in writing of the publisher.

For information, contact State University of New York Press, Albany, NY
www.sunypress.edu

Library of Congress Cataloging-in-Publication Data

Name: Dombrowski, Daniel A., author.
Title: Process mysticism / Daniel A. Dombrowski.
Description: Albany : State University of New York Press, [2022] | Includes
 bibliographical references and index.
Identifiers: ISBN 9781438491356 (hardcover : alk. paper) | ISBN 9781438491363
 (ebook) | ISBN 9781438491349 (pbk. : alk. paper)
Further information is available at the Library of Congress.

10 9 8 7 6 5 4 3 2 1

Contents

Abbreviations of Works by Charles Hartshorne,
Alfred North Whitehead, and Henri Bergson — vii

Introduction — 1

Chapter 1   Concepts of God — 11

Chapter 2   World-Inclusiveness and Nature — 29

Chapter 3   Ideal Power and Tragedy — 49

Chapter 4   Abstract and Concrete — 67

Chapter 5   Whiteheadian Contributions — 87

Chapter 6   Asceticism and Apophaticism — 107

Chapter 7   Visions and Voices — 127

Chapter 8   Bergsonian Contributions — 147

Chapter 9   The Aesthetics of Mystical Experience — 167

Chapter 10 Consequences for Ethics — 187

Bibliography — 207

Index of Names — 219

Abbreviations of Works

Charles Hartshorne

AAP	"An Anglo-American Phenomenology"
AB	"Arthur Berndtson on Mystical Experience"
AD	*Anselm's Discovery*
AW	*Aquinas to Whitehead*
BH	*Beyond Humanism*
BS	*Born to Sing*
CA	*Creativity in American Philosophy*
CE	*Creative Experiencing*
CS	*Creative Synthesis and Philosophic Method*
DL	*The Darkness and the Light*
DR	*The Divine Relativity*
DRA	"The Divine Relativity and Absoluteness"
DWVN	"In Defense of Wordsworth's View of Nature"
EA	*Existence and Actuality*
ERT	"The Environmental Results of Technology"
FVRS	"The Formal Validity and Real Significance of the Ontological Argument"
GR	"The God of Religion and the God of Philosophy"

HB	*Hartshorne and Brightman on God, Process, and Persons*
IO	*Insights and Oversights of Great Thinkers*
IS	"The Intelligibility of Sensations"
LP	*The Logic of Perfection*
MEA	"Metaphysical and Empirical Aspects of the Idea of God"
MMEJ	"Metaphysics and the Modality of Existential Judgments"
MRM	"Mysticism and Rationalistic Metaphysics"
MVG	*Man's Vision of God*
NT	*A Natural Theology for Our Time*
OD	"An Outline and Defense of the Argument for the Unity of Being in the Absolute or Divine Good"
OO	*Omnipotence and Other Theological Mistakes*
PCH	*The Philosophy of Charles Hartshorne*
PD	"A Philosophy of Death"
PPR	"Peirce's Philosophy on Religion"
PPS	*Philosophy and Psychology of Sensation*
PSG	*Philosophers Speak of God*
PUK	"Psychology and the Unity of Knowledge"
RE	"The Aesthetic Dimensions of Religious Experience"
RGW	"Review of Gerda Walter, *Phanomenologie der Mystik*"
RPWP	"Religious Psychology of the Western Peoples"
RSP	*Reality as Social Process*
RSW	"The Rights of the Subhuman World"
SQFT	"Sense Quality and Feeling Tone"
SSH	"Science as the Search for the Hidden Beauty of the World"
STF	"The Social Theory of Feelings"
STM	"Some Theological Mistakes and Their Effects on Modern Literature"

TIS	"Three Important Scientists on Mind, Matter, and the Metaphysics of Religion"
WIG	"Whitehead's Idea of God"
WM	*Wisdom as Moderation*
WP	*Whitehead's Philosophy*
WVR	*Whitehead's View of Reality*
ZF	*The Zero Fallacy and Other Essays in Neoclassical Philosophy*

Alfred North Whitehead

AI	*Adventures of Ideas*
AE	*The Aims of Education*
CN	*The Concept of Nature*
DANW	*Dialogues of Alfred North Whitehead*
FO	"Freedom and Order"
IM	*Introduction to Mathematics*
MT	*Modes of Thought*
PANW	*The Philosophy of Alfred North Whitehead*
PNK	*An Enquiry Concerning the Principles of Natural Knowledge*
PR	*Process and Reality*
RM	*Religion in the Making*
S	*Symbolism*
SMW	*Science and the Modern World*

Henri Bergson

CEV	*Creative Evolution*
CM	*The Creative Mind*
TS	*The Two Sources of Morality and Religion*

Introduction

The term "mysticism" can mean at least two different things. The term can refer to "immediate" or "direct" experience of God (these terms will be analyzed in due course) or it can refer to the thesis that reality is ineffable and can be characterized only in paradoxical ways. These two meanings are quite different because there is nothing in the concepts themselves of "immediate" or "direct" experience that entails paradox or ineffability. In fact, if God is omnipresent or ubiquitous, then we should expect for there to be mystics. If God's existence is pervasive, then what would be paradoxical is claiming that no one can experience God; or at least the claim not to experience God could be seen as just as paradoxical as the claim to having done so. In this regard, the idea that there are mystics about is compatible with some versions of realism in that reality (including divine reality) is experienced because it exists, in contrast to the antirealist view that reality exists because it is experienced. Alfred North Whitehead's concept of reality being "prehended" or "grasped" supports this realist view (MRM 463–69; *RSP* 69).

The purpose of the present book is to explore both senses of what it means to be a mystic from the perspectives of the process philosophies of Alfred North Whitehead, Henri Bergson, and Charles Hartshorne, although admittedly the perspective I will defend is definitely more Hartshornian than Whiteheadian or Bergsonian. I should also admit at the outset that the first sense of what it means to be a mystic (the claim to have "immediate" or "direct" experience of God) is primary, and the second sense (the claim that reality, or at least ultimate reality, is ineffable), although important, is not as crucial as the first. I will nonetheless attempt to find the proper place for the *via negativa* or apophatic religious discourse, which is often either mischaracterized or overemphasized in contemporary philosophy and theology, in my estimation, as Donald Viney also insightfully argues in an article titled "Hartshorne's Dipolar Theism and the Mystery of God."

My aim is not so much to demonstrate that mystical experience is true or veridical as to *understand* in William Jamesian fashion how mystical experience could be possible and how claims to having had mystical experiences can avoid contradiction vis-à-vis the concept of God, specifically a process concept of God with which James was only dimly aware. This effort to understand mystical experience is not meant to compete with other efforts to achieve understanding, as in the recently popular tendency to see mysticism largely in terms of "negative theology" (or the *via negativa* or as "apophatic" discourse). Rather, my hope is to contribute something significant to scholarship on mysticism in terms of process philosophy and theology, which covers the territory in a distinctive and provocative way that is not traversed in other approaches. This novel process approach is meant to supplement and enrich other stances (*DL* 147–49, 152; *HB* 23, 28–29).

Whereas the most common way of preserving divine mystery in classical theism is through the *via negativa* or apophatic discourse, in the neoclassical or process theistic view that will be operative in the present book, divine mystery will be preserved largely through a crucial Hartshornian distinction between divine essence (*what* God is) and divine existence (*that* God is), on the one hand, and divine actuality (*how* God exists), on the other. Whereas the divine essence, as that than which no greater can be conceived, and God's necessary existence can be discussed in rational terms, it is in divine actuality that mystery primarily resides (*CA* 182–83; *PCH* 594).

The obvious data that are readily detected are those that are sometimes present and sometimes absent, as in the sensation of an object that is bright yellow in color or an intense pain or the sudden appearance of a camel. But what is always present tends to escape notice, as in spatiality. It is true that there are different aspects of spatiality and different degrees of distinctness of spatiality, but spatiality is given in all experience. Hence, we have an analogy for the difference between the mystic and the rest of us, the latter of which tend to notice only the obvious data found in bright colors, intense pains, or the appearance of odd objects. Or again, most of us detect spatiality in our experiences of color, but only some of us do so with respect to spatial extension in experiences of sound, even though sound always involves spatiality. I will return to this analogy for mystical experience later in the book, the point of which is to illustrate the idea that the mystic is someone who is explicitly aware of what remains implicit for the rest of us, as in spatiality or God (*DL* 110, 120–21; *EA* xiii–xiv).

One of the key contributions of process thought to our understanding of mystical experience is a critique of the idea that experience is simultaneous with the data of experience. That is, there is a temporal structure to experience such that there is a finite amount of time that it takes for the data to be experienced by the subject, due to, say, the speeds of light or sound. This fact becomes obvious to us only in the case of really distant objects, such as when there is epistemically present experience of a star that burned out light years ago. But the temporal structure of experience applies even in experience of reality rather close to us.

The (implicit) presence of deity in all experience is not unconnected to matters of ethical concern. For example, the greatest happiness of the greatest number is not itself the actual happiness of any individual human being or collection of human beings. We are all naively aware of the fact that other people exist and that our importance is to a large extent constituted by what we contribute to the lives of others and that their importance in part consists in what they contribute to us. As is well known, value is relational. But the true measure of value or importance is something that transcends you or I or all of humanity. Only a theist can identify this additional factor who is the subject of the greatest happiness of the greatest number. Solipsism of the individual *and* the collective solipsism of all of humanity fail to account for the greatest good.

Both the immensity of space and the immensity of value presuppose a subject cosmic in scope. We can think of the extended cosmos as a society of sentient creatures who influence one another via empathic prehensions in patterns treated by the sciences, including physics. Our knowledge of such patterns is always partial and fallible, but because we can falsify certain hypotheses with assurance (in Popperian fashion), our fallible knowledge presupposes a higher kind of knowledge that provides us with a measure or standard. The well-known Quaker mystic who heavily influenced Hartshorne as his first philosophy teacher and to whom he dedicated his intellectual autobiography, Rufus Jones, is instructive in the way he held that the difference between mystics and the rest of us is one of degree and not of kind. The mystic is one who is explicitly aware of what most of us are aware of implicitly: that we are meaningful parts of an immense whole; that our fallible value judgments presuppose a standard of Value that avoids our own defects in judgment, although our confidence that some actions are evil *simpliciter* means that we are not totally in the dark in this regard; and that our slow yet progressive effort to know the world presupposes an omniscient standard that secures for us our strongest intuitions and knowledge claims (*DL* dedication; *ZF* 29, 36; *MVG* xviii; *OO* 107; *PCH* 14).

We will see in Hartshornian fashion that the existence of God is either necessary or impossible in that the contingent existence of God is ruled out by Saint Anselm's great discovery that contingent existence is at odds with the very definition of God as that than which no greater can be conceived. The implication of this view for mystical experience is that either everyone is aware of God at least implicitly or no one is aware of God. If the first option is true, then nontheists are deceiving themselves; and if the second option is true, then it is theists who are mistaken. Either way there is value to be found in the explication of mystical experience, if only due to the fact that some people at least claim to have had an awareness or intuition of God's actuality. Hartshorne himself may have been a mystic, even if he does not spend much time telling us about his own religious experiences. At the very least he tells us that he came "close to" a mystical experience of the finite aspect of God (to be explained in due course) while crossing the Atlantic at the time of the First World War. And he tells us of his fascination with James's descriptions of those who have had religious experiences, which conform to the general tendency of human beings to feel or have experiences first and then think about or interpret them later. The world is given as emotional, although Jones appealed to Hartshorne precisely because he was a *philosophical* interpreter of mysticism who was persuasive regarding the conceptual importance of the existence of love in the world (*DL* 126, also 84–86; *PSG* 499–500, 503–06).

The prominence of aesthetic categories in process thought dovetails with the tendency of mystics to see beauty everywhere in the world, although at times the beauty in question is tragic. To experience something is not necessarily the same thing as knowing exactly *what* one has experienced. After all, *aesthesis* is the Greek word for feeling, in general. Further, there is much in experience concerning which we are not consciously aware and concerning which we can never be fully aware. In the present context it is important to note that it is philosophy's task to see if it is even possible to have the sorts of experiences claimed by the mystics in their feeling of the divine. Although there should be nothing mystical about philosophy's method, the exercise of dialectic might point us toward the (at least partial) intelligibility of the sorts of experiences claimed by mystics. Throughout the present book we will notice that at every turn orthodox theological systems actually contradict what mystics say about God. This is a conceptual problem that deserves attention in that what is given and what is inferred are both of philosophical significance. It is also significant that we intuitively understand the difference between the terms "perfect" and "imperfect," even if such understanding is in need of conceptual fine-tuning.

Granted, there is historical evidence of the biases in metaphysical traditions that limit our understanding of mystical experience. The hope of the present book is that at least some of these biases can be corrected. The examples of mystical experience that will be considered in the book come primarily from the Abrahamic religions. This is due not to any assumption on my part that only these traditions are worthy of consideration but rather to my own limited competency, which is confined to the Abrahamic religions, in general, especially to Saint John of the Cross, in particular. I suspect that comparisons with Vedantism or Buddhism, for example, would be very fruitful indeed. If my focus is somewhat limited, this is due to a hope that it can bore through misconceptions of mystical experience that get in the way of a wider-angle view of the mystical terrain. In this regard it should be mentioned that differences *within* a particular religious tradition are often as great as differences *between* such traditions. Hartshorne, for example, finds one strand of Vedantism in Sri Jiva Goswami more congenial than classical theistic strands in the Abrahamic religions. Or again, Jewish or Christian process thinkers might find the process thought of Mohammed Iqbal more congenial than the thought of classical theistic thinkers in their own respective religious traditions. Further, it seems to me that there is a certain unity in the reports of mystical experiences once adventitious elements from different traditions are removed from them, as Hartshorne (who was once invited to speak at a Trappist monastery) attests (*PSG* 373; *ZF* 39).

If "ineffable" means "not exhaustively describable," then, in a sense, the description of *any* experience in its concreteness and in full detail is ineffable. If to have experience of God means an experience of the one who knows everything logically knowable, then in a sense to know God would mean to be omniscient ourselves, which is ludicrous. However, I will nonetheless argue that there is a sense in which, when we talk about God's abstract qualities, in contrast to God's concrete experiences of knowing and loving the world in its detail, we *can* offer an accurate description. That is, the *abstract* essence of God need not transcend language, or at least not in the same sense that description of God's life in concrete detail understandably does present difficulties regarding accurate description (*RSP* 175–76; *WP* 9–11).

In chapter 1, I will deal with the famous critique made by defenders of mystical experience that "the God of the philosophers" is inadequate to understanding mystical experience. I will argue that it is a particular, yet widely influential, concept of God (classical theism) that is inadequate, not philosophical concepts in general or a concept of God that offers a more nuanced understanding of the greatest conceivable being (neoclassical theism). *Both* metaphysical concepts and religious experience are necessary for a better understanding of ultimate reality, and inadequacy in one will affect negatively our understanding of the other (*PSG* 503–06).

In chapter 2, I will examine the concept of world-inclusiveness as it surfaces in neoclassical theism. Specifically, I will explicate the (Platonic) concept of the World Soul, defended by Hartshorne, so as to better appreciate the testimony of the great mystics that God is omnipresent and that it is possible to have *inter*action with God. The complete denial of divine embodiment in classical theism is criticized in the process effort to overcome the bifurcation of the world. In this chapter I try to overcome the gap that might appear in classical theism between "theistic mysticism" and "nature mysticism." That is, in neoclassical theism the two mysticisms are alternative ways of designating the same sorts of experience (*RSP* 152–53).

Chapter 3 indicates the severe problems with the concept of omnipotence as found in classical theism and shows how these problems get in the way of an understanding of mystical experience and tragedy. Nonetheless, in neoclassical theism, God would, as that than which no greater can be conceived, exhibit ideal power, if not omnipotence. As long as the doctrine of omnipotence is in play, there is a tendency not to be drawn positively to omnibenevolent love but to question why particular sufferings exist.

It is the purpose of chapter 4 to explicate the relationship between very abstract thinking in philosophy about the concept of, and existence of, God, say as found in the ontological argument, on the one hand, and the concrete experience of God found in the mystics, on the other. Special attention is paid to two distinctions that are not often made when trying to understand mystical experience: the distinction between indirect and direct experience and the distinction between mediated and unmediated (or immediate) experience. A big mistake is made when these two distinctions are collapsed, a practice that negatively affects some of the most important philosophical analyses of mystical experience. In this regard the approach of John Smith is shown to be far superior to that of William Alston.

The purpose of chapter 5 is to supplement my largely Hartshornian treatment of mystical experience with the thought of Whitehead. The two are sufficiently different to warrant attention paid to Whitehead's thought, too. The relationship between the two constitutes something of a unity-in-difference that will be productive in the effort to understand the contributions process thought in general can make to scholarship on mysticism (*WP* 111–12, 145, 153).

In chapter 6 there is an attempt to build on the previous chapter in the effort to rescue mysticism from the allegation that it is tied to a dangerous world-denying tendency that is fueled by both ascetical and apophatic negativities. Starting with asceticism, there is no doubt that the Abrahamic religions, heavily influenced by classical theism, have failed to genuinely synthesize "spiritual" and "physical" values, especially by denigrating the latter. It is precisely this failure that plays into the hands of religious skeptics such as Friedrich Nietzsche, who sees in asceticism something body-hating and world-denying. I will respond to this challenge by emphasizing the roots of *askesis* in athletic training in a positive way so as to perform well in big events. Also in this chapter can be found an examination of the ways in which apophatic or negative theology is both defensible and indefensible (*RSP* 163).

Chapter 7 examines the widely-held assumption that mystical experience is to be identified with, or finds its prime exemplification in, flashy claims to having received divine visions and voices. I take a deflationary view of visions and voices in this chapter, but I also try to locate their place in the traditional debate between "the God of the philosophers" and "the God of religious experience." This debate changes dramatically in the transition from classical to neoclassical theism. Further, in this chapter I explore, with the help of John Gilroy, some of the strengths and weaknesses of neurotheology for the topic of divine visions and voices, in particular, and for mystical experience, in general.

Like chapter 5 regarding Whitehead, chapter 8 deals with the distinct contributions to an understanding of mystical experience and the concept of God that are made possible by considering the thought of Henri Bergson, another magisterial figure in the history of process metaphysics. Bergson helps us to realize that mysticism and the concept of God are rooted in social life, broadly conceived. But there are two sorts of social life: closed and open. Each of these is connected to a particular view of God. Very often mystics are those who open us up to a more dynamic and defensible concept of God, morality, and society.

Chapter 9 explores the aesthetic dimensions of mysticism, both in its generic sense, wherein all of us at least implicitly experience ourselves as parts of a meaningful whole, and in its specific sense, wherein God is experienced *as* God. We will see that the Greek word *aesthesis* originally meant nothing other than feeling, or what we today might call "experience." Only later did the word refer to a disciplined feeling for beauty, in particular. I will make use of both senses of *aesthesis* in defense of a view of beauty as a dual mean between two sets of extremes. Both the beauty of abstract ideas and the beauty of concrete experiences, including mystical experiences, will be explored.

In chapter 10 can be found an examination of some of the practical ramifications of process mysticism. I will locate the mystical tradition within a kindred tradition in ethics: the virtue ethics approach, with the theological virtue of love occupying a prominent place in my exploration of the consequences of mystical experience for ethics. The virtue of love has controversial implications for the issue of death; in this regard I will be defending a view called "contributionism." I will also consider a danger in the agent-centered character of virtue ethics. Further, the virtue or vice of anger will be treated, which seems in our especially irascible world to provide an impediment to the life of virtue that is a precondition of the contemplative life.

My focus on mysticism in the Abrahamic religions is *not* due to a commitment on my part to the thesis that different traditions or different historical epochs or even two different thinkers within the same tradition and in the same historical epoch are incomparable. Indeed, I lean in the opposite direction in claiming that well-read and open-minded thinkers *can* fruitfully engage in intellectual comparisons across various boundaries. I will be assuming that abstract disciplines like metaphysics (and mathematics) have extremely wide application across many cultures and that these disciplines are just as important (or almost as important) as those that rely on concrete observations. We do not scrutinize experience one drop at a time but tend to bring various experiences into a system of fallible explanation. In order to make sure we have surveyed all (or almost all) of the possibilities, one must arrange them in a formal way. Johannes Kepler did this when he discovered that the orbits of the planets were not circular, hence he found the need to use a theory of conic sections in astronomy. Likewise, when we find mystics in various traditions and in different historical epochs saying things about God that conflict with established doctrine, we find the need to contrast theory in what I will call classical theism with theory in neoclassical or process theism.

My aim in the present book is to work toward a higher synthesis of various conflicting ideas to be detailed in the book. It will become apparent that I defend a view that can be described as epistemological realism and ontological idealism, a view that has important implications for real (mystical) knowledge of God as psyche. The hope is that progress can be made in metaphysics, particularly in its relationship with mystical experience. Just as there must have been some stage in the development of medicine before which it would have been safer to rely on common sense than on the advice of a physician, so also before the onset of neoclassical metaphysics it would have been better (or at least as fruitful) to listen to the mystics and not to classical theistic metaphysicians if one wanted to learn about God. Throughout the book the term "metaphysics" will refer to the rational (and secular) study of the universal traits of experience and existence. This discipline does not presuppose any special religious experiences, but it should at least be compatible with them. Classical theism is not compatible with such experiences due to its unsocial conception of reality wherein the lowest beings in inanimate nature are seen as inferior to social relations and God is seen as beyond them as unmoved and strictly impassible. What we need is a weighing of reasons in the effort to achieve reflective equilibrium between abstract metaphysics and concrete experiences found in various religious traditions (*RSP* 129–30).

The entire book can be seen as an effort to bring together what is special and very particular in religious experience and what can be said in the most abstract way about experience in general. Validation in metaphysics occurs not through the details of mystical experience but through what is left when we abstract away from all of the details. Nonetheless we will see that *the* metaphysical question can be put from the perspective of a particular standpoint, that of a revised version of the ontological argument. In this regard I will be trying to arrive at truth *through* Whitehead, Bergson, and especially Hartshorne, rather than to communicate the truth *about* these thinkers. The truth in question is compatible with both rationalist and empiricist tendencies in philosophy, neither of which should be denigrated. I want to do justice to *all* of experience so as to secure a place for mystical experience, in particular. It might be too ambitious to claim that I will *prove* something in the present book, an aim that would seem to confuse philosophy with geometry, but the goal of approximating reflective equilibrium might enable me to half-prove something very important (*AD* xii).

A key concept in the book is that of dipolarity wherein reality everywhere has aspects of particularity *and* generality, concreteness *and* abstractness, contingency *and* necessity. To assert that reality consists only in contingency or only in necessity leaves out of the picture something significant. God as supreme reality can be described as dual transcendence: ideally necessary in existence and ideally contingent in response to creaturely feelings (especially suffering feelings). Although the method of philosophy is not mystical, its conclusions are, as we will see (*PSG* 513–14; *PCH* 626). Finally, as a result of the process theism that will be explored in the present book, it can be said that the classical theistic God that many claim is dead never was alive in that no living being can be simply unmoved by other life.

Chapter 1

Concepts of God

It is widely assumed that "the God of the philosophers" is at odds with the God of religious experience. But it will serve us well to be skeptical of the claim that it is the philosophical concept of God per se that is the problem. We would be better served to see what is problematic about the classical concept of God from the perspective of mystical experience, then explore the possibility of there being a concept of God more congenial to such experience.

At the outset I would like to make it clear that by "classical theism" I refer to a view of God in philosophy and theology, not to biblical or scriptural theism. (It is an interesting question, and an open one, whether classical theism or neoclassical theism does a better job of preserving the best insights regarding the concept of God in the Bible.) This classical theistic view involves at least the following five features:

1. Omnipotence (including the related claim that God created the world out of absolute nothingness).

2. Omniscience (in the sense of God knowing, with absolute assurance and in minute detail, everything that will happen in the future).

3. Omnibenevolence.

4. Eternity (in the sense not of God existing everlastingly throughout all of time but rather of God existing outside of time altogether).

5. Monopolarity (to be described momentarily).

It will be to our advantage to be as clear as we can on what we mean by the term "God." In this effort we will be able to see more clearly the strengths and weaknesses of the classical theistic view. I will use the term "God" to refer to the supremely excellent or all-worshipful being. A debt to Saint Anselm is evident in this preliminary definition. It closely resembles Anselm's "that than which no greater can be conceived."

The ontological argument is not what is at stake here. Even if the argument fails, the preliminary definition of God as the supremely excellent being, the all-worshipful being, or the greatest conceivable being seems unobjectionable. To say that God can be defined in these ways still leaves open the possibility that God is even more excellent or worshipful than our ability to conceive. This allows us to avoid objections from those in mystical theology who might fear that by defining God we might be limiting God to "merely" human language. I am simply suggesting that when we think of God we must be thinking of a being who surpasses all others, or else we are not thinking of God. Even the atheist or agnostic would admit this much. When the atheist says "There is no God" there is a denial that a supremely excellent, all-worshipful, greatest conceivable being exists (see especially *PSG* 1–25).

The excellent-inferior contrast is the truly invidious contrast when applied to God. If to be invidious is to be injurious, then this contrast is the most invidious one of all when both terms are applied to God, because God is only excellent. God is inferior in no way. Period. To suggest that God is in some small way inferior to some other being is no longer to speak about God but about some being that is not supremely excellent, all-worshipful, or the greatest conceivable. The dipolar theist's major criticism of classical theism is that it assumes that all contrasts, or most of them, when applied to God are at least somewhat invidious (*PSG* 104–08, 242, 285–86, 306–8, 417).

Let us assume that God exists. What attributes does God possess? Consider the following two columns of attributes in polar contrast to each other:

one	many
being	becoming
activity	passivity
permanence	change
necessity	contingency
self-sufficient	dependent
actual	potential
absolute	relative
abstract	concrete

Classical theism tends toward oversimplification. It is comparatively easy to say, "God is strong rather than weak, so in all relations God is active, not passive." In each case, the classical theist decides which member of the contrasting pair is good (on the left), then attributes it to God, while wholly denying the contrasting term (on the right). Hence God is one but not many, permanent but not changing, and so on. This leads to what can be called the monopolar prejudice. Monopolarity is common to both classical theism and pantheism, with the major difference between the two being the fact that classical theism admits the reality of plurality, potentiality, and becoming as a secondary form of existence, "outside" God (on the right), whereas in pantheism God includes all reality within itself. Common to both classical theism and pantheism is the belief that the categorical contrasts listed above are invidious. The dilemma these two positions face is that either deity is only one constituent of the whole (classical theism) or else the alleged inferior pole in each contrast on the right is illusory (pantheism).

However, this dilemma is artificial. It is produced by the assumption that excellence is found by separating and purifying one pole (on the left) and denigrating the other (on the right). That this is not the case can be seen by analyzing some of the attributes in the right-hand column. Classical theists have been convinced that God's eternity means not that God endures through all time everlastingly but that God is outside of time altogether, and is not, cannot be receptive to temporal change and creaturely feelings. Saint Thomas Aquinas (following Aristotle, who was the greatest predecessor to classical theism) identified God as unmoved. Yet both activity and passivity can be either good or bad. Good passivity is likely to be called sensitivity, responsiveness, adaptability, sympathy, and the like. Insufficiently subtle or defective passivity is called wooden inflexibility, mulish stubbornness, inadaptability, unresponsiveness, and the like. Passivity per se refers to the way in which an individual's activity takes account of, and renders itself appropriate to, the activities of others. To deny God passivity altogether is to deny God those aspects of passivity that are excellences. Or, put another way, to altogether deny God the ability to change does avoid fickleness, but at the expense of the ability to lovingly react to the sufferings of others, a reaction that is central to the testimony of the great theistic mystics (*PSG* 1–25, 270, 289, 297).

The terms on the left side also have both good and bad aspects. Oneness can mean wholeness, but also it can mean monotony or triviality. Actuality can mean definiteness, or it can mean nonrelatedness to others. What happens to divine love when God is claimed to be *pure* actuality? God ends up loving the world but is not intrinsically related to it, whatever sort of love that may be. Self-sufficiency can, at times, be selfishness (*PSG* 99; *RSP* 17–18, 31, 160).

The task when thinking of God is to attribute to God all excellences (left and right sides together) and not to attribute to God any inferiorities (right and left sides). In short, excellent-inferior, knowledge-ignorance, or good-evil are invidious contrasts; but one-many, being-becoming, and the like are noninvidious contrasts. Evil is not a category and hence it cannot be attributed to God. It is not a category because it is not universal, and it is not universal because animals cannot commit it, even if they can be its victims. That is, both animals and God can feel evil, but they cannot commit it, God because of the supreme goodness in the divine nature, animals because of their ignorance of moral principles (WIG 516–17, 519, 527–28, 542).

Within each pole of a noninvidious contrast (e.g., permanence-change), there are invidious or injurious elements (inferior permanence or inferior change), but also noninvidious, good elements (excellent permanence or excellent change). The dipolar, process theist does not believe in two gods, one unified and the other plural. Rather, there is belief that what are often thought to be contradictories are really mutually interdependent correlatives. The good is unity-in-variety or variety-in-unity. Too much variety leads to chaos or discord; whereas too much unity leads to monotony or triviality (*AD* 122; *CE* 93, 117; *CS* 38, 277).

Supreme excellence, to be truly so, must somehow be able to integrate all the complexity there is in the world into itself as one spiritual whole. The word "must" indicates divine necessity, along with God's essence, which is to necessarily exist. The word "complexity" indicates the contingency that affects God through creaturely decisions. In the classical theistic view, however, God is identified solely with the stony immobility of the absolute, implying nonrelatedness to the world. God's abstract nature, God's being, may in a way escape from the temporal flux, but a living God is related to the world of becoming, which entails a divine becoming as well, if the world in some way is internally related to God. The classical theist's alternative to this view suggests that all relationships to God are external to divinity, once again threatening not only God's love but also God's nobility. A dog's being behind a particular rock affects the dog in certain ways, and thus this relation is an internal relation to the dog, but it does not affect the rock, whose relationship with the dog is external to the rock's nature. Does this not show the superiority of canine consciousness, which is aware of the rock, to rocklike existence, which is unaware of the dog? Is it not therefore peculiar that God has been described solely in rocklike terms: pure actuality, permanence, having only external relations, unmoved, being and not becoming? (*PSG* 131–32; *DR* 7, 15, 52, 54, 70; DRA 60).

One may wonder at this point why classical theism has been so popular among theists when it has so many defects. One can imagine at least four reasons, none of which establish the case for classical, monopolar theism: (1) It is simpler to accept monopolarity than dipolarity. That is, it is simpler to accept one and reject the other of contrasting (or better, correlative, noninvidious) categories than to show how each, in its own appropriate fashion, applies to an aspect of the divine nature. Yet the simplicity of calling God "the absolute" can come back to haunt the classical theist if absoluteness precludes relativity in the sense of internal relatedness to the world, including those who enter into mystical union with God (*IO* 60; *MVG* 239, 322; *NT* 44; *OO* 44).

(2) If the decision to accept monopolarity has been made, it is simpler to identify God as the absolute than to identify God as the most relative. Yet this does not deny divine relatedness, nor that God, who loves all, would therefore have to be related to all, or, to use a roughly synonymous term, be relative to all. God may well be the most relative of all as well as the most absolute of all, in the sense that, and to the extent that, both of these are excellences. Of course, God is absolute and is relative in different aspects of the divine nature (*MVG* 290; *PCH* 635; *PSG* 119–20).

(3) There are emotional considerations favoring divine permanence, as found in the longing to escape the risks and uncertainties of life. Yet even if these considerations obtain, they should not blind us to other emotional considerations, such as those that give us the solace that comes from knowing that the outcome of our sufferings and volitions makes a difference in the divine life, which, if it is all-loving (as the mystics attest), will certainly not be unmoved by the suffering of creatures (*CS* 263, 273; *PSG* 103, 460).

(4) Monopolarity is seen as more easily compatible with monotheism. Yet the innocent monotheistic contrast between the one and the many deals with God as an individual, not with the dogmatic claim that the divine individual itself cannot have parts or aspects of relatedness with the world.

In short, the divine being becomes, or the divine becoming is. God's being and becoming form a single reality, and there is no reason to leave the two poles in a paradoxical state: God *always changes*, and both words are crucial. There is no logical contradiction in attributing contrasting predicates to the same individual provided they apply to different aspects of this individual. Hence, the remedy for "ontolatry," the worship of being, is not the contrary pole, "gignolatry," the worship of becoming. God's *existence* is everlastingly permanent, but God's *actuality* (how God exists concretely from moment to moment) is constantly changing (*CS* 291; *LP* 93).

The theism that I am defending is: (1) *dipolar*, because excellences can be found on both sides of contrasting categories (i.e., they are correlative and noninvidious); (2) a *neoclassical* theism, because it relies on the belief that classical theists (especially Saint Anselm) were on the correct track when they described God as the supremely excellent, all-worshipful, greatest conceivable being, but classical theists did an insufficient job of thinking through the logic of perfection; (3) a *process* theism because it sees the need for God to *become* in order for God to be called perfect, but not at the expense of God's always (i.e., permanently) *being* greater than all others; and (4) a theism that can be called *panentheism*, which literally means "all in God." God is neither completely removed from the world—that is, unmoved by it—as in classical theism, nor completely identified with the world, as in pantheism. Rather, God is: (a) world-inclusive, in the sense that God cares for all the world, and that all feelings in the world—especially suffering feelings—are felt by God; and (b) transcendent, in the sense that God is greater than any other being, especially because of God's love. Thus, we should reject the concept of God as an unmoved mover not knowing the moving world (Aristotle); as the unmoved mover inconsistently knowing the moving world (classical theism); or as the unmoved mover knowing an ultimately unmoving, or at least noncontingent, world (Stoics, Spinoza, pantheism) (*SSH* 128–29; *PSG* 176–78, 186–88).

Two objections may be raised by the classical theist that ought to be considered. To the objection that if God changed God would not be perfect, for if God were perfect there would be no need to change, there is this reply: In order to be supremely excellent God must at any particular time be the greatest conceivable being, the all-worshipful being. At a later time, however, or in a situation where some creature who previously did not suffer now suffers, God has new opportunities to exhibit divine, supreme excellence. That is, God's perfection does not merely allow God to change but requires God to change (*CE* 95, 97, 113; *CS* 133; *HB* 49).

The other objection might be that God is neither one nor many, neither actual nor potential, and so forth, because no human concept whatsoever applies to God literally or univocally but at most analogically. The classical theist would say, perhaps, that God is more unitary than unity, more actual than actuality, as these are humanly known. Yet one wonders how classical theists, once they have admitted the insufficiency of human concepts, can legitimately give a favored status to one side (the left side) of conceptual contrasts at the expense of the other. Why, if God is more simple than the one, is God not also more complex, in terms of relatedness to diverse actual occasions, than the many? Analogical predication and negative theology can just as easily fall victim to the monopolar prejudice as univocal predication. To be agent and patient together is much better than being either alone. This is preeminently the case with God, and a human being is more of an agent and patient than is an ape, who is more of both than a stone. Stones can neither talk nor listen, nor can they decide or appreciate others' decisions. The problem is not with analogical discourse regarding God per se but rather with analogical discourse when distorted in a monopolar way (*AW* 25; *CE* 2; *PCH* 672; PPR 341).

It probably does not even occur to classical theists to question seriously the idea that God is wholly immutable and nontemporal in that it is simply assumed that mutability and temporality constitute the order of the created. Or again, classical theists do not see as problematic the seemingly obvious contradiction between a concept of God as not compassionate (because immutable) and the evidence of mystical experience wherein God is eminently compassionate. Somehow or other God helps those in misery without sympathizing with them. It is simply assumed in classical theism that not to suffer is better than to suffer, rather than to think through carefully the dipolar (rather than monopolar) logic of perfection. Further, the positive aspects of passivity are to be distinguished from the obsequiousness often associated in the Abrahamic (and other) religions with the subordination of women, with women as mere helpers (*PSG* 85; *MVG* 123; *DR* 123–24).

In this regard Jewish classical theists (Philo, Maimonides, etc.), Christian classical theists (Saints Augustine, Anselm, Thomas Aquinas, as well as Martin Luther, John Calvin, etc.), and Muslim classical theists (Al-Ghazzali, Averroes, Avicenna, etc.) are saddled with a monopolar metaphysics that is at odds with the great works in mystical theology in these various traditions. Classical theists, in general, have a tendency toward the naked worship of power on the analogy of the political form of coercive power found in the despot, rather than toward responsive love. Or at least they have a tendency to put the concept of responsive love in a position subservient to divine omnipotence (*PSG* 294; *CS* 386; *HB* 74).

The problems of Saints Augustine and Thomas Aquinas are those of all classical theists in creating a monopolar concept of God that is impossible to reconcile with mystical experience. The relations between human beings and God are, from the Thomistic point of view, real to the creatures, but not to God, despite the fact that in mystical experience the mystic senses real relations both ways. Even Immanuel Kant continues the tradition of classical theism by assuming that God is purely nonrelational and eternal. He is imprisoned in the half-truths of monopolarity. And Kant's admirable appeal to the moral law does not enable him to increase this fraction (*AD* 209, 211, 216; *CS* 279).

The doctrine of divine monopolarity is integrally connected to substantialist thinking, with mystical experience by contrast connected to the vision of God as *living* and processual. There is an inverse relationship between classical theism's inability to explain a concept of God compatible with mystical experience in the positive sense of "mystical" and its tendency to proliferate "mystery" in the pejorative sense of the term. Two examples of the latter are: (1) the nastiest version of the theodicy problem created by classical theism's version of divine omnipotence, wherein all of the evils in the world are either sent by, or at least permitted by, the classical theistic God; and (2) the "mystery" of how human beings could be free (and hence responsible for their actions) if God is omniscient even with respect to the outcome of future contingencies such that the classical theistic God knows with complete assurance and in minute detail *everything* that human beings will do even before they act. That is, classical theism inflates "mystery" in the pejorative sense of the term and deflates the positive aspects of mystical experience that are the lifeblood of religious belief (*WP* 84, 86; *PSG* 160–64, 325).

None of the concrete religious experiences of God in the Abrahamic religions are explicated well by classical theistic abstractions. Luckily the long reign of monopolarity and etiolatry (worship of divine causality and denigration of divine receptivity) need not last forever. The hope is that Christian and other varieties of mysticism would find a theoretical home. By focusing on divine eternity (in contrast to divine temporal everlastingness) and divine unchangeableness, the very heart of religion in religious experience is lost or at least denigrated. It is no wonder that the inadequacies of classical theism led to the monumental critiques of Ludwig Feuerbach, Karl Marx, Sigmund Freud, and other thinkers. Freud, in particular, is instructive in pointing out that the alleged omnipotence of the classical theistic God can create severe psychological problems for believers who (erroneously) think that they will be protected from tragic harm. *If* God were omnipotent this hope would not be unreasonable. That is, classical theism breeds a sort of infantilism and wishful illusionism. On the contrasting dipolar, neoclassical theistic view, tragedy is inherent in life itself, including the divine life. One of the key questions regarding neoclassical theism that is being explored in the present book is whether a less infantilist version of religious belief will take away the emotional appeal of theism itself. To the contrary (*PSG* 470–71, 473, 477–79, 481–82, 485; *IO* 137; *MVG* 341; *NT* 66).

The problems with classical theism are ultimately metaphysical in that they involve a defective understanding of the relationship between being and becoming, the abstract and the concrete. Although religious experience itself is not to be identified with metaphysical thinking, it may very well be the case that the latter is needed to accurately illuminate the former. The proper indictment of classical theism need not imply a veto on all religious belief. Instead, such an indictment can be seen as part of the effort to purify religious experience and belief (*CA* 59; *DR* vii).

A changeless being cannot love, at least if the love in question is even remotely analogous to what we human beings understand love to be. This is why the greatest conceivable being could not be changeless, despite the entrenched concept of God that is inherited by many religious believers. Granted, if we abstract from all of God's contingent qualities (as in God's particular responses to those who have had religious experiences), the rest of the divine reality is described somewhat accurately by classical theists in that some aspects of God (e.g., God's everlasting *existence*) are in fact unchanging. God is both contingent and necessary in different aspects of the divine life, and classical theists are to be thanked for the intellectual progress made with respect to description of the latter aspects. The gradual collapse of classical theism from the time of the Enlightenment until the present is due in large measure, however, to classical theism's inaccurate description of God's contingent aspects. Indeed, these are denied (*AD* 30; *AW* 8; *IO* 87–89; *MVG* 128; *ZF* 24).

God's superiority to us, on classical theistic grounds, is that God only acts and does not interact. This unfortunately eliminates *any* analogy between God and creatures, despite the insightful Thomistic emphasis placed on the doctrine of analogy. The lack of such interaction would, if it occurred, ring the death knell for mystical experience. Luckily there is a dipolar alternative to monopolar classical theism.

To worship Being (or the absolutely independent) is to worship an aspect of God rather than God. When classical theists do precisely this, they should not be surprised that they do not provide a warrant for mystical experience. By confusing the divine fullness with an abstraction such as being or absoluteness, classical theists no doubt think that they are doing the concept of God a favor, but what is more likely is that they will make classical theism increasingly unbelievable. Nonetheless, we should thank classical theists for offering us a first approximation, albeit a one-sided one, of the concept of God. At its worst this concept leads to idolatry. Likewise, classical physics was a first approximation to truth in that discipline, with relativity and quantum theories supplementing the original theory in crucial ways (*CS* 43–44; *DR* xii; *PSG* 146; *WP* 167).

If there can be nothing greater or more worshipful than preeminent love, then there is something especially misleading in the classical theistic identification of divine love with strict independence and nonrelativity (i.e., absoluteness). This sort of being would not even be minimally loving, much less worshipfully so. The chief contribution of classical theism is its emphasis on permanence, but the permanence *of divine love* is not explicated well on a classical theistic basis. As before, God *always changes*, and both words are crucial. If one prays to the classical theistic God, or if one enters into mystical union with such a God, the divine being is in no way influenced because the God of classical theism influences all but is in no way influenced. Aristotle accurately saw the consequences of God as an unmoved mover and more consistently owned up to these consequences than classical theists. Aristotle's God knows only itself, does not care for others, and cannot be affected by them, whether positively or negatively. So much the less for the notion that God is an unmoved mover. How can a "God" who is in no way changeable, is not capable of growth in any sense, is in no way open to influence or enrichment by the creatures, and is wholly self-sufficient, nonsocial, and nonloving (or at least is not loving in any way we can understand or feel) nonetheless be the God of religion and religious experience? (*PSG* 279).

The basic axioms that underly divine monopolarity are seldom questioned by classical theists, which is why neoclassical theists provide such an important function in the effort to understand mystical experience. In all cases of knowing that we are able to understand, the knower conforms to and partially depends on the known. However, in classical theism God is made an exception to this understandable view by making the known conform to and depend on the divine knower. To say that God knows the world in classical theism is to say quite ironically that the world is known by God.

The flourishing of various mystics in Judaism, Christianity, and Islam, despite the lack of theoretical support from classical theism for their religious experiences, indicates the vitality and resilience of mystical theology. The attempt to blend total self-sufficiency and nonreceptiveness, on the one hand, with a God of loving relatedness to creatures, on the other, is inherently futile. The fact that God is totally devoid of compassion (or even passion) is a skeleton in the classical theist's closet that is an embarrassment in the face of the long history of mystical experience. Love and compassion need not be seen as signs of weakness: to the contrary! To say that God is an unmoved mover *and* a preeminently loving being is to reduce the analogy between human love and divine love to the vanishing point.

The classical theistic world is one devoid of chance due to its view of divine power. This mistaken view acts like a corrosive acid with respect to any effort to extricate the classical theistic God from responsibility for the intense suffering that pervades human history. Or, more charitably, if the half-truths of classical theism were recognized as such, rather than confusing them with an approximation to the whole truth, then there could also have been a closer approximation of a concept of God compatible with the testimonies of the famous mystics. It is quite amazing that the definition of God as immutable perfection without remainder has held sway for two millennia (*OO* 15; *IO* 97, 208; *LP* 6).

The view I am defending in this chapter is that classical theism is an incorrect translation of the central religious ideas (e.g., love) into philosophical categories. The goal is to preserve, and perhaps even enhance, religious experience while avoiding contradictions and paradox. Theological paradoxes, it should be noted, tend to be contradictions applied to the divine case. To repeat an example from classical theism itself, if a dog is superior to a pillar because the former is capable of internal relations, whereas the latter is capable only of external relations, and if a human being is far superior to the dog in terms of capacity for internal relations, is it not a "paradox" that the greatest conceivable being was thought to be wholly devoid of internal relations? If God is purely absolute (i.e., purely unrelated), then the only being that God could enjoy is divinity itself, and we cannot, even in mystical experience, be related to such a God.

The classics in mystical theology give testimony not to a God unrelated to creatures but to a God *supremely* related to creatures. A rock has no internal relations to others, a dog has some, a human being is internally related to a far greater number than a dog and in a qualitatively superior way, and God is either unrelated to creatures in a reversion back to a rocklike existence (as in classical theism) or supremely related to creatures both quantitatively and qualitatively (as in neoclassical theism).

To be known or felt by all subjects is just as distinctive as to know or feel all subjects, on the dipolar view. Whereas classical theism legitimately emphasizes the status of God as the subject-for-all-objects, it is a distinctive feature of neoclassical theism to see God as the object-for-all-subjects. Neoclassical theism contributes to mystical theology by emphasizing not only that God knows us but also that we can know and feel God. Our contributions to divine awareness can even be enjoyed by us as such. Preeminent activity *and* passivity should be included in any adequate description of deity.

The seeking of simple explanations for complex issues can indeed prove to be useful as a first step on a long journey. But there is no virtue in engaging in a method of tenacity in defense of traditional simplifications. Experience does not exhibit the essential inferiority of the contrasting terms to classical theism's preference for permanence and activity. That is, change and receptivity are often *experienced* as positive, as in listening very carefully to someone who thinks that her point of view has been trivialized or ignored in the past.

Whatever happens in the contingent world of becoming must be a matter of indifference to the entirely impassive God of classical theism. This is equivalent to denying that God can love. *Nothing* that we can do or suffer makes a difference to a God, who is immune from all passivity and who is identified *simpliciter* with coercive power and sheer causation. Further, this classical theistic worship of naked power has had a negative effect on ecclesiastical polity. Although classical theists in the Abrahamic religions have historically *said* that God is personal, and although they have traditionally derided pantheists because of their impersonal deity, such derision, although understandable, is misplaced given the classical theist's own inability to make room for personal traits in deity. That is, the personal qualities of deity *as articulated by* classical theists are pious fictions.

Another oddity in the classical theistic view is its attempt to appropriate for itself biblical theism, with its obvious emphasis on divine passivity, love, mutability, and personality, as in the attribution of mercy to God in the Psalms and elsewhere. Although some scriptural passages can, in isolation and out of context, be used to support classical theistic monopolarity, the weight of the biblical tradition is better supported by the dipolar view. Origen is one major figure in the Christian tradition who implicitly recognized this in his emphasis on divine possibility and mutability. And Anselm, although himself a classical theist, has offered a definition of God as that than which no greater can be conceived that facilitates the transition from classical theism to neoclassical theism: It is an open question whether divine perfection is necessarily to be equated with perfect stability or can include as well perfect changes. For Christians, Jesus himself was obviously changeable, hence the need in this tradition to figure out a way to relate his changeableness with the permanent aspect of deity. The process approach to this problem is to emphasize that deity is preeminent change as well as preeminent permanence, to the extent that, and in the ways that, both change and permanence are excellences. In addition to problems trying to render consistent classical theism with the best in biblical theism, there are related problems trying to render it consistent with trinitarian theology, where personhood is central. What sense can be made of the concept of a person who is in every sense unchanging? Wherein lies a believable analogy to human persons? (*MVG* 70–71; *RSP* 24; *PSG* 34, 36–38).

God must have a pattern of emotions if God is a person, a pattern that presumably would include both suffering and joy in light of the realization that the greatest conceivable being would share not some of, but all of, the sufferings and joys of the creatures. Whereas we are likely to be overwhelmed by the sufferings and joys of others, the greatest conceivable being would be able to sympathize with *all* of them in a qualitatively superior way. Even the least sorrows of creatures would be compassionately felt by the all-worshipful being, as in the biblical line regarding even the fall of a sparrow not escaping divine notice (Matthew 10:28).

To extricate God from all suffering is to (perhaps unwittingly) attribute ignorance to God regarding the suffering of creatures. Process mysticism contains the idea that we are in fact accidents in the divine life, in contrast to the classical theistic view that there are no divine accidents: God is pure actuality. There is quite a difference between claiming, as in neoclassical theism, that there is real process and becoming in God and claiming, as in classical theism, that there is only real process and becoming outside God. Although the language of the mystics is sometimes cloudy and fanciful, they clearly indicate a view closer to neoclassical theism than to classical theism. Our decisions contribute to divine development. It is true that, lacking familiarity with the dipolar alternative to monopolar classical theism, many of the great figures in mystical theology either give up on "the God of the philosophers" altogether or give half-hearted support to classical theism on the assumption that this was the only intellectual option (in addition to pantheism, which has its own problems). Jacob Boehme is one famous mystic who was skeptical of what I am calling classical theism, hence it should not surprise us that Friedrich Schelling and Nicholas Berdyaev have consolidated Boehme's insights in their own versions of dipolar theism that prefigure in many ways the work of Alfred North Whitehead and Henri Bergson and Charles Hartshorne.

Classical theism and pantheism each have complementary strengths and weaknesses; and neoclassical, dipolar pan*en*theism tries to reach a higher ground where the strengths of these two views are preserved and the weaknesses eliminated. That is, it should not be assumed that a theistic critic of classical theism automatically ends up with a pantheist view. The task for the dipolar panentheist is to make sure that when contrasting predicates are applied to God they apply to different aspects of the divine life so that these contrasting predicates do not degenerate into contradictories, as in the aforementioned claim that on the neoclassical view divine *existence* may be permanent, but God's *actuality* (or *how* God exists from moment to moment) can be constantly changing. Likewise, by way of analogy, there is no contradiction involved in saying that a particular human being is always honest even if his/her individual utterances constantly change.

On the dipolar view, divine omniscience involves ideal memory such that God exhibits a meticulous care that nothing be forgotten. It must be admitted that the heavily sedimented concept of God is such that the very use of the word "God" immediately leads a great number of people to think in classical theistic terms, but an emphasis on these tender aspects of the divine process can mitigate the damage done by classical theism. Failure to even consider a concept of God other than that found in classical theism is one of the greatest errors in the history of ideas in that the concept of God affects all others, either directly or indirectly, as in the long and dehumanizing history of determinism in the sciences, which is rooted in classical theistic omniscience. At base all determinism is theological in that the determinist is claiming to have, or at least aspires to have, the sort of foreknowledge (with absolute assurance and in minute detail) of how future "contingencies" will be determined that is claimed for the God of classical theism.

Obviously there have been many intellectually honest classical theists, but this does not mean that they have done an adequate job of fairly examining their basic assumptions. Thomas Aquinas, for example, vigorously played the devil's advocate for various theorems, but not for alternative fundamental axioms that underlay the theorems, as in the very abstract preference for permanence over change, hence the resulting idea that God is *completely* unchanging. Any sort of intimate mystical experience of God is at odds with such preference, hence my desire to articulate a concept of God that at least reaches rapprochement with religious experience (*AW* 2, 4).

When classical theists refer to "God," what they should say is "God in one aspect." With this simple move the gap between classical theism and neoclassical theism could be narrowed significantly. Without this move, however, a large gap remains because in classical theism God is treated as an immobile, impersonal object, not as a subject. Unmitigated classical theism leads to contradiction at every turn: God is a power over the utterly powerless, a will that cannot change, a knower of the contingent yet wholly necessary in such knowledge, a lover who is completely unaffected by the subject loved, and so on. Only by distinguishing two different aspects of God—abstract existence and concrete actuality—can such contradictions be avoided.

Another sort of limited thinking is found in the assumption that there are two and only two alternatives: either belief in the classical theistic God or some sort of religious skepticism. This dichotomy does mystical experience a disservice because the conceptual difficulties found in classical theism are assumed to discredit mystical experience as well. A conceptually cogent view of God would help to get religious experience itself a fairer hearing than it has received in recent centuries. Contrary to popular belief, even in philosophical and theological circles, the problem of theism, including the problem of how to assess mystical experience, is a remarkably new one that has come into focus only as a result of the prominence in the past century of the higher synthesis offered by neoclassical theism, which preserves the best and eliminates the worst in both classical theism and religious skepticism, as well as preserving the best and eliminating the worst in classical theism and pantheism (*MVG* 28).

It is understandable why, upon first hearing, many classical theists are turned off by neoclassical theism. It is quite a cipher for them how God could be, say, maximally independent *and* maximally dependent. But the apparent contradiction is removed when the neoclassical distinction between *existence* and *actuality* is kept in mind. There is no contradiction in God being maximally independent in existence, but *how* God exists (i.e., God's actuality) largely depends on the creatures, and this due to divine omniscience and omnibenevolence. God's existence, on this account, is less than the entirety of the divine life. The abstract fact *that* God exists is quite different from concretely *how* God exists, hence contrasting predicates applied to existence and actuality involve no contradiction.

The biblical command "Be ye perfect!" (Matthew 5:48) obviously does not mean "Be ye immutable!" The reason for this is that there can be such things as perfect changes, say in response to others. It is for this reason that we should hope not only to develop an adequate concept of God ("the God of the philosophers") and an adequate understanding of mystical experience ("the God of religion") but *both together* as part of the overall effort to overcome the bifurcation of nature that has been the hallmark of modernity from the time of René Descartes and Galileo until the present. This effort also includes the neoclassical realization that the following features of classical theism tend to mutually reinforce each other, hence the need to rethink classical theism as a whole: the priority of being over becoming, the reduction of creaturely freedom to the mere reiteration of items decreed by divine fiat, the denial of chance or randomness in the world, and the complete immutability of deity (*NT* 18; *DR* 1).

In order to break up the block universe that is implied in classical theism (even if this implication is seldom noticed), it is necessary to affirm the theory of time as objective modality. Although the necessary features of reality that always are (as indicated in the proposition "Something exists") in a way escape the temporal flux (or better, are omnitemporal), the contingent features of reality are inherently temporal: the past is fixed and determinate, the future is at least partially open and indeterminate in that it is not here yet to be determined, and the present is that fleeting region wherein immediately future determinables are rendered determinate. An omniscient being, on this neoclassical view, knows everything that can be known, but no being, not even divinity, can know how future determinables will be rendered determinate before such determination occurs regarding the contingent features of reality. God is not to be conceived on the neoclassical view as a mere *eternal* spectator but as an *everlasting* existence who enjoys and/or suffers all that occurs in temporal process. God is as great as possible at any particular time, but new events bring with them new possibilities to exhibit divine knowledge and benevolence. In this regard, it makes sense to see God as ideally perfect*ible*. Concrete actuality, even in the divine case, is always contingent, even if divine existence is in itself abstract and immune to coming to be or passing away (*IO* x).

It is crucial to emphasize that God's dependence is just as unique and remarkable and admirable as God's independence. So also regarding the other dipolar contrasts. To cite another pair: God's passivity (say with respect to those who seek mystic union with God) is just as unique and remarkable and admirable as God's activity. We are affected by only a relatively few fellow creatures, and intermittently so, and qualitatively in a manner mixed with our own egoistic concerns. God is affected by *all* creatures *all the time* and in a qualitatively superior way. Hence it is one of the biggest mistakes in classical theism to think of independence-dependence and activity-passivity as logical contradictories rather than as correlative pairs that mutually reinforce each other. This mistake is due to a failure to consider the possibility that these contrasting pairs apply to different aspects of the divine nature, thus avoiding dreaded logical contradiction. Further, there is nothing in dipolar theism that diminishes that aspect of God that classical theists did isolate and explicate rather well, as in God's envisagement of various conceptual objects, which makes our inferior envisagement of such conceptual objects possible (*PSG* 395).

Because an understanding of mystical experience has been hampered for many centuries by a defective metaphysics, it can be said that a central *religious* problem is metaphysical. An advance in metaphysical thinking that would aid in the understanding of mystical experience would involve a distinction within the Anselmian concept of that than which no greater can be conceived. There is a crucial difference between God being unsurpassable by another being (the neoclassical theistic view) and God being unsurpassable even by Godself (the classical theistic view). The latter involves the inability to change *simpliciter*, even if such change is by way of addition or enrichment. One model for deity ignored altogether by classical theism is that of dialogue. The classical theistic view has God speaking but not hearing. This is the (supposedly benevolent) dictator view of deity that is surpassed by a view wherein God is both preeminent speaker *and* listener on the analogy of an ideal human dialogical partner (*PSG* 110; *PCH* 571).

Monopolarity is actually a type of idolatry rather than a prominent feature of the worship of deity properly conceived. Even the suggestion that God is infinite in every respect and in no way finite is problematic. It makes sense to see God as infinite in the temporal reach of divine existence, but it also makes sense to see God as finite, yet preeminently so in the way that God relates to *particular* creatures here and now. The positive sense of finitude is related to the concept of determinateness and intimacy, in contrast to an indeterminate blob of relatedness to others. In this regard the ancient Greeks are instructive in the way they see the infinite (*apeiron*) as in a sense inferior to the finite (*peras*). The greatest conceivable being, on the neoclassical theistic view, would be excellently infinite and excellently finite in the ways that both of these are excellences. Mere infinity is empty, formless; nor could the merely infinite (or necessary) know finite (or contingent) things. This is why "infinite" is not a synonym for "supremely good," nor is "finite" a synonym for "not supremely good." In this regard it should be noted that the one mystical experience reported by Hartshorne himself in his autobiography *The Darkness and the Light* concerned his coming to realize in a very particular, intimate, indeed idiosyncratic way the finite aspect of God (*DL* 126; *NT* 134; *OO* 116, 131; *PSG* 234).

A God who gives everything and receives nothing is a radically deficient being, as least if God is one whom we serve. By concentrating too much on the question of the *existence* of God, rather than on the *concept* of God, philosophers and theologians have done a disservice to religious thought. In fact, without an adequate concept of God the very issue of the existence of God seems quite beside the point. The religious view of the world, I assume, is one where God not only loves but also is loved by others, who contribute to the actuality of God in process. Although God is the necessarily existing individual who is better than those who do not exist necessarily, this does not mean that God is *exclusively* necessary, because such a being would be incapable of love and being loved by others and hence would be at odds with the virtue of omnibenevolence. Although mystical experience can give us insight regarding the quality of divine love and of God being loved, it cannot help us to clarify the thorny conceptual issues entwined within classical theism that give rise to the problem mystics have had historically with "the God of the philosophers." In a way, classical theists never really believed in what they said in that, from a pastoral point of view or when talking about the Trinity, etcetera, they have always insisted on a personal (or tripersonal) God of love who reacts to us and to our suffering. But such insistence cannot be based on their own metaphysical views (*MVG* 219, 241, 247).

Of course, just as the greatest being cannot be pure actuality, it is also true that a perfect being cannot be pure potentiality. Likewise regarding divine activity-passivity, etcetera. This highlights the great achievement of classical theism *within its own limited sphere*. But the dual transcendence that characterizes neoclassical theism means that there is twice as much transcendence in this view than is found in monopolar theism. God is transcendently permanent as well as transcendently changing, transcendently active as well as transcendently passive, and so on. Contrary to the familiar charge made against process theism, it is actually the classical theistic God who is too small (as Bernard Loomer argues) by one-sidedly exhibiting abstractions rather than the fulness of deity. In the dually transcendent God there is admittedly transcendent unity, but also a sort of divine inclusiveness of all of the diversity of creation. Likewise, in the dually transcendent God there is eminent permanence of existence plus eminent (and endless) novelty. To be universal cause *and* effect is far better than being either alone (*PSG* 150, 152; *PCH* 686).

Chapter 2

World-Inclusiveness and Nature

It is a commonplace among theists, in general, that God is omnipresent. It is something of a surprise, therefore, that classical theists have typically asserted in monopolar fashion that God is pure spirit and is in no way embodied. A more defensible neoclassical view would suggest, once again, that classical theism fails to follow through consistently with its own doctrine of analogy. Granted, there is a danger in *univocal* discourse regarding God in that if terms used to describe creatures are employed in exactly the same sense they are used to describe God, then there is a real possibility that we would end up with an attenuated view of divine reality. It should also be granted that there is the opposite danger in *equivocal* discourse that if the terms we use to describe creatures have meanings that are completely different from when these same terms are used to describe God, then we would have no idea what we are talking about when discussing the concept of God. Our best option, as Thomas Aquinas rightly emphasized, is to split the difference, so to speak, between univocity and equivocity by speaking of creatures and God in *analogical* terms wherein there are some similarities and some differences in the use of terms. The hope is that both the uniqueness of God and the intelligibility of our discourse would be preserved.

Rather than judiciously apply the doctrine of analogy to the issue of divine embodiment, classical theists give up entirely in the effort, influenced as they are by the logic of monopolarity: They deny altogether divine embodiment. The greatest conceivable being, on the neoclassical view, would be *both* preeminent mind or soul *and* preeminent body. Just as each one of us hylomorphically animates this or that body, so analogously God hylomorphically animates body. But God does not animate this or that particular body but the body of the world or the cosmos in general. This cosmic hylomorphism relies, quite ironically (in that it is Aristotle who is usually identified with hylomorphism), on Plato's doctrine of the World Soul, which was discussed in at least five of his later dialogues, especially the *Timaeus* (*OO* 133–35; *PSG* 40, 50, 53; *ZF* 88).

A four-term analogy might help in the effort to understand the neoclassical concept of divine world-inclusiveness:

P1 : P2 :: P2 : P3

P2 refers to psyche per se as found in sentient animals such as ourselves and other animals with central nervous systems. P1 refers to microscopic psyche as found in sentient or self-active cells. P2 is spread throughout the body such that if one's cells (P1) are harmed, the sentient individual as a whole (P2) is harmed. The point to the above four-term analogy is to indicate that in relation to God (P3), we are like living cells, and that for God there is no external environment (*BH* 198, 239; *CA* 274; *CE* 16; *CS* 284–85; MEA 187–88; *MVG* 186–87; *OO* 61, 80; *PCH* 597, 617–18, 700; *PSG* 377; *ZF* 91).

Rationality can lead us to seriously consider the concept of God: Because we are obviously fallible, we are led to inquire about what it would be like to be infallible (like God); because we are finite in time, we are led to inquire about what it would be like to live everlastingly (like God); and especially important for the topic of the present chapter is the realization that we are obviously fragmentary in spatial extension, hence we are led to inquire about what it would be like to be omnipresent and ubiquitous (like God). There is no logical dependence of natural theology (or metaphysics or philosophy of religion) on revealed theology, such that uninhibited theoretical activity itself leads to the concept of God as one of its products. Of course, it might be understandably objected that while the *concept* of God might arise by theoretical procedures, the *existence* of a corresponding reality is another matter. The point I am trying to make here, however, is that, in addition to the concept of God arising quite naturally when thinking of the topics of knowledge, time, and space, some people generally, and mystics even more so, *feel* themselves as fragmentary parts of a mighty, cosmic whole (*ZF* 28, 71; *PD* 87; *LP* 245; *CA* 67).

Of course, some other people feel alienated from the world and do not see it as their home. But the pervasiveness of the sense that we *are* at home in the world, indeed that we are organically included in a benevolent whole, should not escape our notice. Although there are perhaps a greater percentage of people today than in the past who do not sense, even implicitly, divine world-inclusiveness, the fact that this sense was the dominant one in previous ages should alert us to what might still be the case. Plutarch, for example, informs us that *all* of the ancient philosophers (except for Aristotle and the atomists) believed in God as the World Soul who animated the cosmic body (*Plutarch's Morals* 3:133). Throughout history there have also been Abrahamic theists (e.g., Philo, Origen, Gustav Fechner, Otto Pfleiderer) who have continued this belief, which alternatively can be seen as a philosophical or as a mystical truth (*PSG* 77, 80–81; *PCH* 645).

Both God's omniscience and omnibenevolence require that God be spatially extended. Mystics are typically transformed by the realization that they are to God as microscopic reality (say sentient cells) are to us; they typically have a sense that it is possible as a result of such transformation to make the world a better place (*PSG* 319–20, 382).

God as the World Soul knows the world both by knowing the world-inclusive divine nature itself (analogous to a human being's self-knowledge) and by knowing the constituents of the cosmos (analogous to knowledge we might have of our cellular constituents). God includes or embraces us, on this model, but not without residue, as would be the case in pantheism. There are also admittedly disanalogies, as in the fact that we experience both an internal environment and an external one, whereas God as the World Soul would not experience anything external to the whole that is the divine body. Nonetheless there is much at stake in the metaphors chosen to depict our place in the uni-verse (note, not pluriverse): To say that we are as mere specks of stellar dust is quite different from saying that we are as living cells within the great cosmic bodily becoming. On the latter view, God is the perfect Person who animates a genuinely *organic* community that involves more than mere backslapping congeniality. This community is not always pleasant in that pain in one part of the cosmic organism can be felt by other parts, as the religiously sensitive have always attested (e.g., in terms of the mystical body of Christ) (*PSG* 255, 285, 400–01; *CA* 45; *DR* 62, 76; *HB* 31–32, 75–76).

It is noteworthy that very few religious skeptics have taken the time to critique neoclassical theism and its favorable implications for mystical experience. That is, they have assumed that classical theism *is* theism and have tarred mystical experience with a classical theistic brush. David Hume is an exception in that he (unlike Kant) had a very open-minded view regarding the concept of God and the World Soul, whatever his own view regarding the existence of God might have been. To the extent that sympathy is spread generally throughout the cosmos, we have an inkling of what the mystic feels. As before, mystics *feel* the universe more as an organic whole than as a mechanical object or collection of mechanical objects. Further, the World Soul, it should be noted, implies dipolarity in turning away from monopolar insistence on God as pure spirit that is in no way (supposedly) tainted by body. Just as in a human being, wherein personal coherence and bodily coherence are two inseparable aspects of one (hylomorphic) reality, so also in the divine/cosmic case God is not something additional to natural order or supernaturally added onto the natural world but animates it throughout. The mystic claims to feel that human valuations are included in an all-embracing Love (*PSG* 423–24, 433; *PCH* 695).

To be a theist is to believe that we are "in" God (via omniscience properly conceived and omnibenevolence); mystics *really* believe this. Indeed, the very word "God" stands not only for the greatest conceivable but also for the analogy between a feeling/thinking animal and the cosmos itself conceived as animate. Not only is the asymmetry between a human being and God not compromised in panentheism, it is enhanced and made intelligible. The way in which cellular feelings in our bodies participate in the feelings of a human being as a whole (think of localized pleasure or pain) is to be distinguished from the way in which human feelings in general affect those of cells (think of psychosomatic illness). A single cell makes only a negligible difference to the human being as a whole, but a single human individual can affect all of the cells in his or her body. Analogously, God should be seen as both effect and cause, albeit as Supreme Effect and Supreme (although not omnipotent) Cause. The problem with classical theism was not that it found a place for asymmetry between human beings and God but that it fostered a falsely simple asymmetry. Likewise, not only is there a significant place for transcendence in neoclassical theism, it actually entails a dual transcendence superior to classical theism's monopolar transcendence (*DR* 79–80, 90; *HB* 46).

We have experience of the power of agents over other agents, as when a human individual sways bodily constituents by, say, eating well or poorly, drinking well or poorly, avoiding unnecessary stress or stoking it, etcetera. The fact that our persuasive power over our cells can be positive enables us to have a glimpse of a being who would be not merely benevolent in persuasive power but omnibenevolent (*BH* 45).

Interpersonal relations—such as parent to child or ruler to subject—have traditionally provided in classical theism the basis for most analogies regarding the divine-human relationship. One problem with the parent-child analogy is that as soon as a child is born the process of separation from the mother starts, a defect that is avoided in the panentheistic model of God as a World Soul, which captures the cliché among mystics that God is nearer to us than breathing. Another limitation of the parent-child or ruler-ruled analogies is that they do not help us to understand the *categorial* inferiority we have with respect to a God whose influence is cosmic in scope and everlasting in temporal duration. God is the individual integrity *of the world* and does not exhibit our fragmentariness (even if God is in some respects "finite" in the honorific sense of the term) (*OO* 54; *CE* xii).

No disrespect is shown to us by comparing us to cells in the divine organism when it is realized that cells are, like us, sentient individuals, tiny animals. They are constantly reorganizing their parts and repairing damage. Cellular feelings most prominently concern the internal relationships they have with, and stimuli they receive from, their neighbors, say in nerve cells across synaptic connections. We have direct evidence that our cells feel, once again as evidenced in the experience of localized pain. Although we cannot identify the cellular microindividuals themselves that have had intense heat rip open their cell walls, *our* suffering largely consists in an immediate sharing in, and sympathy with, the suffering that occurs at the cellular level. Our cells respond to our feelings, and we respond to theirs. The sympathetic intimacy discussed here provides us insight into the lives of the great mystics in their relationship with God and God's relationship with them. The Pauline way to put the point is to say that we are members of one another (Romans 12:5) when we are seen as cellular constituents of the cosmic divine life (*BH* 163; *CS* 220–21; *OO* 108, 120, 123; *WP* 56; *ZF* 15).

Deity is the highest form of inclusion of others in the self. Whereas our inclusion of cellular lives into our lives is largely indistinct and unconscious, God's inclusion is both distinct and conscious, indeed personal. As omnibenevolent, God participates more fully in our happiness than we participate in the suffering of others, as the symbol of the cross in Christianity indicates. Further, the biblical ideal to love the other as one loves oneself starts to become intelligible with the idea of God as world-inclusive on the analogy of our own inclusion of cellular others in our bodies (*PSG* 270).

If God is the soul for the world, then the material world in general is the divine body. If the material world is everlasting, then there is nothing analogous to cancer cells that could threaten continued divine existence, although the suffering of creatures indicates that God as omnibenevolent suffers, too. Our defect is not so much that we are finite, given the honorific as well as pejorative aspects of finitude, but that we are fragmentary. The World Soul, by contrast, does not "begin to exist," nor is the World Soul confined spatially to only one place. When a human or other animal dies, there is no chaos involved, merely a return to the types of order indicative of the cosmic body. The World Soul can (at least) vicariously suffer with the suffering members, but it cannot suffer in the sense of passing out of existence altogether. Individuals can influence God, but they cannot pose any real threat (*RSP* 21; *PSG* 249; *MVG* 278; *LP* 204; *DL* 26–30, 309).

The contrast between more or less essential body parts arises from an animal's having an external environment, but because God has no external environment, each creature becomes, as it were, not merely a cell but a nerve cell in the divine body. The cosmic analogue of a brain is simply the entire system of things as immediate and internal to the divine mind. Plato noted in his day that the cosmos does not need limbs to move about because it is its own place, no digestive system to transfer matter from without in that there is no without, no lungs to take in air from without for the same reason, etc. All of the parts are internal to the divine life (via omniscience and omnibenevolence) and communicate directly with God as the World Soul. The implications for mystic experience are significant in that they make intelligible what would otherwise be a real cipher: how the two-way bridge of sympathy or feeling can occur between God and creatures (*STF* 91–92; *PCH* 659; *NT* 95; *LP* 197–98; *BH* 202).

For as long as classical theism flourished there was an understandable sense that religion had to be cosmic in scope, but it is not as clear in classical theism as it is in neoclassical theism how this could be so. The universe as one *is* God, analogous to the way that each one of us *is* our respective bodies. In addition, the philosophical problem of other minds is illuminated in that this "problem" is analogous to the experienced relationship between different cells (or different groups or kinds of cells) in the body. One experiences the pleasant or unpleasant feelings of one's own bodily cells, as when we tell the difference between a headache and a sore toe. And our cells, however dimly, feel us. God, in a superior fashion, feels us and we feel God, albeit the mystic does so with greater acuity and vivacity than the rest of us (*CE* 24; *DL* 369; *MVG* 190, 204–5; *NT* 97; *PSG* 337).

It would be a mistake to think that my approach is based exclusively on the move from *concepts* like world-inclusiveness, necessary existence, and unsurpassibility to God. In addition, it makes sense to move from the mystical *experience* of a loving God to concepts like world-inclusiveness, necessary existence, and unsurpassibility. These two approaches can be seen as mutually reinforcing. One of the greatest defects in classical theism is that it assumes a concept of God as unmoved and necessary in both existence and actuality that precludes a God who could love in any way analogous to human love. *Starting* with the religious experience of love has beneficial consequences that help us to improve on the classical theistic view.

Abrahamic theists, in general, are rightly dismissive of Aristotle's concept of God wherein the only thoughts God can have deal with the divine nature itself. There has to be a place as well for divine thoughts about nondivine things, they think, quite legitimately. But they do not consistently indicate how this could be the case.

Although nature is a sublime totality and human beings a tiny fraction of the whole, this need not mean that we are meaningless parts. Any organism is a society of parts, but there are two sorts of society. One sort may be called *democratic* in the sense that it has no dominant member, as in plants. The other sort of society does have a dominant member who synthesizes the feelings of the parts. In such a *monarchical* society (like a human organism) the entire group acts as a functional unity. The real agent here is always momentary, with an abiding sequence of such moments constituting personhood. In this sense the neoclassical doctrine of the World Soul can mitigate the fears of those who worry about hegemonic holism in that the whole changes as each new moment comes into existence; not even divine life is *totum simul* or all at once but is enhanced constantly. That is, there is nothing "totalizing" in the pejorative sense about the World Soul due to divine and creaturely dynamism. The dynamic unity of the World Soul is monarchical *in the sense that* the cosmos feels and acts as a functional whole. However, the monarchical society in question refers to a cosmological principle, not a political one. God does not rule over the world from the outside, like a (classical theistic) tyrant, but provides coordinating influence (*LP* 182, 200–201; *WM* 90; *RSP* 38–40).

Some may be skeptical regarding the claim that the cosmos is genuinely and organically one. In response we should note that when *anything anywhere* happens, its effects are communicated at the speed of light or sound in all directions. Further, the same basic modes of action pervade all of space, as detailed by physics. There is no secession from the cosmic community because there is nowhere to go from the uni-verse.

Without an everlasting community, our action is only "a passing whiff of insignificance," to use Whiteheadian language. To render our actions everlastingly significant, something more is needed than the pseudounity provided by a state or group-mind. In fact, the significant choices made by "group minds" tend to be driven in actuality by a small group of individuals or an individual. What is needed is a nonlocalized mind, cosmic in scope, and perfect in memory, a mind with whom the mystics make contact. The remedy for narrowness of experience is provided somewhat by political commitment, but the remedy ultimately resides in the "ocean of feelings" (another Whiteheadian commonplace) that is the divine life (*RSP* 34, 61–62).

There is no opaque mystery in sympathy in that we all experience it both interpersonally (as in love of one's family members) and intrapersonally (as in the feeling of pain when one cuts one's finger). Both social and organic relations involve sympathy, hence it makes sense when thinking religiously to involve *both* social relations and organic ones in order to analogize fruitfully when discussing the relationship between human beings and God. Our relationship to a radically superior, divine mind is analogous, I have suggested, to the relationship between cells in our body and us as persons. In exceptional, yet not unbelievable, mystic states some people have more adequate experiences of God than most of us can muster, even if they fall short of complete adequacy. To have complete adequacy would be to have the divine mind itself.

The idea that a cell (in Greek, *neura*, a nerve) is in the person as a person is in the cosmos, we have seen, goes back to Plato and several other ancient Greek thinkers, as do the social *and* organic analogies used to understand God. But the ancient Greek tendencies toward monopolarity (from which Plato partially escaped), immutability, and impassivity have to be properly contextualized in order for the ancient concept of the World Soul to be properly understood. Admittedly, the further away one gets from human personality, the harder it is to express in language the psyche in question, whether one is going downward from animals with central nervous systems to cells or upward from heroes or angels to God. But this is quite different from an aggressive version of ineffability, which is more dogmatic than it is humble. That is, hubris comes in many forms.

Plato himself made it clear in the *Republic* (462c–d) that if one has pain in one's finger (note, not the whole hand), the whole community of bodily members is adversely affected, just as, if one of us is harmed, a whole greater than us is adversely affected. The experience of pain in one's finger is, in a way, one's own experience and, in another sense, is the experience of others (i.e., of cells in the finger). This Platonic example illuminates the partial autonomy of the mystic who exists within the divine, cosmic whole (*HB* 67; *LP* 192; *MVG* 153; *PPS* 264).

Even Isaac Newton referred to space as God's sensorium. The sort of world-inclusiveness defended by neoclassical theists is an attempt to understand what this might mean, especially in the context of various mystics' testimony regarding the variegated sensory evidence: visual, auditory, tactile, gustatory, and olfactory. Nothing, it seems, abides forever except the cosmos seen as the divine sensorium. If we are like ganglia within the whole, this implies an organic conception of the world to which the questions of theism and mystical experience refer. By contrast, classical theism is tied to a view of God as strictly *super*natural and divorced from nature and sensory experience as a result of the monopolar prejudice. The debate here is between classical theists and religious skeptics, on one side, and neoclassical theists, on the other: Is the universe to be regarded as the mere sum of all individuals or as itself an individual, cosmic in scope? (*MVG* 273; *BH* 45).

To speak more cautiously, it is not obvious that the universe is *not* an organism, given its organization and habits (popularly referred to as laws of nature). That is, it is at least possible that psychology can be generalized so as to apply to the simplest, subhuman, microscopic elements of the universe as well as to the cosmic mind itself. What is mysterious in the pejorative sense of the term is how we are to account for the fact that the world *is* a universe, a cosmos, without the World Soul hypothesis. Of course, the feelings of the World Soul are only analogous to, and not identical with, our feelings in that they would be cosmic in scope and undeflected by bias caused by partiality. It would be unduly anthropocentric to say that a non-human animal would first have to become a human in order to suffer when caught in a trap. Likewise, it would be unfair to restrict sentiency at the highest level to *us*. Psychological understanding of P1, P2, and P3 involves vicarious experience of psyche-variables of an infinite range, from simple to complex. It is only the fully conscious and clear/distinct aspect of human experience that is finite; we faintly feel ourselves in semiconscious fashion as parts of an infinite temporal and spatial whole. The infinite existence we dimly feel, mystics more distinctly than the rest of us, is God.

The world as a whole is held together by certain habits (once again, commonly called laws of nature) that hold sway over the local habits of us as individuals. Neoclassical theism is an elaboration of this deathless (but not changeless) cosmic individual. At the local level sympathy without antipathy would signal a complete merging of selves, just as antipathy without sympathy would signal a complete lack of interaction or influence among local selves. Because local selves do not completely merge, and because they do interact with and influence each other, we can be confident that both sympathy and antipathy characterize the lives of local organisms. The presence of antipathy helps us to understand how the World Soul cannot guarantee perfect harmony among the creatures. The function of mind, even divine mind, is to give each organism both a certain degree of unity as a spatiotemporal individual and to appreciate aesthetic and moral *quality* in a limited way.

Often those who prohibit discourse about the universe as a whole contradict themselves in Bertrand Russell–like fashion by talking about the piecemeal and higgledy-piggledy nature of *the world* (presumably as a whole). The telos of divine persuasion of *the world* would be to keep the member parts predominantly, though not possibly completely, healthy and in harmony with other parts as well as to share sympathetically in the values of these parts. No other purpose is needed in order to have a meaningful world (*BH* 216; *IO* 307; *PCH* 571; *WM* 133; *PSG* 495; *DL* 391; *MVG* 330).

Although there are some obvious problems with preliterate animism, it is not necessarily an improvement to extinguish this view altogether so as to replace it with modern mechanism, where the world as a whole and we as individuals are seen as machines composed of submachines. Classical theism prepared the way for modern mechanism by setting up a two-tiered universe wherein God supernaturally hovered above the natural world with its changes and passivities. On this classical theistic view, mystical experience occurs when a human being somehow pole-vaults, as it were, out of this natural world into a supernatural one. It is no wonder that many late modern and postmodern thinkers find this view unbelievable and exorcize the ghost that hovers above the universal machine, just as they are willing to exorcize the human ghost from the human body viewed as a machine (*BH* 312–13; *DR* 28).

Mechanism is opposed to a society of cellular psyche relating to each other, whether the society in question is our own bodies or the cosmos. It is one thing to be all-inclusive, quite another to be absolute in the sense of being unrelated to others. Or better, God can be absolute in existence yet supremely relative and social in actuality. To know all is, in a way, to include all; so, too, regarding caring for all. God as an effect is superior to all other (somewhat defective) effects, just as God as cause is superior to all other (somewhat defective) causes; the classical theist admits only the latter. When the universe is patterned after the ideal of sentient, rational animality, the superiority of dipolarity to monopolarity becomes readily apparent. The God who creates and the divine inclusion of creation are one God, albeit with two different aspects.

As before, it would be a mistake to assume that all versions of divine world-inclusiveness are types of pantheism in that the neoclassical view is not that God is "merely" the cosmos. The pan*en*theist stance is that God is neither exhausted by the cosmos (because God could hylomorphically animate a different world from the one that exists at present) nor completely independent of the natural world, as in classical theism. Or better, although God is independent of this particular world, due to the fact that a partially new world will be brought into existence in the next moment, this does not mean that we have to hyperbolize divine independence in classical theistic fashion by postulating a God who could exist alone without any world at all.

Philosophy itself should be seen as an attempt to understand and justify value judgments that are as free as possible from bias and provinciality. This escape from the merely local inexorably leads us to consider forms of valuation cosmic in scope, a consideration engaged willingly by the mystic. The cosmic soul would be unborn and undying, to echo the language from the Buddhist tradition regarding the reality that underlies local changes. The task when trying to understand psyche—microscopic, mesoscopic, and cosmic—is to avoid at least two fallacies. The fallacy of division is committed when it is assumed on the (supposed) evidence of the insentience of the whole that the microscopic parts are also inert and lifeless. And the fallacy of composition is committed when it is assumed on the (supposed) evidence of the insentience of the parts that the whole is also inert and lifeless. The type of world-inclusiveness found in panentheism analogizes an animal body and the cosmos when both the parts (cells) and the whole are sentient, although some of the microscopic parts are aggregated into larger, insentient, mesoscopic parts that are the sources for the mistakes made by mechanists.

It is quite common to read of mystics who claim that the soul of the universe dwells in their own souls or pervades the cosmos the way one's own psyche pervades one's body. On this view, both monism and pluralism have a legitimate role to play. Each one of us contributes to the Whole without losing our individual (albeit processual) identities.

The idea of God being related to the cosmos as the human mind is related to its nerve cells is a valuable analogy in part because it is strong where interpersonal analogies (parent-child, ruler-subject) are weak. This is because the interpersonal analogies do not indicate at all the strength of a panpsychist view wherein psyche goes all the way down to the microscopic level, nor do they indicate well the concept of divine world-inclusiveness via omnibenevolence and omniscience (properly understood). Hurt my cells and you hurt *me*. Likewise, hurt me and the greatest conceivable being is adversely affected, but not threatened with nonexistence. We have seen that it is not mere infinity that distinguishes God from creatures but rather the unique dipolar excellence of God's infinity (of existence and essence) *and* finitude (making possible actual relations with flesh-and-blood individuals, especially the mystics). It should be noted that my point in the present book is not to examine mystical experience so as to "prove" divine existence but rather to remove what would otherwise be a lack of coherence: If God is omnipresent and animates not this or that body but the body of the whole universe, it would be a real cipher why we could not actually experience such a divine reality.

In one sense God as the World Soul is an individual, and in another sense God is universal. God is the only universal individual. Contradiction is avoided because to be God would be to be related to reality as such and yet be a singular, integrated reality. "God" both names an individual and refers to universal properties like unsurpassibility. The Cosmic Observer does not move to another place because this individual is already everywhere on the analogy of a human consciousness whose reach extends throughout a whole body rather than being localized into a point. It would be a mistake, however, to think that it is only a one-way influence that is top-down, which is a real hazard if God is analogized exclusively in terms of interpersonal analogies such as ruler-subject or parent-young child. Cells influence us, and we influence God, a consideration that is crucial in the effort to understand the processual terms found in the writings of the mystics (*AD* 292–93; MMEJ 117; *NT* 34; *OO* 59, 69, 110; *PSG* 493).

There is a significant difference between being a quotidian particular individual and a divine universal individual in that only the latter involves a sequence of concrete states of consciousness connected with the others in the most ideal way through omniscient memory and steadfastness of purpose. These divine characteristics are what make at least somewhat intelligible the *inter*action between God and humans in mystical experience.

The doctrine of the World Soul is not a "mere" metaphor or analogy because it is connected to metaphysical issues surrounding the defects in monopolarity and the strengths of a dipolar analysis of contrasting terms such as being-becoming, psyche-matter, activity-passivity, etcetera. Further, our ability to compare a toothache and a stomachache not only helps us to analogize regarding God's relationship with two different suffering beings in different parts of the world, it also helps us to understand the relationship between minded body or embodied mind, the two phrases being rough equivalents. To be God would entail having perfect access to all concrete feelings, an access felt analogously by mystics who are aware of their own past feelings and those of their cells (*BH* 110–22).

There is a problem with saying "There is a God" *and* "There is a world" in that there would then need be a third, inclusive reality that includes God and world. I am claiming in the present chapter that God *is* the world-inclusive reality and that all is in this God via omnibenevolence and omniscience. We cannot adequately understand the fragmentariness of our experience and its fallibility and confusion unless there is a contrast with an Experiencer who is fully adequate to the scope of the whole. There is no bifurcation of the world in neoclassical theism, as there is in classical theism, but there is bi-level experiencing both at our level (cellular feelings felt by *me* at a higher level) and in the universe at large (my feelings and those of the Cosmos conceived and perceived as personal). This is not pantheism because of the signal difference between saying there is nothing that is not in *every* sense God (pantheism) and saying that there is nothing that is not in *some* sense God (panentheism) (*PCH* 716–17).

Or again, God is all-inclusive not only because aware of all of the parts but also because God will survive them so as to both remember them and any parts that replace them as they come to be and pass away. Regarding the criticism that the cosmos is being overpersonalized in the view I am explicating, there is the reply that there is also the danger that we would underpersonalize intelligent agency wherever it is found, as when reductionistic materialists even deny that *we* are persons and insist, or at least imply, that we are machines. Nor does the criticism hold that, on the panentheistic view, God would become responsible for evil, in contrast to the classical theistic view where God is above and beyond the natural world of changes. The proper response here should be that to feel the sufferings of others is, in fact, to suffer, but to feel the volitions of others is not to will them. Each one of us, God included, is both agent and patient, and our creaturely willing involves activity that is somewhat different (but not totally different) from divine agency or activity, even if God is affected by our volitions. We are parts of God now, not parts of how God could have been if our or God's volitions had been different (*ZF* 159).

Some readers may be more comfortable with the language that we "intuit" God, rather than talking about mystical experience of God. Here I have no quarrel. The present chapter has emphasized the point that it is common, when experiencing our fragmentariness, to also experience a sense that we are (cared for) parts of a mighty whole; that we influence the whole and that we are influenced by it, just as our cells influence us and we influence our cells, contra epiphenomenalism. In defending neoclassical theism, one need not fear being accused of the pathetic fallacy if the accuser is equally vulnerable to what can be called "the apathetic fallacy," wherein feeling is denied even when evidence points toward its existence. Indeed, in explicating the World Soul, I very much want to avoid an animistic fairyland, but I also want to avoid the view of the cosmos as a giant machine. All three views involve analogical reasoning, so no easy escape from analogy is likely. Much of the universe *is* mysterious, it seems to me, and our best bet is to use analogy responsibly in the effort to understand the real, or at least in Popperian fashion to push back the darkness a bit further. I, for one, do not feel my own psyche illuminated well by machine-like metaphors (*ZF* 159; *IO* 250).

However, it should be clear by now that I see the most fruitful analogy to be that between our prehensions of our bodily cells (and their feelings of us) and divine prehension of our feelings (and our mystical or intuitive feelings of God). Minds without bodies make no sense, as I see things in Merleau-Ponty–like fashion. As Plato realized long ago, this is true even with regard to the divine mind in relation to the divine body, *the* body, the cosmos. To put the point in Pauline terms (Acts 17:28), it is within divine reality that we "live and more and have our being" (*CE* 126; *CS* 149).

It should be clear at this point that there is no wide gap in neoclassical theism between "nature mysticism" and "theistic mysticism," as there might be in the sort of mystical theology that arises in classical theism. However, there is also a close connection in neoclassical theism between "mysticism" and "romanticism," which is not surprising given the fact that the poetry of William Wordsworth exerted a heavy influence on both Whitehead and Hartshorne. In fact, the title of Hartshorne's intellectual biography (*The Darkness and the Light*) alludes to a famous line from a Wordsworth poem ("The Simplon Pass"). Nature mysticism consists in a certain feeling for nature in which nature is seen as basically beneficent, even when it threatens us with a sort of sublime beauty, in contrast to the prettified beauty with which we are perhaps more familiar. Nature lovers are never really alone when in close proximity to natural beauty. One advantage in highlighting the close relationship between process mysticism and nature mysticism is that the feeling of being at home in nature and in never being lonely in nature cuts across several religious traditions and many cultural barriers. Being a nature lover makes sense not only in the Abrahamic traditions and preliterate animistic traditions but also in Taoism and Hinduism and many other repositories of mystical literature (*CA* 48, 260; *CE* 135; *DL* 397–99; ERT 71; *MVG* 215, 259, 320; *OO* 30, 125; *PSG* 294–95; PUK 87; *RSP* 177; STM 61).

The romantic nature mysticism that is compatible with neoclassical theism reinforces the efficacy of the four-term analogy discussed above:

P1 : P2 :: P2 : P3

Wordsworth's poetry is replete with poetic images for the panpsychist view in which microscopic sentiency (P1) plays a significant role. To take just one example, consider Wordsworth's statement:

> The budding twigs spread out their fan
> To catch the breezy air
> And I must think, do all I can,
> That there was pleasure there. ("Lines Written in Early Spring")

Notice that it is the twigs, not the whole tree, that are sentient, which I assume is Wordsworth's poetic way of illustrating P1. So also, P3 is illustrated by Wordsworth's language regarding the cosmos as "one mind" rather than as a mechanical aggregate. Nature is not as dull as mechanists make it out to be. All of the parts of nature are understood and cared for by an omniscient being who is also omnibenevolent (*DL* xiii, prologue, 80, 158, 372–79; DWVN 85–87; *LP* 218; OD 233; *PCH* 12–13, 694; *RSP* 83–84; *ZF* 35).

The romantic view of nature with which neoclassical theism agrees has the following features:

1. Throughout animate nature there is feeling.

2. So-called inanimate nature is not really inanimate; rather, the widely held view that nature is largely inanimate is due to the attention paid to aggregates of sentient parts, to beings that are as wholes inanimate, as in rocks.

3. Nature as a whole exhibits a supreme life or mind of which lesser lives or minds are constituents.

4. The evidence for points 1 through 3 is found in human experience itself, often called mystical experience.

5. However, many or most people are not consciously aware of points 1 through 3 due to the fact that after childhood there is a tendency in many people to become preoccupied with (supposedly) more practical concerns and to drift into a facile belief that the cosmos is largely composed of dead matter (see especially DWVN 81–82).

Nature mystics are opposed not only to mechanists who are reductionistic materialists but also to mechanists who are dualists. The latter make an exception to mechanism for human beings and some of the higher animals, but most of the world in the dualist view conforms to the mechanistic model. Nature mystics, by contrast, experience feeling not only in human beings but also in active singulars spread throughout nature and in Nature as a whole. Their view is at once a type of micropsychism, mesopsychism, and cosmopsychism.

It is typical of nature mystics to feel God in everything, but historically they have not been much help in sorting this out conceptually. The concepts of dipolarity, dual transcendence, and world-inclusiveness are crucial in this regard such that agents in nature have their own feelings *and* these feelings do not aggregate into a mere cosmic machine. Everyone is familiar with the aesthetic experience of natural beauty, but neoclassical theists are reluctant to view this experience as strictly subjective: There are feelings in the objects of our aesthetic experiences, too. The nature mystic *experiences* nature as alive when aesthetic value breaks into our perceptions, as when the agony of a dog penetrates into our auditory perception when we hear the whine of the animal struck with a sharp object, or as when the aesthetic delight of a bird in spring reaches us via birdsong. Our perceptions of nature are suffused with *value* in various forms: pleasant sights, unpleasant feels, etcetera. The value of a color of a flower is not merely in us (although it is at least that) in that it is intuited to be "out there" as well (say in the living cells of the flower). From the perspective of the nature mystic, this is nothing short of obvious (OD 236, 239, 255; *PCH* 17–18, 722–24; *ZF* 137).

Nature mysticism involves a description of nature and of how we experience nature when we are not distracted by pragmatic considerations or scientific abstractions, as important as these are. This is an inversion of the popular view that natural beauty is in the eye of the beholder first and is then projected onto the object. An accurate report of what is actually experienced includes value given in the object; nature comes *to* us as constituted by feelings. That is, lifeless matter is a construct; a useful construct, perhaps, but a construct nonetheless. In this regard one can easily understand the historical tension between nature mysticism and classical theism. In the latter the key relation is that between human beings and God, although this relation is not a real relation to God. In nature mysticism, however, by way of partial contrast, the key relationship is that between God and nature (with human beings included in nature), with the relationship real at both ends. Wordsworthian seeing "into the life of things" refers not only to human beings and other higher animals but also to pleasurable feelings in the sentient constituents of things; this is what makes it possible to dance with (the living cells of) daffodils. The limits to our ability to see into the life of things are at times self-imposed, as is evidenced by nature mystics, who at least partially overcome such limits. Even Kant (who was, along with Descartes, the quintessential dualist) admitted in *Dreams of a Spirit-Seer* that either we must remain agnostic about what the things we experience are in themselves or agree with Gottfried Wilhelm Leibniz and other panpsychists that they consist of individuals with psyche of a subhuman kind.

Of course, physicists do not even consider the possibility that there are feelings in nature; nor even is the physicist interested in feelings in human beings! But equally obvious is the fact that this neglect does not prove that there are no such feelings. It only shows that for the very limited purposes of predicting measurable changes in the "inanimate" parts of nature, consideration of how things feel is irrelevant. Physicists *are* interested in the problem of order-in-disorder in nature, but they tend to shy away from the possibility that the disorder is due, in part, to feeling constituents who add to spontaneity and regional unpredictability. Nature mysticism is characterized by the belief that there are deep truths about nature discovered by scientists *as well as* deep truths about nature left untouched by them.

By concentrating on the more important and obvious types of creativity in human beings, we might overlook the humbler sorts that are always there spread throughout nature, like the character in Molière who did not know that he had been speaking prose all his life. On the neoclassical view, nature, indeed Nature, should be understood as a living, ever-growing organism, and knowledge of nature (or Nature) supplements whatever else we might claim to know about God. It is not without reason that Wordsworth and other nature mystics speak of a "natural piety." One advantage of this natural piety is that it can help to narrow the gap between the theist and the atheist in that the difference between them concerns the proportion of conscious life in the cosmos; everyone, including the atheist, should admit that there is at least *some* conscious life in the cosmos (*CS* 6).

Nature mysticism is compatible with the view that all of nature should be viewed behavioristically from the outside, hence it is compatible with both the natural and social sciences. However, it is also the case that all of nature should be viewed for possible traces of psyche. Viewing nature physically and psychically are, it should be noted, analogical operations starting from human behavior and human psyche and then moving outward, downward, and upward as far as possible. Natural law, after all, should include a careful consideration of *human* nature. Henry David Thoreau speaks for nature mystics in general when he says that he is always on the alert to find God in nature, to discern the divine lurking places, and to attend all of the oratorios in nature. This Wordsworthian or Thoreauvian view would definitely improve our aesthetic appreciation of nature, but it also might enhance our knowledge of it.

From the above it should be clear that the familiar charge of "escapism" regarding mystical experience deserves scrutiny. Indeed, a supposed flight from the natural world would in fact be escapist. But the sort of theism defended here finds God in the natural world, hence the charge of escapism is avoided. Further, it is not often noticed that there is another sort of escapism to be avoided: obliviousness to, or an active attempt to obliterate, the possibility that the cosmos is a meaningful whole animated by a Presence far more deeply interfused into the fabric of nature than is supposed by religious skeptics. However, religious skeptics are insightful in their critiques of theistic versions of petitionary prayer wherein it is assumed that mountains can be moved without exertion on our part. We are fortunate in the realization that the mistakes of religions in the past—East and West, North and South—need not be repeated in the future (*BH* 39, 50, 83–84, 95–97).

In addition to petitionary prayer, the prominent place for miracles in various theisms also deserves scrutiny. Much depends on what one means by "miracle." It should be clear that there is no place for "supernaturalistic" miracles in neoclassical theism as there is in both classical theism and various other theisms. But there are "acts of God" in neoclassical theism, including divine influence regarding what happens habitually in nature (the neoclassical version of the "laws of nature"). Widespread experience of the divine lure, intensified in mystical experience, makes it possible for things we did not expect to happen to actually (in a way, miraculously) happen (*BH* 77).

It would be correct to conclude that mysticism contains within it an implicit monism, which is very close to the surface of the doctrine of the World Soul defended in this chapter. Of course, a standard objection to monism is that it makes the *variety* of things experienced inconceivable. But to say that all things share in one life is not at all to say that all things are simply one. It is only to say that in mystical experience there is a sense of an all-embracing Interest upon which we depend. Neither sheer identity nor sheer nonidentity can account for the individuals we experience in everyday life. Mystic monism is not necessarily to be equated with the former, although the monisms of F. H Bradley or Fa Tsang do seem to make this mistake (*CE* 67; *DL* 313; OD 1, 26–27, 37; *PCH* 677; *WM* 5).

The cosmic unity articulated by neoclassical theists is not extreme due to another reason: its simultaneous affirmation of panpsychism. Since the time of Leibniz, panpsychists have been aware of microscopic *organisms* that can be understood only through some sort of analogy with ourselves as active singulars. Rather than the problematic bifurcation of nature into mind and mindless matter, the neoclassical view includes a distinction (not an ontological bifurcation) between different levels of experience, from microscopic to mesoscopic to macroscopic (cosmic). Minimal levels of experience include feelings, or better, feelings of feelings as parts of a thoroughly relational worldview.

One of the unexpected reasons to consider seriously the doctrine of the World Soul is the recent rise in philosophy of mind of a view called "cosmopsychism." Although there is no necessary connection between this view and theism, it is nonetheless true that this view is compatible with theism. The thesis is that, on certain scientific evidence of uniformity throughout nature and of the relational connections of different well-established scientific hypotheses, the cosmos as a whole exhibits psyche-like or phenomenal properties. Authors such as Freya Mathews, Philip Goff, Yujin Nagasawa, and even David Chalmers have popularized this view in philosophy of mind, a development that could not have been anticipated a generation ago.

Chapter 3

Ideal Power and Tragedy

The purpose of the present chapter is to indicate the severe problems involved in saying that God is "omnipotent" and to also indicate how these problems get in the way of understanding more clearly tragedy and mystical experience. Indeed, the title to one of Hartshorne's books (*Omnipotence and Other Theological Mistakes*) is illustrative of how central a critique of omnipotence is in neoclassical theism. Nonetheless, in neoclassical theism God would, as that than which no greater can be conceived, exhibit ideal power, if not omnipotence (*MVG* 30).

There are at least three general reasons to be critical of the doctrine of omnipotence. The first is that it creates the nastiest version of the theodicy problem in that every intense pain and moral evil is, on the omnipotence hypothesis, either sent by God or at least permitted by God. For example, the excruciating suffering experienced by a young child with a birth defect could, on the doctrine of omnipotence, be prevented. Religious skeptics are correct to point out that the doctrine of divine omnipotence is at odds with the doctrine of divine omnibenevolence. Given a forced choice between the two, neoclassical theists think that omnibenevolence is the easier doctrine to render consistent with the logic of perfection. In short, omnipotence is an impediment to belief in an all-loving God. This is because so long as the doctrine of omnipotence is in play, there is a tendency for the religious believer not to be drawn positively to omnibenevolent love, as the mystic is, but to question why particular sufferings exist (*CA* 28; *DL* 385; *NT* 59; *PCH* 666, 676).

Second, omnipotence is at odds with the Platonic metaphysical claim defended by process theists that being *is* power (*dynamis*—see *Sophist* 247e), specifically the dynamic power to both exert influence on others and to receive influence from others, in however slight a way. This is a major theme in process theism. If omnipotence refers not to the quite intelligible abilities to influence all and to be influenced by all, as neoclassical theists believe, but rather to the ultimate possession of *all* power, then the concept of God becomes unintelligible. That is, if each existent has *some* dynamic power of its own to influence and to be influenced, in however humble a fashion, then no being, not even a divine being, could have *all* power because such power would render everything else powerless, that is, nonexistent. But beings other than God *do* exist, hence the unintelligibility of omnipotence. If being *is* power, then if being is divided, power is divided as well. This means that a thing is where it acts *and* is acted upon in some partially indeterministic way (*BH* 311; *CS* 1, 3, 114; *IO* 367; *MVG* 14, 89, 198, 294; *WP* 100; *ZF* 72; *OO* 21; *PCH* 650; also *AI* 120–21).

Third, the concept of omnipotence has been closely connected historically to the doctrine of creation ex nihilo. However, this doctrine makes no sense due to the fact that, although *relative* nonbeing or otherness makes sense (as in the claim that a carrot is nothing like a corkscrew), *absolute* nonbeing or nothingness is a contradiction. To say that absolute nothingness *is* is to talk gibberish and to turn absolute nothingness into somethingness, yet the doctrine of creation ex nihilo says precisely this. It comes as a surprise to many classical theists to learn that the biblical account of creation at the beginning of Genesis is not ex nihilo but rather consists in a shaping or luring of order out of the aqueous, disorderly muck that is there everlastingly on the scene along with the persuasive agency of God (see Levenson, *Creation and the Persistence of Evil*; May, *Creatio ex Nihilo*). This is creation *ex hyle* (out of matter) rather than creation ex nihilo. In the remainder of this chapter, I will be exploring the importance of these three criticisms for tragedy and mystical experience (*PSG* 268, 274–75, 288; *WP* 194–95).

It must be admitted that a world without an omnipotent God involves risks in that a universe that involves creative agency contains no guarantee that the creative agents will not get in each other's way. That is, a world without risks is not genuinely conceivable in that a totally risk-free universe would be a dead one without living agents; but there are living agents. On the neoclassical view, by way of partial contrast with the classical theistic view, God's power consists primarily in divine unsurpassable love. In Whiteheadian terms congenial to mystical experience, God's power consists in the worship and love that divinity inspires (*DL* 49–50; *DR* 154; *RSP* 158).

Of course, the classical theist will respond to the neoclassical critique of omnipotence by claiming that the neoclassical theist "limits" God and that the neoclassical God is not that than which no greater can be conceived. But the overall point to the above three criticisms of classical theistic omnipotence is to suggest that omnipotence is a false, indeed an unintelligible ideal, hence it is ironically the classical theistic view of God that is limited. In classical theistic omnipotence, evil becomes inexplicable, yet evil obviously exists; in the classical theistic view the power of creatures is eliminated, despite the fact that such power clearly exists at several different levels; and in the classical theistic view creation ex nihilo is affirmed, despite the logical contradiction involved in the claim that absolute nothingness is (or at least was) (*OO* 17; *PSG* 361).

Classical theists are much more willing to claim apophatic ignorance of God's goodness than of God's (allegedly) coercive power. The alternative neoclassical view of God's *ideal* (not omnipotent) power is both that God's persuasive agency influences all and that God's admirable patiency is influenced by all, in dipolar fashion. *If* by all-powerfulness or omnipotence one means the highest genuinely conceivable form of power, then the neoclassical theist has no quarrel. We have active power over only a small corner of the world; likewise regarding our ability to passively receive influence. But because many or most people think of all-powerfulness as coercive omnipotence, it is perhaps safer to altogether drop the word "omnipotence" in descriptions of divine perfection. On the contrasting neoclassical view, God has power uniquely excellent in quality and scope to influence all and to be influenced by all (*AD* 82; *CA* 57–58; *DR* 137–38, 156; *HB* 32; *PCH* 614; *PSG* 234; *RSP* 41).

The classical theistic view in reality involves a concept of a tyrannical God who leaves no room for chance, despite the chance elements that characterize contemporary explanations of reality in evolutionary biology and quantum physics. Intrinsic value gives power to affect others and to be affected by them. Neoclassical theists feel the force of an old dilemma: Either divine love or divine coercive power has to be rethought. Classical theists should be more forthright than they have been historically in the admission that they really worship divine power and apophatically claim ignorance of divine love. Further, there is much to be said in favor of the view that the historic problems with the concept of God involved not how much power God had but what kind of power was divine. Not even perfect power, on the neoclassical view, can guarantee perfect harmony. In their individuality the details of the world can only be influenced, never completely coerced or determined. According to the Hartshornian maxim, power is influence and perfect power is perfect influence (*CE* 98; *CS* 292; *MMEJ* 114; *OO* 24–26; *WM* 85).

To have perfect power over all individuals is not to have all power over them, on the view I am defending. The greatest power *over individuals* cannot leave them utterly powerless but rather must leave something for them to decide as individuals. *All* power in one individual is impossible because power must be exercised with respect to something that exists with some powers of its own to influence others and to be influenced by them. The real cannot be merely inert for the reason that anything that has no active or passive tendencies at all would be nonexistent (or at least completely beyond our ken). If the something that is acted upon is itself partially active, then it must offer some resistance, however slight, to ideal power. In short, power that is resisted cannot be omnipotent. An analogy from friendship is appropriate here: A friend does not dictate the terms of the relationship down to the last detail. Rather, friends respect the independence of friends. If someone decided on all of the details of another's life, this person would not really be a friend but a tyrant who aspired to totalitarian rule (*MVG* 105; *CA* 214; *LP* 154; *PSG* 444; *WM* 74; *WP* 164; *ZF* 2).

As before, being *is* power. The fact that God cannot "make us do" certain things does not really "limit" God's power because there is no such thing as power over the powerless or power to do nonsense. Power over us would not be power over *us* if our being counted for nothing. The mystic, in particular, counts for something in his or her active/passive powers.

Divine providence consists not in the complete elimination of chance (as if this were possible) but in the optimization of chance, in eliciting the best from a plurality of powers at play. It is the very reality of chance that makes divine providence significant; it would not really be significant if God already controlled *everything*. Two extremes are to be avoided: omnipotent control over all of the details of our lives, belief in which inadvertently makes God the source of our woes, or no divine influence at all over our lives. On the moderate neoclassical view, the details of our sufferings just happen and are not the results of divine decisions (*PSG* 430; *OO* 67; *CA* 30, 242).

Talk about neoclassical theism's "limiting" of omnipotence assumes that the concept of omnipotence without such limitation makes sense. But the world contains local agents making their own decisions. Instead of saying that divine power is "limited" in neoclassical theism, we should say that it is maximally possible power, the ideal power, given the thesis that being *is* power. Deity is the supreme case of *social* influence that takes account of the freedom of others (*IO* 76; *RSP* 94; *MVG* 282–83; *WIG* 526–32).

Tragedy is not an accidental byproduct of evolutionary history but is integrally connected to the concept of being (as power). Power that is not responsive to the tragedies of others is irresponsible and is not the greatest conceivable. The last thing we should do is to engage in abject worship of coercive power. This is because the ultimate power is that of sensitivity to others. The worship of divine attractiveness, otherwise known as divine persuasion, is intelligible to us because we are already familiar with the power a human being can have over another through the value the second individual recognizes in the first. Hence it is not so much that God "makes us" be what we are as that we at least partially make ourselves while considering divine beauty and goodness as inspiration, as various mystics in different traditions attest. In a sense (and this is the strongest way to make the point of the present chapter), God's power on the neoclassical view is actually *greater* than sheer omnipotence or sheer making by fiat. This is because divine power fosters other powers who are self-active agents (*PSG* 280–81; *RSP* 190).

One can agree with the idea that greatness involves omnicapacity, so long as one adds the qualification that it is omnicapacity that is genuinely conceivable. Social power, even if it is perfect, is still social in the sense that it must adjust to the power of others, but it cannot destroy it altogether. The theodicy problem in its most acute form is actually a pseudoproblem that depends on a defective notion of divine power, specifically on the notion of omnipotence. On the neoclassical view, however, divine control of human affairs must confront the nuanced relationship between freedom and risk: When more freedom is in play, risk is also greater, as good statespersons in politics realize in their own more limited domains (*EA* 111; *CS* 239–40; *RSP* 152; *PSG* 149).

If what it would mean to be God would be to exhibit perfect or ideal love, as the neoclassical theist holds, then we have reason to be skittish about the effort to divinize coercive power, and arbitrary coercive power at that. Perfect power is something quite different from absolute coercion of the world or absolute dictation. There is something perverse in the view that God decides when sentient beings will suffer and how much they will suffer or endure. Equally perverse is the view that evil is in some way good or that an omnipotent being could turn evil into good. In neoclassical theism, mystics can be steered away from several blind alleys mapped out in classical theism.

To ask why God sent a horrendous evil to an innocent person, as classical theists sometimes do, is to clearly ask the wrong question, from a neoclassical point of view. At the very least one can hope that the *question* of the nature of divine power should be on the table for consideration and that we should not be too quick to think that the received view is the correct one, as Job and his friends were reminded at the end of the book in the bible named after him. Both classical theism and traditional atheism simply assume that the greatest conceivable being would have to be omnipotent, thus inadvertently encouraging distrust of those who have had mystical experiences. Is it obvious that "ideal power" is synonymous with "monopoly of power"? I am claiming that theists need not make this identification. Monopoly of power is not so much an ideal as a nightmare (*NT* 117–19, 122).

The word "omnipotence" paralyzes both thinking about God and religious experience in ways that "divine lure" or "divine persuasion" do not. One example of this concerns the theodicy problem, which is either an insoluble project (as in classical theism) or a confusion (as alleged by neoclassical theists). Although many classical theists define "omnipotence" as the power to effectively choose that any possible world be actual, they are notoriously unclear and unconvincing regarding the world we actually live in: How could an omnipotent God have chosen *this* world? In order to render theism intelligible, and to explicate a worldview that provides a home for mystical experience, it is crucial to point out that critique of the concept of power monopoly or decision-making monopoly does not involve a limiting of God in any pejorative sense of "limitation."

"Almighty" is an ambiguous word and is not as objectionable as "omnipotent." If this term refers to the ideal case of power assuming a division of power in the universe, then the neoclassical theist has no objection. The maximal concentration of power compatible with distribution of powers among a plurality of beings is precisely the neoclassical view. Almightiness is problematic only if it refers to a God who has *all* the power, which, once again, would have to refer to power over the powerless, that is, over the nonexistent. Neoclassical theists do not so much "limit" God's power as point out that there is a social or relational element in the very idea of power. Power is relative in the sense that it entails the capacity to deal with antecedent decisions or the capacity to use data to make new actualities.

Rather than see the God of neoclassical theism as "weak," we should focus on ideal strength as something other than a monopoly of power so as to make the conceptual terrain fruitful for human (mystical) experience of a genuinely relational, caring God. In Whiteheadian fashion, we should be suspicious of metaphysical compliments given to God that backfire (like omnipotence). It makes much more sense to accommodate ourselves to the pervasiveness of partial creativity in nature as a result of the reality of being as power, of the reality of each individual exerting an influence on the world, whether positive or negative (WIG 524).

The tyranny of the theodicy problem need not continue if the transition from classical theism to neoclassical theism takes hold. This would involve an acknowledgment of the reality of chance as well as the reality of order, thus redirecting attention away from the goal of complete, divinely imposed order that has gotten in the way of religious experience for centuries. It is not merely that classical theists have attributed too much power to God; they have also attributed the wrong kind of power. They have misunderstood power, hence they have misunderstood what it means to enter into mystic union with God. At least from the time of Charles Darwin, the defects of omnipotence should have been readily apparent: If God controls *everything*, then God is responsible for monstrosities like two-headed calves and nonhuman animal suffering, in general, which are not covered by the "free-will defense" offered by many classical theists to shore up a theodicy hampered by belief in divine omnipotence. That is, a consideration of Darwin (see Rachels, *Created from Animals*) can help to awaken classical theists from their dogmatic slumbers, not so as to abandon theism itself but to abandon a certain version of theism that has disastrous consequences (*IO* x; *CA* 131; *CE* 8).

Although some classical theists will be offended by the neoclassical critique of omnipotence, there is something gained by speaking forthrightly about the fact that someone who leaves nothing for others to decide is a tyrant, not an admirable ruler. The word "omnipotent" stands for a theoretical mistake, indeed, for one of the greatest mistakes, considering its practical ramifications for political doctrines such as the divine right of kings. Christian mystics such as Thomas Merton, along with Mohammed Iqbal in Islam (as well as several other mystics in other traditions), would, in their own idiosyncratic ways, agree with this critique.

To think that the existence of evil in the world disproves the existence of God presupposes the classical theistic concept of God, hence classical theism and many versions of religious skepticism have more in common than is routinely thought. What is held in common is the assumption that divine power would arrange all things, down to the last detail. This is in contrast to the neoclassical view wherein power is an aspect of love, the means by which love is efficacious. To be all-powerful in the sense of influencing all and being influenced by all is not to be all-determining. So also, to be ideally powerful is to be unsurpassable in the scope of power and in the quality of power, but it is not to be all-determining (*AD* 161; *CA* 116; *PSG* 343, 437, 439, 462; *RSP* 110; *STF* 92).

The great mystics, even those who (often reluctantly) used the philosophical concepts inherited from classical theism, are in agreement that it is a mistake to separate divine power, on the one hand, from divine knowledge, goodness, and beauty, on the other. This view is amplified by the realization that God is as powerful as a singular agent could be in a universe with an immense plurality of agents. But God *is* a cosmically influential ordering power, as the mystics also acknowledge, on the evidence of the general regularity of the universe.

Dipolar, process theism is an attempt to achieve technical metaphysical expression of the idea of a suffering deity (symbolized in Christianity by the cross, a symbol cherished by many mystics, including John of the Cross) and of a tragic sense of life (as defended, say, by Nicholas Berdyaev). The contrasting view that there can be a complete escape from tragedy is a part of the classical theism that haunts religious history. Tragedy is inherent in the freedom of several lives in possible conflict with each other. Conflict seems inevitable. This is not the Patripassianist view regarding divine *existence* in that God's everlasting existence cannot be terminated; but it *is* Patripassianism regarding divine *actuality* in that God *does* suffer along with the suffering creatures. In Whiteheadian terms, God is the Fellow-Sufferer Who Understands, whereas we are fellow sufferers who partially understand. As Abraham Heschel asserts in his famous book on the Hebrew prophets, God is not an unmoved mover but is the *most* moved mover (*DR* xi; *HB* 95; *PSG* 152, 159, 286; *WP* 188; *ZF* 6).

When classical theists posited immunity from suffering in God, they perhaps gained a vicarious sense of escape from it themselves, but no one *really* escapes it. Once something terrible has happened, this evil becomes woven into the fabric of the real so long as there are those with memory to preserve it. What is admirable is not sequestering oneself from suffering but trying to alleviate suffering in others. The greatest conceivable being has maximal *non*immunity to suffer in the divine actuality. Concern for the concrete and individual itself, in contrast to concern for the abstract and universal, throws us into the tragedy of life. The dubious assumption that the goal of life is to altogether escape from suffering is at odds with what it means to love. Even the experience of beauty involves tragedy, as the ancient Greek tragedians and Shakespeare realized (WIG 553–54; *WM* 54, 86; *WP* 108; *RSP* 42, 99, 106–7, 148; *PSG* 15, 163, 167, 174, 243, 283–84, 290–91, 297, 313; *OO* 35; *LP* 13–14, 314–16; *DR* 149).

It is a mistake for classical theists to put wickedness and suffering in the same category in that although God cannot do evil, God can experience it in the form of suffering. There is no good reason to think that because God is in no way wicked, God would in no way suffer. Although there is no *erasure* of suffering in neoclassical theism, it is *transformed* when it is felt intensely by God and gathered into the everlasting divine life. This transformation is due, in part, to the fact that these sufferings are added to the divine storehouse of all previous sufferings, thus allowing in theory the possibility to understand immediate suffering against a wider background that includes both intense suffering and joy. The only way to eliminate the tragedy in the divine life is to eliminate pervasive creativity (i.e., pervasive existence) itself. This theodicy is dramatically different from those found in classical theism. Indeed, it is a sublime view that avoids classical theism's cold-bloodedness in that evil springs from indeterminacy that divine providence cannot banish due to the wide range of existences (i.e., powers) in play (*DR* 47, 74).

Although there are several different ways that the great mystics in different religions approach God (which are not the focus of the present book), all of these ways are enhanced through the experience of sorrow and suffering on the part of the mystic. It is one of the chief aims of this chapter to argue that the greatest conceivable being, who would certainly be omnibenevolent and omnicaring, could not remain unmoved and indifferent to such sorrow and suffering.

An imagined realm beyond the reach of chance and hence tragedy is in reality a mirage. This does not exclude every version of divine providence, but providence should not be seen as a simple alternative to chance, as it is in classical theism, but as a luring or persuading or channeling of chances that lie between, as it were, the riverbanks of what is possible. The function of divine providence is not so much to maximize the ratio between good and evil as to maximize the ratio between chances to do good and chances for suffering and evil to occur. Alleged utopias are often achieved conceptually by reducing risk, which thereby reduces vitality, indeed by extinguishing life. That is, escapism is very often the alternative to facing the tragedy of existence (although escapism is, in a different way, tragic in itself), even in the divine life. Although tragedy in general may be inevitable, the details are always open to idiosyncratic prehension and creative response. But to ameliorate the tragedy of life by eternally punishing perpetrators of evil in hell is actually a type of sadism.

To use some terms familiar in popular culture, the neoclassical view is one that exhibits a qualified cosmic optimism that is fully cognizant of the legitimate claims made by pessimists. Happiness and awareness of tragedy should not (in fact, cannot) be conceived as contradictories. God saves what can be saved, but God also commiserates regarding what remains regrettable. There is no question in neoclassical theism of eliminating all evil, either instantaneously or in the long run. Each new moment brings with it new possibilities for enjoyment but also new possibilities for evil or at least for a clash of freedoms.

It is not only human beings who exhibit novelty in the neoclassical view, nor only animals, in general. Creativity goes all the way down, thus enabling us to understand suffering that is not caused by misused human freedom, as in clashes of viruses (including corona viruses!) with other protoplasmic stuff. When and how we die, for example, does not depend on the decisions of any single agent but of innumerable creatures, including ourselves, other people, and countless subhuman agents, all interacting in partially chance-like ways. Life is something of a perpetual gamble such that someone who gets cancer should not ask (in classical theistic fashion) why God sent the cancer, in that it is the cancer cells themselves, if not even smaller realities, that have caused the disease. There is also the psychosomatic possibility that it is a person as a whole whose stresses altered the lives of an individual's cells (*BH* 169; *DR* 146; *MVG* 109; *OO* 12–14).

If one believes that creatures' lives can be (or should be!) completely determined by God, then tragedy becomes not only painful but also inexplicable. The hope in neoclassical theism is that tragedy would at least become understandable, and hence somewhat more bearable than it would be within a classical theistic worldview. Nor does it help much for the classical theist to predict that the tragedy will be completely ameliorated "in the end" if there is no end to the creative process and its inherent risks. Having no monopoly on decision making, in the neoclassical view, God is not responsible for tortuous suffering, as God would be on a classical theistic basis.

"To be is to create" (*CS* 1). That is, every concrete individual creates and could not fail to do so. "Creativity" here refers to a certain degree of unpredictability and to a condition of incomplete determination. It means that there are constant additions to the definiteness of reality. This also means that emergence is not a special case but is the general principle of process. This view of universal creativity works against creation ex nihilo because an alleged first state of the world would be unlike anything we can conceive; what it means to be is to prehensively receive influence from the past and then to creatively advance, in however humble a fashion, beyond such influence. This is what it means to exist temporally. What is commonly called "unfreedom" or "determinism" actually refers to an unduly narrow range of alternatives for the existence in question. The *apparent* determinism of inorganic nature is due to the extremely limited degree of creative power found there. Causal conditions can limit what can happen to a range of possibilities such that one can speak legitimately of a hierarchy of degrees of indeterminacy. The past is different from the future at the very least because the latter cannot in principle be known in detail, whereas the former can in principle not only be known but known in detail. This is because the details of the past have actually occurred. We may forget these details, but the fact that they have happened radically distinguishes the past from the future (*WP* 39, 132, 175; *LP* 189; *MVG* 268; *CA* 19, 49; *BH* 151).

God's temporal existence exemplifies the basic characteristics of nature. Growth and development are essential. The power behind an alleged creation ex nihilo is "mysterious" in the pejorative sense of the term in that it refers to needless conundrums brought about by a defective concept of God. Both creatures (who are actually creators in their own right) and Creator are in the grip of the ultimate metaphysical ground: the creative advance into novelty. In fact, we have seen that human beings are part creators of God, not of God's essential nature and existence, but of God's actuality, God's accidental qualities that are the results of human decisions. When human beings do sleezy things, God grieves. Very real human dependence on God is not an entirely one-sided relation, as it is in classical theism. Rather, there is always a divine influence found in human decisions and a human influence in divine ones.

We have seen that the determinist (even in science) is always a theologian by leaving to (classical theistic) omniscience the observations that could give real meaning to the concept of determinism itself. The deterministic God who "does not throw dice" is a poor candidate to explicate the God of religion in that one wonders why someone would yearn for mystical experience if the having or not having of such experience would already have been "in the cards" from eternity. Neoclassical theism is an attempt to rescue theism and religious experience from the wreckage of Newtonian determinism (*BH* 151; *IO* x).

We have seen that a defensible concept of God returns to Plato when interpreted in a dipolar way and when his idea of the World Soul is emphasized. Many of the problems with classical theism are due to Aristotle's interpretation of Plato and the heavy influence Aristotle has had on philosophers who are commonly referred to as "Neoplatonists." Although Aristotle himself obviously did not defend the doctrine of omnipotence, he may have unwittingly aided in the development of this doctrine through his monopolar scheme wherein activity is prioritized over passivity, the formal over the material, and the permanent over the changing. Another consequence of Aristotle's view is that the influence of his indifferent deity made it easier for classical theists to prioritize omnipotence over omnibenevolence, a prioritization that I am arguing violates both the logic of perfection and the intuitions of reflective religious believers in the history of mysticism. One of the oddities of the history of ideas is that, whereas Aristotelian theism died out due to its inability to fulfill religious demands, classical theism as a philosophical/theological view endured. Such endurance occurred because these demands were outsourced to mysticism and popular piety (*AW* 14–15; *IO* 42–45, 51, 53–54, 176, 366; *OO* 8; *PSG* 58–60, 66–67, 73).

Aristotle realized that if God is entirely without contingency, God does not know all that is logically knowable. If God really is omniscient, however, then we have to admit that becoming is not an inferior form of being. By dropping Plato's view of God as the World Soul, with the concomitant notion that soul is self-*moved*, Aristotle was left with gods who were unmoved. This is in contrast to Abraham Heschel's aforementioned neoclassical view of God as the *most* moved mover, a view that is more conducive to understanding the interaction that occurs in mystical experience (*ZF* 6).

Of course, Aristotle was a genius for whom we have much to thank. For example, one has the distinct sense that his thoughts about God could have gone otherwise in that he was perhaps the discoverer of the idea that time is objective modality. It is not human language that introduces possibility and necessity into the universe. Modal concepts like necessity, possibility, and impossibility are built into the temporal structure of the universe in terms of two contrasts: (1) between the direction forward in time and the direction backward in time; and (2) between some things existing only for a relatively short time and some things existing everlastingly for all time. Regarding (1) we should notice that any occasion of experience, including mystical experience, presupposes its causal antecedents, but an earlier experience does not presuppose what comes after it. The two directions in time are modally distinct. The possible is not bound to occur. Hence, the existence of a particular, contingent mystical experience is not inevitable. There is, at best, only a conditional necessity regarding the future. For example, it may be necessary that each of us will die, but how and when we will die are not "in the cards" already. Agnosticism regarding the details of the future is not due to ignorance so much as it is due to the contingent nature of the future itself. And regarding (2) it can be asserted that no everlasting existence, as in God's existence, could be contingent. If some mystics speak as if God is strictly necessary in every respect, this should be seen as a defective *interpretation* of mystical experience encouraged by the assumption that necessity is in every respect superior to contingency (*AD* 141).

The necessary as such is extremely abstract and lacking in definite content. The necessary as such is the common factor found in all contingent, concrete reality. By contrast, we are indeed agents with respect to our descendants, but we are patients with respect to our ancestors, including previous moments of experience in our own lives. It is this patiency status that Aristotle denies to deity and that is (disastrously) denied by classical theists as well. Neoclassical theists, in partial contrast, try to analogically exalt both agency and patiency. Whitehead may very well be correct in *Adventures of Ideas* that the doctrine of divine omnipotence may be due to a misguided attempt to emulate the coercive power of Caesar and other despotic rulers. But it should not escape our notice that, in addition to the cultural and political roots of the concept of omnipotence, there are also conceptual roots found in certain monopolar preferences that are not defensible merely because they have been around for a long while.

The defects in the doctrine of divine omnipotence are not unrelated to the steady decline not only of classical theism but of theism itself, since the time of the Enlightenment. The most virulent atheists actually *hate* theism, at least in part because of the belief that the worst aspects of human misery have either been sent by, or at least permitted by, an omnipotent God. But some of the greatest advances in the history of philosophy have been made when thinkers listen respectfully to skeptics, as when Kant listened to Hume. That is, the challenge offered to classical theism by religious skeptics might commendably force theists to pay more careful attention to terms such as "absoluteness," "omnipotence," 'infinite," etcetera, than has been paid to them historically by either classical theists or religious skeptics. The (over) reaction of religious skeptics is, after all, understandable given the defects in classical theism, especially those defects that are the result of the doctrine of omnipotence (*RSP* 13).

The way forward involves, at the very least, an escape from the false dilemma exploited by Jean-Paul Sartre and other famous atheists: *Either* omnipotent divine power settles everything, and so is responsible for every evil as well as every good, such that human beings have no freedom whatsoever, *or* we have all of the freedom, hence there is no God, or at least there is no God worth worshipping. Neoclassical theism provides a way around this false dilemma by showing that both horns of the dilemma are defective. Very often those who allege to have "seen through" religion have only trashed one of its expressions, and not one that helps us to better understand mystical experience (*WVR* 15–16).

It should be noted that the dipolar concept of God that I am defending, a concept that is conducive to a critique of omnipotence because of the introduction of passivity and change into God, is not to be confused with Nicholas of Cusa's famous or infamous "coincidence of opposites." It must be admitted that Cusa may have pointed toward a dipolar view of God, but he does not really get us there. (Hartshorne, relying on the interpretation of Rudolph Otto, thinks that Meister Eckhart came much closer to neoclassical theism than Cusa.) The active and passive (and other) contraries or correlatives are not really coincident, if what it means to be coincident is to be identical or indistinguishable. To speak of elements in contrasting pairs as identical *does* lead to contradiction, which dipolar theists want to avoid at all costs. To say that both activity and passivity are in God is not to say that they are the same in God. In fact, the contrast between the elements in the two poles is not less but incredibly *greater* in God. This is because God's activity exceeds that of all other activities because God influences all (not some or most) realities; and God's passivity exceeds that of all other passive powers because God is influenced by all (not some or most) realities. Neoclassical dual transcendence, rather than classical monotranscendence, makes the process concept of God ironically much "bigger" than the half-sized God of classical theism. This insight is worth emphasizing when the neoclassical critique of omnipotence is attacked by classical (and other) theists (*CS* 237; *IO* 92, 108; WIG 522).

The neoclassical critique of omnipotence is not unrelated to major concerns in feminist theology in that some of the worst aspects of classical theism concern its deification of a tribal patriarch whose every whim is law (see Christ, *She Who Changes*; Case-Winters, *God's Power*; Davaney, *Feminism and Process Thought*). Even when classical theism avoids its most extreme forms, as in Manichean and Gnostic horror of the earth and women, it nonetheless tends to deemphasize the tender qualities that are most admirable in human beings, such as love and compassion. Although these qualities often resurface in popular religion, they tend not to find a logical home in the classical concept of God. For example, such qualities are often instantiated in popular versions of Catholicism in Mary, if not in God the Father. These qualities are nonetheless crucial in what mystics experience in and with God (*PSG* 331–34; *DL* 399; *AD* 147).

In many cultures around the world, masculinity is associated with mastery and other versions of active power, stability, and absoluteness, that is, with what I have throughout the book called monopolarity. Equally prevalent is the tendency to have a deflationary view of traits historically associated with femininity, such as passivity and fluidity, becoming and relativity. The viciously overly masculine traits located in the classical concept of God, which are very much at the root of the concept of omnipotence, tend to hide not merely the fact that the supposedly feminine traits are legitimate facets of the logic of perfection but also the idea that the traits traditionally associated with femininity, especially responsive love, are in reality *superior to* traits like rigidity and absoluteness when these traits stray from their legitimate home in the divine existence and (disastrously) migrate to divine actuality.

Although God is not indebted to us for divine existence, God is indeed indebted to us in divine actuality. We can escape scorn from classical theists regarding this claim by noting that because God as omnibenevolent is not conceited or envious, there is no divine motive to escape or deny this indebtedness. It is envious human beings who have a motive for such an escape when they feel threatened by a critique of divine omnipotence.

I would like to be clear that it is not only the concept of omnipotence that needs clarification but that of omniscience as well, although in neither case should the concepts be trashed altogether. Ordinary language presupposes both theism and the concept of omniscience. We cannot avoid an idea of "the truth," even if only by way of our falsification with assurance. That is, some views (in science, politics, etc.) are simply false. But to falsify with assurance presupposes the truth as an ideal limit, and "the truth" presupposes an omniscient standard. To say, as we often do, that we cannot be absolutely certain about X is to say that *we* are not omniscient or infallible, as would be the greatest conceivable: To be is to be known by God. Each of us is vaguely what divine omniscience is distinctly (*LP* 152–54).

But to say that God is omniscient is *not* to subscribe to the classical theistic idea that all truth is known by the divine timelessly. This doctrine would make creaturely freedom a mere illusion; however, we *do* have experience of having made free choices. According to classical theists, omniscience does not mean divine actualization of all that happens, only eternal divine (fore)knowledge of what happens. This stance involves paradox in that it is by no means clear how that which is not eternally actualized can be eternally known. By way of neoclassical contrast, "knowledge of all things" means knowledge of each thing as it is: the merely possible as merely possible, the future as future, and the past as past. Thus, "knowledge of all things" means an absence of error, but it does *not* necessarily mean a "knowledge" of future possibilities as already actualized. We can understand that we simply cannot understand the detailed content of omniscience; at the same time, we can understand an impossibility as such. A future contingency would not be such if it were known already as an actuality (*WP* 34–35; *LP* 152–54, 157, 159; MMEJ 114; *IO* 83; *CA* 60; *CE* 87, 90; *CS* 137, 166).

Predestination is a nightmare for theodicy, for our sense that our actions count for something in the world, and for any hope for a better future. We must rest content with the ideas that the definite past can be known as well as the partially indefinite future as precisely that. The point is not that God is first ignorant and then knowing, but rather that first there is no definite fact of any kind to know, then there is the fact that *can* be known. Here the critique of omnipotence and that of omniscience intersect. Trying to apprehend the future differs essentially from trying to apprehend the past, on the asymmetrical view of time fostered by neoclassical theism. Hence, mysticism need not, ought not, be tied to any sort of fatalism. God *is* omniscient, as the great mystics attest, but not in the classical theistic sense. We need to get out of the (classical theistic) habit of thinking of the future in terms of the Doris Day cliché: What will be, will be. The past is settled in ways that the future is not. Ideal divine power and ideal divine knowledge need not be distorted in the classical theistic ways of thinking of these concepts.

Just as we ought to avoid the problems associated with belief in divine omnipotence, so also we ought not move from a legitimate concern that God be world-inclusive to a pantheistic conclusion, say as found in Plotinus or Sankara, on Hartshorne's (in contrast to Henri Bergson's) interpretation of these thinkers. Although the thesis that Plotinus was a pantheist is controversial, it is nonetheless safe to say that there is a dramatic dominance of unity over diversity in his thought. "The One" indicates a negation of the manifold; and divine foreknowledge of the future in Plotinus ensures that there is a block universe articulated in his thought that operates both spatially and temporally. Further, the World Soul in his thought operates as a lesser deity, which renders his thought susceptible to monopolarity. Granted, without unity we could not understand diversity, but the reverse is also true, contra Plotinus's monopolar view. Likewise regarding the relationship between the abstract and the concrete, the intellectual and the bodily, etcetera. One of the ironies of Plotinus's thought is that, despite his scorn for the physical, such that embodiment in all its forms is denied of God, his symbols and analogies for God rely more on physical things (such as objects that are seen or smelled) than on more obviously spiritual things (such as love and memory) (*IO* 58–59, 312; *PSG* 211–12, 215–16, 219–21, 223–24).

Quite apart from what Plotinus's views may have been, there is the question to be asked of pantheism regarding why diversity is more illusory than unity, why mutability is more profane than permanence. On the dipolar view opposed to both pantheism and divine omnipotence, there are two contrasting, yet complementary, aspects of deity: a unitary, immutable aspect (existence) and a supremely diverse and changing aspect (actuality). That is, diversity and change are not merely the results of our ignorance. These defects are crucial to consider if only because once the defects in an omnipotent God are exposed, some thinkers try to rescue theism by turning to pantheism. One of the problems with this move is that change is not an illusion; it is experienced as *real*. One does not arrive at unmitigated monism through experience but through certain (mistaken) intellectual categories and prejudices, the monopolar preeminent among these. If one understandably sees problems with the externality of the world to God found in classical theism with its omnipotent God, pantheism is not the only theistic alternative. It must be admitted, however, that the concept of divine world-inclusiveness itself is not the problem, as Spinoza showed when he delivered the first significant blow to classical theism, an attack from which it has not recovered. However, Spinoza also showed a preference for necessity over contingency; indeed, the latter does not exist, as he sees things. Along with monopolarists, in general, including classical theists that Spinoza would otherwise want to criticize, pantheists continually avail themselves of the pole they deny. How could one move through the world on a daily basis without presupposing temporal change and the fact that some events occur contingently? (*PSG* 30, 165, 169, 173, 176, 189–90, 193, 195–96, 208–9, 326–28, 411; *NT* 17; *CS* 270; *CA* 44; *AD* 173–75; *AW* 12).

It is common for pantheists to make a distinction between the one, necessary substance and the many, contingent modes of the substance. Here the pantheist is close to Hartshorne's distinction between necessary existence and contingent actuality, but the pantheist then tends to speak in terms of necessary modes or modifications of reality. But what exactly is a necessary modification or qualification of reality if not the essence of the thing all over again? The supposed flourishing of mysticism in pantheism is just as misleading as its alleged flourishing in classical theism. The famous saying of Spinoza that if we love God, we cannot expect God to love us in return is contradicted by the testimony of mystics in the Abrahamic religions, including Judaism. "The God of the philosophers" is just as much a problem in pantheism as it is in classical theism. God does not lose perfection if passively affected in a loving way by the creatures. Once again, it is not world-inclusiveness per se that is the problem, rather it is world-inclusiveness tied to monopolarity that causes the difficulties.

What is most attractive about pantheism is the idea that there is an unbreakable union with God, but the "union" in question is destructive of divine personhood and of any sense of gratitude. That is, pantheism seems to be tied to an amoral naturalism, despite the fact that at times pantheists talk about "God." Pantheists are also to be thanked for defending the idea that one cannot escape from this (the only) world. The parts are indeed contained in a mighty whole that cannot be avoided. Just as tiny batteries can be arranged in a series so as to accumulate a high voltage, so also feeble psychic flashings can be compounded into something much more considerable. But calling the world "God" does not amount to much if the whole in question is impersonal and hence uncaring. Pantheists might commit to a graduated, panpsychist view of affectivity/mentality, but they do not commit to the supreme affectivity/mentality experienced by the mystics (*PSG* 374).

There is more than a verbal flourish found in the distinction between "God is all things" and "God includes all things (via omniscience and omnibenevolence)." The former points to pantheism, the latter to panentheism (the belief that all is *in* God, again via God's knowledge and love). It is true that Spinoza's necessitarianism rescued the ontological argument from the assumption that it could be used only in the context of classical theism, but its use by neoclassical theists is much more fruitful than its use in Spinoza in that neoclassical theists, rather than pantheists, get us closer to an adequate conception of divine perfection as personal and all-loving and (at least in divine actuality) contingent. Strict necessitarianism is hardly a religious doctrine in the sense that it trivializes the experiences of the mystics. Hence there is a need for nuance when all versions of divine world-inclusiveness are mistakenly seen as versions of pantheism (*RSP* 120). That is, we ignore the panentheist option at our peril.

Chapter 4

Abstract and Concrete

It will be the purpose of the present chapter to explicate the relationship between very abstract thinking in philosophy about the concept of, and existence of, God, on the one hand, and the concrete experience of God found in the mystics, on the other. The most famous example of the former is found in the ontological argument, one version of which can be stated as follows:

1. Modality of existence is a predicate (in that saying that X exists necessarily or contingently or impossibly, rather than merely saying that X exists, is surely to predicate something significant about X).

2. There are three (and only three) modes of existence: (a) impossible (cannot exist); (b) contingent (may or may not exist); and (c) necessary (must exist).

3. 2b contradicts the logic of perfection (which is Saint Anselm's great discovery in chapter 3 of *Proslogion*) because a being that existed only contingently in some circumstances but not others would not be the greatest conceivable.

4. Therefore, the existence of God—the greatest conceivable being or a perfect being—is either impossible or necessary (preliminary conclusion).

5. The existence of God is not impossible (which is the conclusion from other theistic arguments and from mystical experience itself).

6. Therefore, the existence of God is necessary; or, at the very least, the nonexistence of God is inconceivable (ultimate conclusion).

One of the most common mistakes that occurs when interpreting the ontological argument is to assume that what must be inseparable from the concept of God is not only the bare *existence* of God but also God's full *actuality*. There is nothing arcane about this mistake in that, if philosophy's most important function is to clarify the religious question (as Charles Hartshorne thinks), then as much clarity as possible regarding the concept of God is crucial. In facing first and last and cosmic things there are the twin dangers of fanatical faith and cynical despair. Regarding mysticism, in particular, these twin dangers surface in terms of either unquestioned acceptance of whatever is claimed within a specific religious tradition, on the one hand, and skepticism regarding, or sheer indifference toward, the very idea of mystical experience, on the other (*AD* 20, 38; *DR* 87; *EA* 109–10).

In ordinary cases of existence, not only is the particular concrete actuality contingent but also it is contingent whether there is any existence embodying the predicate. On the basis of the ontological argument, however, God's existence is necessary or inevitably actualized, although the particularities of God's actualization at any particular time are contingent and open to human (and other) influence. In different terms, in our case existence and actuality are contingent, whereas in the divine case only actuality is contingent in that God's necessary existence means that divine existence is always somehow actualized, the details being contingent. Nothing concretely actual can be necessary, which helps us to locate the modal status of mystical experience (*IO* 98–100; *PPR* 339–40).

We have seen that neoclassical theists are in agreement with classical theists that to be God would mean being the universal *subject* of knowing in that all knowing presupposes God as omniscient. But neoclassical theists also claim that God is the universal *object* of knowing in that all knowing presupposes God as objective standard. This latter claim narrows the gap between the experience claimed by, or on behalf of, the mystic and our own quotidian experience. Of the three forms of modality, it is *contingency* that characterizes human experience of, or knowledge of, God. This is because such experience or knowing is, in our case, neither *necessary* nor *impossible*. Or better, the point to the ontological argument is that, although it is impossible to conceive the nonexistence of God, it *is* possible to conceive of the possible existence of God. Further, mystics claim to *experience* God, which is not surprising given the conclusion of the ontological argument to the effect that *if* God's existence is conceived, it has to be conceived as existent. Although having a *concept* of God and having *experience* of God are quite different things, the two are compatible. In neoclassical theism, a defense of the ontological argument makes it possible to understand the complementary roles of the conceptual and the experiential in the religious life (*ZF* 95, 107; *AD* 46, 172; *CS* 171).

The idea that the divine existence is entirely extraconceptual and must be experienced, rather than conceived, is extreme, as is the opposite view that the divine actuality can be deduced via logical argumentation. Of course, some thinkers claim that one cannot have a concept of God without religious experience. If this claim were true, then we would all (theists, atheists, and agnostics) have to be mystics before we could discourse about the concept of God! This seems hyperbolic. In a different sense, however, an appreciation of the concept of God itself *is* a religious experience, say when one achieves the Anselmian realization that God's existence could not be contingent. Indeed, all thought about God is close to the ontological argument in that, if we really are thinking about God, we could not be thinking about merely an additional fact about the world (*MMEJ* 117–18; *MVG* 274; *PCH* 665, 713).

To grasp what the concept of God is one needs no special historical reference or special perceptual (mystical) experience, only the intelligence to be able to understand the most universal aspects of any kind of history or experience. God is a datum for human thinking *and* feeling, with the former highlighted in the ontological argument, while the latter is the stuff of mystical experience. One of the advantages of Anselm's way of thinking is that it can liberate us from traditional ways of thinking about God. "Greatness" refers to whatever properties it would be better to have than not to have, and it is by no means clear that thinkers in previous ages have avoided mistakes regarding what properties the greatest being would have. Monopolizing freedom and power might not be great (*MVG* 303; *AD* 202).

We have seen that if God exists necessarily and ubiquitously, then as a result it follows that *all* experience must have God as a datum at least implicitly, even if the datum may not be amenable to clear or easy detection. It is the concreteness of divine actuality, in partial contrast to the abstractness of divine existence, that is difficult to appreciate, although the great mystics make this task easier. The perfection of God is the heart of religious thought *and* feeling, feeling *and* thought. In Whiteheadian terms, the ontological argument (despite Alfred North Whitehead's own skittishness regarding the argument) deals with God as primordial, whereas mystical experience affects God's consequent nature (or better, nature*s*, in that there is a partially new consequent nature at every moment) (*MVG* 15, 315).

As a result of the ontological argument we can say the following: We must be contradicting ourselves when we deny the existence of God. This argument is a way of making clear the intuition of deity in mystical awareness. God is a reality that either always exists or never has existed, on the basis of the ontological argument. Religious experience warrants the intellectual effort to understand the concept of God just as neoclassical efforts to understand the concept of God provide warrant for taking claims to mystical experience seriously. In this regard it is worth noting that the agreement of concepts and percepts is the test of *all* truth, including truth in religion. Mystical experience provides, I am claiming, a percept of the World Whole of which we are parts (*AD* 60; *CA* 215; *LP* 106).

It is often objected to the ontological argument that we normally do not analyze our thoughts to find out what exists. But questions regarding existence are at least sometimes analytic. For example, we can know by conceptual analysis that a round square cannot exist, that Abraham Lincoln could not vote to impeach Donald Trump, etcetera. The objector is, however, correct that the effort to find out what exists contingently cannot be determined analytically. Anything definitely conceivable is either contingent or necessary, and, if necessary, necessary positively or negatively (impossible). If contingency of existence is shown (à la Anselm) not to apply in the case of a perfect being, then the key question is whether the positively necessary existence is conceivable. Pervasive testimony from various religious traditions and from every historical epoch of mystical experience offers strong support for the claim that God's existence is at least possible. It must be admitted that disproving atheism does not itself establish the conceivability or logical possibility of God. Once again, this reinforces the importance of this pervasive testimony (*AD* 64–65, 74, 125–26).

A monolithic version of empiricism popular today would discredit both theistic metaphysics *and* the sort of experience claimed by the mystic. The thesis of the present chapter is that the intellectual approach to God found in the ontological argument and mystical experience mutually reinforce each other. These are two ways in which God can be "verified" by finite (or better, fragmentary) human beings. It has long been noted that the different rational arguments for the existence of God mutually support each other in that where one is weak, the other is strong. But I am trying to accomplish something a bit different by urging the mutual reinforcement intellect and experience can give to each other in the religious life, a neoclassical version of something attempted (only partially successfully) in the medieval synthesis on a classical theistic basis (*AD* 178; *CS* 280).

Of course, it might be objected that if we really did have a coherent insight into the nature of perfection, which is what the ontological argument requires, then we would have no need of the argument in that we would know that God exists as a result of the mystical experience that made the insight possible. This objection is tempting, but it should be emphasized that the conceivability of God that the ontological argument requires is a logical conceivability that avoids the contradictions found in classical theism. The argument does *not* require that we have an intuition into divine actuality such as that experienced by various mystics. That is, there is no need to beg the question in favor of the ontological argument by *requiring* the sort of experience mystics claim to have (*MVG* 79; *FVRS* 238).

One advantage in thinking of the ontological argument and mystical experience together is that we can be free of the familiar misconception that this argument moves illegitimately from the abstract to the concrete. Nothing could be further from the truth. The necessary existence of God that is the result of the argument is itself very abstract. The argument tells us about the abstract divine existence (which is either necessary or impossible), but not about concrete actuality, which must be either felt in mystical experience or, in Wittgensteinian fashion, shown but not said. The divine existence discussed in the ontological argument is unspeakably less than God as actual. The more concrete can never follow from the evidence in the less concrete. Concrete actuality is always more than bare existence. *That* the divine nature exists is one thing, *how* this nature is concretely actualized is another. Granted, classical theists who defend the ontological argument conflate the move from God's perfection to God's necessary existence with the move from abstract existence to concrete actuality, but there is no good reason for such conflation, from a neoclassical point of view. Or again, to affirm abstractly that God is all-knowing is one thing, but to claim to know the contents of divine knowing is something quite different (*AD* 24, 41, 228; *CS* 258).

The doctrine of *haecceity* from the Middle Ages (especially in Duns Scotus) points toward an important truth about concrete actuality: its idiosyncratic, unique, very particular quality, in contrast to abstract truths discussed in mathematics and physics and philosophy. God is abstractly perfect *and* perfect in concrete details, which are experienced by mystics. The great achievement of the ontological argument is the conclusion that we cannot conceive perfection as nonexistent, but this conclusion does not tell us *how* a perfect being reacts at any particular moment to the current actual occasions in their own concreteness (*IO* 104).

The point to the ontological argument is not that existing is better than not existing, hence the unsurpassable being must exist. It is rather that a being who cannot be conceived not to exist is better than one who can be conceived not to exist. Of course, this argument assumes that we *can* develop a concept of God that is possible, in contrast to the classical theistic view wherein there are contradictions at every turn, as has been argued above. Do we really know what we mean when we talk about "God"? The debate between classical theism and neoclassical theism is an attempt to clarify such meaning so that we can also understand what it would mean to *experience* such a being. Or again, although the ontological argument deals with the *concept* of God as a formal, necessary truth, the concept of God used by classical theists is quite different from that used by neoclassical theists in the effort to accommodate both divine concrete actuality and human experience of such (*EA* 38, 41; *PCH* 572).

The neoclassical stance and its relationship with mysticism can be enhanced, I think, by appeal to two distinctions within concrete experience. It is common to have mystical experience referred to as "direct" experience of the divine, in contrast to an "indirect" approach to God by way of rational argumentation. And it is often assumed that "direct" is a rough synonym of "unmediated" (or "immediate") and that both are meant to contrast with their opposites: "indirect" and "mediated." However, John Smith, the great defender of the concept of experience developed by major figures in the history of American philosophy, insightfully distinguishes between the indirect-direct distinction and the mediated-unmediated (immediate) distinction. By separating these two distinctions, I claim, we can better understand the major differences between the classical theistic account of mystical experience and that typically found in the works of neoclassical theists.

The distinction between indirect and direct experience is that between experience that relies on rational inference and that which does not, respectively. By way of contrast, the distinction between mediate experience and immediate experience is that between experience that requires some medium in order for the encounter between the experiencer and that which is experienced to occur, on the one hand, and experience that is (if this were possible) medium-free, on the other, respectively.

Putting the terms under consideration here in a position matrix, four options (not two) are possible. It should be noted that this position matrix is not meant to be logically exhaustive, as are many of the position matrices used by Hartshorne, but rather to open up certain differences between rival accounts of mystical experience that might not otherwise come to light.

	unmediated (immediate)	mediated
indirect	A	B
direct	C	D

It is hard to know what to make of (A), at least if the experience in question is religious in character. What would it mean to have a religious experience that was not in any way dependent on a medium (not even on a linguistic or conceptual medium), on the one hand, and yet be an experience that was the result of rational inference, on the other? Not much promise is to be found here. Quite understandably, this is not what theists (whether classical or neoclassical) mean by mystical experience.

Further, it is not likely that theists (whether classical or neoclassical) would see mystical experience along the lines of (B). Nonetheless, those theists who defend the ontological argument place a great deal of importance on (B) because they think that through the media of language and logic one can legitimately infer the existence of God, or at least the unintelligibility of the nonexistence of God. But theists tend not to identify consideration of this argument with mystical experience, even if this and other arguments for the existence of God must be rooted in *some* way in experience (*AD* 230).

The debate with which the present section of the chapter is concerned is that between defenders of (C) and (D). The classical theistic attempt to understand mystical experience is usually along the lines of (C) in that mystics are alleged not only to experience God directly (i.e., not merely by way of rational inference) but also without the media of language, logic, or even embodiment. This view of mystical experience (hereafter: mystical experience-1) goes hand in glove with the classical theistic concept of God because this lack of mediation by language, logic, and embodiment is possible only when God is seen as a *super*natural being who transcends time and history (and hence language, logic, and embodiment). The mediating influences of *this* natural world are transcended by the mystics, it is alleged by classical theists, when spiritual contact is made with *that* world that exists beyond this one. To cite a representative example, the mystical *theology* of John of the Cross, heavily reliant on the Thomistic concept of God, favors this sort of understanding of mystical experience-1.

I will not say much more about (C), which has been widely discussed by scholars. But I do hope to reflect light on (C) in the more detailed analysis I will offer of (D). In this regard there is a crucial background distinction that is needed between the sacred and the profane. Robert Neville is a noted scholar who helps to explicate Smith's point of view on this topic, which is very much supportive of the neoclassical view. Not all dimensions of life are holy, despite the doctrine of divine omnipresence explicated above in terms of the World Soul. Many aspects of life are profane, in contrast to those aspects that push against or break boundaries, e.g., birth and death, coming of age, sickness, and tragedy. Holy or sacred events give rise to questions about ultimate reality and the very meaning of human life. These events lead one to wonder not only about one's own *telos* but also about general questions of contingency (and necessity) as such. The religious dimension of life acknowledges these questions and helps us to respond to them.

We should be skeptical of mystical experience if this refers to mystical experience-1. Here it might be better to talk instead of the religious dimension *of* experience (or mystical experience-2). The immediate experience of God alleged in mystical experience-1—that is, (C)—would be unmediated by any signs, hence it is unlikely if we could ever know we had it! This is because, if we had such an experience, we would not be able to distinguish it from any other immediate experience. That is, the prehension of God in experience comes through the use of signs. Although these signs are fallible, they are nonetheless needed as media through which God can be present to us.

The religious dimension of experience, or mystical experience-2 (in contrast to a "religious experience" that transcends mediating nature, language, logic, and embodiment—i.e., mystical experience-1), involves an encounter with the presence of the holy, a presence famously described by Wordsworth in "Tintern Abbey" that had a profound effect on Hartshorne:

> And I have felt
> A presence that disturbs me with the joy
> Of elevated thoughts; a sense sublime
> Of something far more deeply interfused,
> Whose dwelling is the light of setting suns,
> And the round ocean and the living air,
> And the blue sky, and in the mind of man:
> A motion and a spirit, that impels
> All thinking things, all objects of all thought,
> And rolls through all things.

It is crucial to realize that the presence in question is not something merely human. Rather, it is *encountered* as something that transcends the human, even if the human is enveloped by it. Further, the presence in question seems to burst upon us in an instant (*exaiphnes*), as in the experience of Beauty itself in Plato's *Symposium* (210e).

Intellectually honest religious believers do not have to accept everything at face value, but they do have to accept what they find. Many individuals encounter a holy presence *in* the world. These encounters, however, are always experiences both of God or the holy as well as of something else at the same time. That is, these direct experiences are never absolutely immediate. The medium through which religious encounter occurs is thus intimately related to the reality it discloses. This should not be surprising to those theists who are Christian in that in this incarnational tradition (which grew out of Jewish earthiness) it has historically been believed that the best clue we are likely to get regarding the divine nature comes through a being who is fully human, and hence characterized by the linguistic, the logical, and the embodied.

Further, the special times (Wordsworthian "spots of time") when mystical experience-2 is likely to occur are, although extraordinary, nonetheless thoroughly natural rather than supernatural (see Griffin, *Reenchantment*). The special times in question include those that involve initiation, vocation, marriage, birth, suffering, and death. These events elicit in many people a very real experience of being judged, or at least of being watched. And these experiences often force those who have them to conclude that the experiences of ordinary life, when the "world is too much with us," as Wordsworth put it, are banal and that one must come to terms with life in its *depth*. God is not so much constituted out of these crisis events as experienced *within* them.

It should not be assumed that (C) or mystical experience-1 better accounts for mystical experience than (D) or mystical experience-2 because it is time honored and has tested positively against the testimony of a long line of famous mystics. Actually (C) has failed the test. To take the same prominent example that was mentioned earlier, although the *theology* of John of the Cross conforms to (C), his mystical *poetry*, which comes closer than theory to the concrete reality of the mystical experience that he was trying to convey, conforms to (D). Indeed, most of the figures in the history of Abrahamic mysticism have at some point or other complained in a Pascal-like way about the God of the philosophers or theologians.

I should be more precise: their complaint concerns the God of classical theism as traditionally defended by many philosophers and theologians.

John of the Cross's poetry, in contrast to his theology, involves bodily (even sexual) metaphors for the intimate contact with the divine. And although he (along with Saint Teresa of Ávila) at times describes his experience of God as ineffable, even this claim is mediated by language and is artfully contradicted by his (and her) many writings. In fact, John of the Cross is the national poet of Spain, indicating that mediation through language used at a sophisticated level and driven by passion is not only not at odds with mystical experience, it is its lifeblood.

The logic of the term "revelation" requires relationship. What would it mean to speak of divine revelation if there were no one to whom the divine was revealed? Divine presence is always disclosed through a medium (not necessarily in the "spiritualist" sense) that makes possible the relationship between the God who is revealed and the person to whom this God is revealed. God is experienced as present in both natural events and persons, hence attentiveness to these events and persons involves an intimate relation with God. By way of contrast, the classical theistic God (the "God of the philosophers" castigated by many mystics) is unmoved and unchanged by creatures, and hence is not internally related to them, contra the claims of the great mystics. The experience of intimacy with the divine is, in principle, ruled out on the classical theistic view.

Criticism of the supernaturalistic assumptions of classical theists, and of the negative effects these assumptions have on attempts to understand mystical experience, does not lead to an invidious egalitarianism wherein each natural being is as likely as the next to best understand the religious dimension of experience. Just as some beings run faster than others, play the piano better than others, etcetera, so also some beings (e.g., Moses, Jesus, Mohammed, Teresa of Ávila, George Fox, Dorothy Day, and many others) seem to be especially suited both to experience this dimension and to report on such experience. Their own bodies, the historical conditions of their age, and the language they use to report their experiences to others are all mediating influences.

The Judeo-Christian tradition has been especially insistent on the idea that God is encountered in historical events: the Exodus, the Incarnation. Every disclosure of God is also simultaneously a disclosure of something else. This is in contrast to (C), where we supposedly have immediate experience of God in a timeless unity beyond all media. Smith is helpful in his emphasis on the idea that to say that God is revealed through a historical medium is to say that God is directly, but not immediately, experienced. Further, in mystical experience God is encountered, not inferred. God is not immediately prehended because God is known only in and through the medium; yet God need not be inferred if present in the medium experienced.

We are all familiar with how a self can be present to another self and yet require a medium through which the disclosure takes place. This provides us with evidence regarding how personal experience of God takes place. It is a mistaken view that suggests that we first encounter a collection of actions, spoken words, gestures, and facial expressions and *then* infer that there is a person who is encountered. We do not so much infer the presence of another person as we acknowledge the existence of another person at the beginning of the encounter. Similarly, a revelatory situation is one where God is directly present and encountered but not immediately known as such (*CS* 169).

The medium of the suffering servant has historically been fecund ground for the religious element in experience, whether in Isaiah, the Christian scriptures, or in personal lives today. *Here* we encounter God, in contrast to the utter denial of divine historicity in the Docetists, the Gnostics, and sadly to a great extent in classical theists. Because the experience of God is mediated through signs and symbols, it is amenable to (or better, requires) rational interpretation of some sort. And because we are such insistently intellectual beings, we need to make the experience of God intelligible in some way, whether in terms of mystical experience-1 or mystical experience-2. But only the latter comes close to success in this regard.

The great mystics implicitly admit this. John of the Cross, for example, tries to make his experience of God intelligible to us through now famous symbols: dark night, flight to the beloved, intimate union, and the living flame of love. And Teresa of Ávila's experience of God is conveyed to us through the medium of marble by Bernini in his famous statue in Rome. Without the media of rational thought, language, poetic symbols, stone, etcetera, there would be no mystical experience, nor, a fortiori, would there be reports of such.

The view I am defending does not depend on but it is nonetheless very much consistent with the view that suggests that there are severe problems with the fideistic strict separation of faith and reason. Rather than such a strict separation, we should instead speak of relatively unreflective faith, which nonetheless presupposes *some* minimal understanding, and a more reflective, intellectualized faith. Not even the content of the former is mere gibberish in that it is mediated by intelligible language and *some* concepts, however inadequately they are understood. All faith is incipient understanding, as Smith argues. And mediation through language and concepts is unavoidable.

But such mediation provides no good reasons to deny that many people experience a disclosure of a divine reality that is not reducible to our own. That is, mystical experience-2 or (D) is a *living* reality.

Defenders of mystical experience-1 or (C) will no doubt have several objections. One of these can be stated in terms of the following argument:

1. Mystical experience is something quite remarkable.

2. But mystical experience as explicated by neoclassical theists is no longer anything remarkable.

3. Therefore, there is something defective about the neoclassical theistic explication of mystical experience.

The argument is valid (i.e., the conclusion follows from the premises), but is it sound in the sense that the premises are true? I think not because, although premise (1) is defensible, premise (2) is not.

Direct experience of the divine is remarkable at the very least because it requires true solitude, which is rare, and a level of concentration not found in ordinary experience. This is why I have claimed above that mystical experience is extraordinary even if it is not supernatural. We have seen that the most readily detectable realities are those that are sometimes present in an insistent way and sometimes not, as in redness or pain. What is always given, however, tends to escape notice. For example, notice how difficult it is for most people to feel the feeling of individual cells in their bodies, unless, perhaps, localized pain alerts them to cellular feelings, as when cell walls are ripped open through intense heat.

I am pointing toward the remarkable, yet perfectly human, ability of the mystics to directly experience God, albeit mediately. The difference between mystics and others is not an absolute one. The former are consciously aware of experiencing what we all experience implicitly. Most human beings "prehend" God in the sense that they grasp implicitly meaning in the world. They feel as an inchoate object of experience that they are parts of a meaningful whole, that there is a concrete fact of relatedness between themselves and the divine personal force at work in the cosmos. But the mystics have an explicit, remarkable, conscious apprehension of this relatedness. They exhibit an acuity, as it were, that the rest of humanity possesses only potentially. In short, I think that the objection can be countered.

Consider the famous example of mystical experience reported by Thomas Merton in his classic *The Seven Storey Mountain*. Merton is like most mystics who are classical theists in complaining about the God of the philosophers, but what he says about mystical experience actually supports the case for process or neoclassical theism. His experience of God, elicited by the *sounds* of a children's choir and the *sight* of the raised chalice at the Eucharist during a visit to a church in Cuba, struck him like a thunderclap and with a light that was so bright that it neutralized every lesser experience. Here we are reminded of many similar experiences described in William James's equally famous classic *The Varieties of Religious Experience*. Yet Merton goes out of his way to inform us that the light was in a certain sense ordinary. It was a light (and this most of all was what took his breath away) that was offered to all and there was nothing at all strange about it. Further, the God experienced by Merton (despite his Thomism) was anything but an Unmoved Mover or Pure Actuality. Rather, the God of the mystics is the Most Moved Mover (to once again use Abraham Heschel's phrase) with a boundless potential to enter into relations with a person of faith.

One of the hallmarks of process or neoclassical theism is its opposition to the Boethian *eternity* of God, wherein God is seen as transcending time and history altogether. Instead, process or neoclassical theists defend divine *everlastingness* or *sempiternity*, wherein God is seen not as outside of time and history but as omnitemporal. God exists necessarily in the sense that the divine being could not not exist at any time. I used to think that belief in divine everlastingness radically distinguished process or neoclassical theism from other theisms, but a significant number of analytic philosophers who are theists (e.g., Richard Swinburne) have been won over to the cause of divine everlastingness, which perhaps indicates that the patient efforts of process or neoclassical theists to plant the seedlings of divine everlastingness in the minds of philosophers and theologians have started to bear significant fruit. Unfortunately, it is still widely assumed, however, by both theists and religious skeptics alike, that to believe in God is to believe in a supernatural realm.

The concept of God I am defending includes the idea that God experiences our prayers and sufferings; mysticism consists in becoming aware of God doing this. However, it also consists in the awareness that our prayers and sufferings that are prehended or grasped by God are transformed or transfigured (in that they are incorporated into the life of an omnibenevolent and omniscient Being-in-Becoming), and it is this transformed or transfigured character of prayer and suffering that the mystic experiences (see Suchocki, "Charles Hartshorne") and that gives the mystic's life a certain lightheartedness and ludic quality, as I have argued in *Contemporary Athletics and Ancient Greek Ideals*.

The mysticism I am talking about is also evidenced in the common aesthetic experience of the world as neither monotonous nor chaotic (i.e., as in some sense beautiful, despite its obvious flaws). The religious dimension of aesthetic experience in general involves an appreciation for the harmonies and intensities of everyday experience as parts of a mighty (yet not omnipotent) Whole. This appreciation itself is a type of beauty that is more sublime than pretty, a source of excess that is captured artistically by Bernini in his aforementioned famous statue of Teresa of Ávila in ecstasy. On the process or neoclassical interpretation, however, the literal ecstasy here does *not* refer to displacement in some supernatural realm, *sub specie aeternitatis*, as if that were possible. Rather, it refers to a detachment from our normal place, characterized by the usual tendentiousness, bias, and prejudice of human existence; it refers to at least a vicarious view of the cosmos from the perspective of the greatest conceivable living being, one who could not fail to exist at any time (*PCH* 576).

I would be remiss if I did not indicate how the view I am defending in the present chapter is similar to, and yet different from, that of William Alston in his now classic work *Perceiving God*. By doing so I hope to make apparent in a more precise way what I take to be the process-pragmatist contribution I am trying to make to the philosophical understanding of mystical experience.

Although Alston was a strict adherent to the methods practiced by analytic philosophers, he nonetheless adopted Charles Sanders Peirce's view (without explicitly mentioning Peirce) that, rather than clinging to the Kantian metaphor that an argument is only as strong as its weakest link, we should accept the metaphor that an argument is like a cable that is made stronger by adding several argument strands together that mutually reinforce each other in the service of the overall argument. This is a cumulative approach of mutual support. The mutual support in question involves both religious experience and natural theology (including the argument from religious experience, which is different from religious experience itself). Theists may place more or less emphasis on one strand or other, but a significant price is paid if one or the other strand is eliminated. There is wisdom in the Kantian cliché regarding percepts without concepts being blind and concepts without percepts being empty (*MVG* 338–39).

We should take direct perception of God seriously, although we should not follow Alston in taking "direct" and "immediate" perception to mean the same thing, nor should we think that "indirect" and "mediate" mean the same thing. On Alston's parsimonious basis he distinguishes among three sorts of mystical experience: (1) "Absolute immediacy" occurs when we are aware of God through nothing else, not even through a state of consciousness. (2) "Mediated immediacy" occurs when we have direct perception of God without the aid of rational concepts but through a state of consciousness. And (3) "mediate perception" occurs when we are only indirectly aware of God by way of something else, as in an awareness of another act of perception or as a result of a rational inference.

Six comments are in order. (a) It is correct to be suspicious of "absolute immediacy" in that this type of mystical experience is similar to what I have above designated as (C) or mystical experience-1, which I have criticized. Alston himself sees this as "extreme mystical experience." Although it is not clear what he means here by "extreme," it seems that it refers to what Jacques Maritain in *The Degrees of Knowledge* claims about the "absolute immediacy" of the beatific vision. (b) That is, mystical experience in *this* life, in contrast to the otherworldly character of the beatific vision (if there is such), is most likely a sort of "mediated immediacy." This position bears a striking resemblance to what I have designated as position (D) or mystical experience-2. (c) However, by not making the two distinctions I have made above (between direct and indirect experience of God, on the one hand, and between immediate and mediate experience of God, on the other), but only one distinction, Alston confuses matters by oxymoronically describing the perception of God that he is considering "mediated immediacy." Less confusion is caused, I think, by using the less oxymoronic language I have employed.

(d) There is much to be learned from Alston's view of mystical experience, despite the misleading way in which he labels it. What we are both trying to understand philosophically are the experiences wherein God is directly *present* to the experiencer, the sort of presence found in infused contemplation when God is given to the experiencer in such a way that we can profitably use the Russerlian language of acquaintance rather than description. (e) Indeed, Alston is astute to notice that to speak of "indirect presentation" is to contradict oneself. This is why in point (b) above I alleged something similar (with less hyperbole) by claiming that there is something oxymoronic, if not contradictory, about "mediated immediacy." In effect, at times Alston sees no inconsistency in the position he defends, while at other times he quite readily points out the inconsistency. Most importantly (f), despite the appropriateness of Alston's skepticism regarding "absolute immediacy" (i.e., what I have called position "C" or mystical experience-1), it is not clear to me that he can consistently maintain the more defensible position (i.e., what I have labeled "D" or mystical experience-2). The reason for this difficulty concerns the defense of classical theistic divine attributes like *super*naturality and complete *im*materiality. If the experience of God, albeit direct, always occurs mediately through nature, history, and society, then how could a strictly supernatural and immaterial God be experienced? If God is strictly supernatural and immaterial, it seems that experience of God can occur only in something like the aforementioned beatific vision.

Alston does a significant amount of intellectual work on the parsimonious basis of his single distinction between mediate or indirect justification, on the one hand, and immediate or direct justification, on the other. One question is: Can we be justified in believing that mystical experience could be *purely* immediate? Alston responds to this question in the affirmative, although he conveniently covers his tracks here by suggesting that most mystical experiences are (once again, oxymoronically) partly immediate and partly mediate. It is the partly mediate part that is hard to understand if God is not found in the mediating world of nature, history, and society. A panentheistic God, in contrast to the classical theistic one, would not run into these difficulties. Here we can once again see the evidence for the claim that there are rival versions of mystical experience.

It should be noted that Alston does not completely close the door to naturalistic panentheism in that he makes it clear that when he rejects naturalism he is confining his attention to materialist, nontheistic versions of naturalism, which he correctly notes are the most common and particularly prevalent forms of naturalism at present. But there are also theistic versions of naturalism. Although the evidence is unclear here, it seems that Alston rejects Whitehead's and Hartshorne's panpsychism, which is integrally connected to their religious naturalism and panentheism.

My critique of Alston is compatible with related critiques by Nathaniel Barrett, Wesley Wildman, and Benjamin Chicka. Alston has an instantaneous snapshot approach to perception, in general, and to mystical perception of God, in particular. What is needed is a more dynamic account in which the perceiving subject is not completely passive and in which unmediated perception is impossible. The perceiver (mystic) is a living organism in an environment and with a history who is not purely supine but who *interacts* with the perceived in a dynamic engagement. Presentation includes involvement with what is presented. Here both constructivists and realists have legitimate contributions to make in an account of perception in its various forms.

In sum, neoclassical theists can expect only partial rapprochement with classical theists on the topic of how to account philosophically for mystical experience. Both sides can agree that the supposed ineffable quality of mystical experience largely consists in the difficulty of describing such experiences in ordinary terms; spiritual metaphors work better. And both sides can complain about the prejudice in philosophy against the unanalyzable, which is unfortunate if some of what we experience is directly presented to us. Finally, both sides can agree that to directly experience God is not to experience the divine essence. In Hartshornian terms, it is only to experience the divine actuality. But looming behind these agreements is the disagreeable classical theistic view inherited from Boethius of God as *totum simul*. If mystical experience is mediated by nature, history, and society, then it is difficult to see how such experience of God could occur if God is completely outside of nature, history, and society (*CS* 132; *CE* 106–7).

It is common among process thinkers to see metaphysics as the central concern of philosophy, with "metaphysics" referring to the search for universal and necessary truths of *existence*. (By contrast, mathematics and logic search for universal and necessary truths, but not about existence.) An unconditionally necessary truth affirming existence is one whose denial leads to contradiction, as in "something exists," or, via the ontological argument, "God exists." Metaphysical statements are not descriptions of particular things, yet without them no description of anything is complete. On the metaphysical level, coherence guarantees correspondence with reality; in this regard it is important to notice that classical theism is incoherent, for the reasons detailed throughout this book. A coherent view is one that does not contradict at least the possibility of mystical experience. On the Whiteheadian and Hartshornian view I am defending, just as physics is the rational interpretation of the data of sense perception, metaphysics is the rational interpretation of the data of religious experience. That is, metaphysics is the rational approach to theology. By clarifying what it means intellectually to ask about God is, in a way, to contribute in a very abstract way to the understanding of mystical experience itself. This is because, in a way, it is not merely true that metaphysical realities can be experienced, but they are *always* experienced at least implicitly (*ZF* 34; *WM* 66; *IO* x–xi; *HB* 44; *CE* 43, 45, 83, 87, 91, 123).

Although it makes sense in ordinary cases to distinguish between truth as correspondence and truth as coherence, in metaphysics coherence ensures correspondence and incoherence ensures impossibility. This is because in metaphysics we are not dealing with contingent truths that apply in some circumstances but not others. But I am certainly not claiming here that all truth is necessary or that all truth is metaphysical, in that most of the truths that are available to us are quite contingent and dependent on very particular circumstances. Metaphysics is, like logic, limited in its content and in its usefulness. But by getting clear on the necessity of the claim that "God exists" we are then able to focus on the contingent nature of claims to religious experience of divine actuality, of how God exists in particular circumstances. Because our understanding of the future concerns probabilities, at best, we cannot guarantee that there will be mystical experiences in the future, even if we can have some degree of confidence in the metaphysical claim that God will be there in the future in *some* actual fashion. Some truth is necessary, but not the truth of particular mystical experiences, hence we should avoid too much intellectual work being done by appeal to the mystics. That is, extreme defenders of mysticism ought to be resisted along with religious skeptics (*CE* 98; *AD* 148, 228, 230).

Resistance to the work of the present chapter is offered by Richard Jones in his two books on mysticism, who thinks that faith in God is based on experience, not argumentation. On this view, we should reject the infringement of the secular upon the sacred. There is much to be learned from Jones's approach, but he nonetheless ironically gives evidence of assuming a *concept* of God indebted to classical theism. An example is when he says that the process concept of God's ideal power, as opposed to classical theistic omnipotence, is obviously not the greatest conceivable property. It is not obvious to me, however, that the logic of perfection necessitates belief in divine omnipotence, as I have argued elsewhere in this book. Or again, Jones seems to adopt a monopolar rather than a dipolar approach to the permanence-change contrast. Change is seen as necessarily inferior to permanence. However, in an earlier chapter I have shown the advantages of a dipolar approach.

Jones is correct in noting that the neoclassical use of the ontological argument in Hartshorne is very abstract and falls short of the concrete experiences found in the lives of the great mystics. This lack can be explained, however, in terms of the distinction in Hartshorne between divine existence and divine actuality, with the ontological argument dealing with the former. Perhaps what is most troubling in Jones's very learned approach is the assertion in a chapter in his book *Mysticism Examined* that considers the ontological argument that the very concept of God is relativistic and that the Feuerbachian thesis that *we* create the concept of God is defensible.

It is the purpose of the present book, however, to give *reasons why* one concept of God (the neoclassical one) is superior to another (the classical one), while nonetheless preserving the best in classical theistic permanence, especially to the extent that such permanence understandably influences the great mystics. That is, there is no need to settle prematurely for relativism. Nor need we succumb to Jones's belief that ultimate reality is *wholly* other than what is made intelligible by concepts. I am not as comfortable as Jones is with a Tertullian-like admission that religious beliefs are irrational (*credo quia absurdum est*).

My hope is that the concept of God and experience of God could mutually reinforce each other, rather than remain in completely separate spheres of influence. The concept of God, that is, can help to *clarify* the experiences we have of ultimate reality (and this is no small accomplishment) even if there is no substitute for having the experiences themselves. Further, the ontological argument can prepare the way for mystical experience, as apparently it did for Anselm himself. An inference can plow the ground for fruitful experience, just as the experience of divine presence can in some cases facilitate logical inference. At the very least, as Jones and Graham Oppy (*Ontological Arguments and Belief in God*) seem to admit, the ontological argument is strong enough to establish that it is *reasonable* to believe in God, even if some critics militate against the conclusion that such belief is rationally inescapable.

Chapter 5

Whiteheadian Contributions

Previously I made it clear that the process interpretation of mysticism that I am defending is primarily reliant on the thought of Charles Hartshorne. Although Hartshorne's thought is generally compatible with Alfred North Whitehead's, the two are sufficiently different to warrant attention paid to Whitehead's thought, too, regarding the topic of the present book. The relationship between the two constitutes something of a unity-in-difference that will be productive in the effort to understand the contributions that process thought can make to scholarship on mysticism.

As a mathematician-philosopher, Whitehead was alert to the mysterious quality of infinitely small quantities in nature and infinitely small numbers corresponding to them. Because of his opposition to the bifurcation of nature, this mysterious quality is not unrelated to larger religious concerns. In a processual worldview there is attentiveness to the possibility that the infinitesimal smallness of each moment of experience will fade into insignificance. Alfred Tennyson illustrates the problem in his poem "Blow, Bugle, Blow" (*PNK* 200; *IM* 169):

> Blow, bugle, blow, set the wild echoes flying,
> And answer, echoes, answer, dying, dying, dying.

The fear is that each momentary advance of creativity will pass and fade. The remedy for this problem lies with some sort of preservation of that which has occurred, a preservation intimated on a human level in some lines from Wordsworth in "The Solitary Reaper":

> The music in my heart I bore,
> Long after it was heard no more

It should be emphasized that what is being defended here is not a view that can be called the annex theory of value wherein mind is dragged in after the fact to add value on an otherwise valueless perception or an otherwise valueless object. This annex theory of value is a quintessential feature of the bifurcation of nature found in various forms of dualism. By contrast, the process view, we have seen, is that nature is suffused with value, as in the greenness of trees, the songs of birds, and the warmth of sunlight. This value is brought within the perceiver, it is grasped or prehended by the perceiver, it is preserved by the perceiver. Some perceivers/preservers do a better job of this than others, with mystics far surpassing those who are largely inattentive to achieved value. Of course, divine preservation of such value far exceeds even that of the mystics due to both divine omniscience and everlastingness (*BH* 284–85; *CA* 104, 106–7, 112, 148, 198–99; *CE* 14, 71–73, 89; *CS* 89; *IO* 112, 117, 137, 160, 263, 289–90, 327, 344–45, 347; *OO* 27, 33–34; *PCH* 573; PUK 84; *WP* 103, 125–26, 158–59, 172, 192; *WVR* 3, 5–7, 10).

Just as education has several recurring phases—*romance* in the sense of initial contact with some subject matter that is exciting, the drive for *precision* with respect to understanding of such content, and the attempt to place such content within a *generalized* scheme—so does the religious life. Typically mystical experience is followed by rational analysis (rather than preceded by it), both of which in turn can be placed within a reticulative whole. Imposed routine is transfigured by the romance of religious experience. Indeed, the vitality of religion involves the escape from routinization of religious education and dogma (*AE* 33, 39).

As before, Wordsworth and the other great romantic poets are helpful fellow travelers in this regard. Whereas modern science in a way leaves human beings helpless in the face of the mechanism of nature, classical theism plays into this deterministic view via a stance regarding divine omniscience as including assured divine knowledge in minute detail of everything that will happen in the future. Religious experience rescues us from this nightmare. We should be morally and aesthetically repulsed by mechanistic determinism. We can be shaken loose from such mechanism by experience of the brooding presences of things, with biology detailing for us the larger organisms, and physics pointing toward the smaller ones (*SMW* 77, 92).

God as an unmoved mover would have no motive to be concerned with human experience, mystical or otherwise, but would instead be compelled to follow only the divine metaphysical train of thought itself (as Aristotle realized). As a result, the continued influence of this classical theistic view has led to the gradual decay of religious influence in many people's lives, with each religious revival touching a lower peak than its predecessor, and each successive valley going a bit deeper than the one that went before. On the Whiteheadian view being examined in the present chapter, religion has tended to degenerate into something of a formula that decorates a more or less comfortable life. Further, religious *thinkers*, in general, are more or less in retreat. The situation need not be as grim as it seems, however, so long as religious thinkers offer a vision of something much greater than ourselves, whether individually or collectively, of something that surpasses fleeting value, of something that truly inspires worship, and of something that encourages an adventure of the spirit. What is needed is the illumination of concrete fact by what is reticulatively relevant. In this regard God is something of a mirror that discloses to each occasion of experience its own greatness (*SMW* 173, 188; *RM* 44).

Hard-headed versions of rationality in the contemporary world recoil from discourse regarding mysticism, in particular, and from symbolism, in general. But once expelled, mysticism and religious symbols ever return. Although the facts of social life are crucial in religion, so are moments in solitude. Mystical experience depends on what one *does* with one's solitude. Perhaps what one will do is reject it and succumb to collective enthusiasms and the outward trappings of religion. Or perhaps one will take advantage of true solitude, as did Prometheus on his rock, Jesus on the cross, Mohammed in the desert, and the Buddha while meditating. The solitude that is conducive to mystical experience should not be confused with quietism or apathy. At least temporary detachment from immediate surroundings enables one to more easily understand one's place in the world and how to act effectively, rather than spinning one's wheels (*MT* 19; *RM* 16–17, 19–20, 47, 137, 139; *S* 60–61).

The mystic in solitude is capable of direct insight into the real, albeit mediated insight, as argued previously. There is value in self, others, and in the Whole; the first of these should not be trivialized, nor should the world loyalty implied in the last two of these. If we assume mystical experience as a fact, a fact facilitated by solitude, then inquiring minds will be interested in determining how such a fact fits within a metaphysical scheme, with "metaphysics" referring to the discipline that tries to discover the general concepts that are indispensable to the analysis of everything that happens, including mystical experience itself. Among these concepts are those in dipolar relationship with each other as articulated above: being and becoming, activity and passivity, et alia. What we want is as broad and abstract an understanding of mystical experience as possible, and as particular and concrete a familiarity as possible. The topic of religion is solitariness-in-community along with understanding that is both abstract and concrete (*MT* 86–88, 117–18; *RM* 59–60).

One of the most common mistakes in the effort to understand mystical experience is to assume that there must be some sort of special religious sense along with sight and touch, etcetera. But the truth disclosed in mystical experience relies on the ordinary senses of sight, sound, touch, taste, and smell *as these are exercised* at their highest pitch of discipline. That is, the common mistake mentioned above encourages a retreat into abnormal psychology. What I am seeking, by way of contrast, is an articulation of truth in depth as exemplified in particular sensory instances (*RM* 123; *WP* 151–52, 177–79).

We become most aware of what religion means when we consider the endless succession of drops of time/experience passing by. It is this religious aspect of a changing world that haunts mystical literature. Apart from a religious view, human and other life is but a flash of intermittent enjoyments that are punctuated by misery and pain. The mystic focuses on that which endures *within and through* the passing flux. It is characteristic of each occasion of experience to receive influence from the past, to achieve an individuality of its own in the present, and to be drawn into the divine superindividual (*SMW* 191–92; *MT* 46, 53; *PR* 208, 244).

The God I have been discussing cannot without qualification be called "infinite." Or more precisely, the God in question *is* infinite in existence, but because all value is the gift of finitude and determinateness, the infinite cannot be the whole story in the logic of perfection. That is, the infinitude of possibility acquires meaning and value by embodiment in finite experiences, which are felt in the divine actuality. The infinite is vivified by the finite, especially the finite experience of God described in mystic literature. However, no finite perspective can shake itself loose from its connection with the infinite whole or infinite background of possibility (*DANW* 160–61; *PANW* 674–75, 681–82).

It is true that religious intuitions run the risk of being interpreted in light of existing social practices, even if these latter are not especially admirable. The hope is that the people who direct these practices will eventually be persuaded to move in a direction that is the best possible. The remedy for this problem of mystical experience being distorted by existing assumptions and practices is *not* to abandon the world. This move would play into the hands of those who assume the worst concerning mysticism. It is not impossible to join the experience of tragedy in the world and mystic tranquility and equanimity. Everlasting greatness is compatible with *a certain degree of* despair with the world, as least if one places such despair into a reticulative whole and so long as one has abandoned classical theistic belief in omnipotence. The Abrahamic religions show the scars caused by this belief and the refusal to abandon it (*AI* 85).

Problems arise both as a result of classical theism *and* due to a type of mysticism that resists any sort of rationalization. Luckily there have been throughout the centuries mystics in the Abrahamic religions who have adopted a vaguely Platonic worldview such that, although they may not themselves have offered rationalization of their religious experiences, they made it possible as a result of this worldview for others to try to do so. I am one of these others (*AI* 118; *AD* 199; *CS* 92–93, 130; *LP* xiv, 4, 49, 100; *NT* 1–2; *PSG* 293; *RSP* 23, 171, 173; *WIG* 535–40, 551).

But which parts of Plato should be emphasized? The Platonic doctrine of the World Soul, which Whitehead does not adopt but analogously refers to as "the community of the whole," enables us to better understand the all-embracing character of ultimate reality, of nature or *physis*, which Whitehead translates as "Process." That is, the universe is at bottom living, even if the *precise* character of the living parts of the universe, and of the universe itself as a singular individual, are somewhat mysterious. This mysteriousness is due, in part, to the fact that it is always somewhat unclear how the past can be, *in its details*, prehensively included in the present. These problems in process theism regarding how *exactly* to understand the influence of the past on the present and the influence of the present on God's consequent, receptive aspect are quite different from the far more severe incoherence of classical theism: how God could love and yet be completely unmoved by the beloved, how God could know contingent beings and yet remain strictly necessary in every respect, how God could know with absolute assurance and in minute detail everything that will happen in the future and yet have human beings who are free, and how a God with classical theistic attributes could be compatible with the gratuitous pain and monumental evil in the world, etcetera (*AI* 149–50, 166–67; *DANW* 214; *PR* 42).

Of course, things look quite different in neoclassical theism, where divine agency (and patiency) is persuasive rather than coercive, loving rather than vindictive. By "drawing the long bow of mysticism" we can both concretely reinforce and amplify the insights of process theism as a philosophical theory. As before, the very worst aspect of belief in unqualified divine omnipotence in classical theism is the accompanying doctrine that God is responsible for *every* detail of the world (*AI* 25, 169).

Neither philosophical thought nor mystical experience arises in a vacuum. The growth of each involves an adjustment of thought and feeling to an already active reality. Mystical experience, in particular, involves a direct prehension (or perhaps apprehension) of real *value*. This intuition or grasping of something worthwhile in the sense of goodness or beauty is later amenable to rational analysis and critique, but it should be noted that emotion vivifies ideas. Hence, we should be wary of any hegemony of metaphysics over religious experience (and vice versa). Two especially important virtues of philosophic thought are that it can help to both *clarify* emotion and place particular experiences within a certain *pattern*. Because general patterns among particulars are the subject matter of mathematics, there is a role for this discipline to play in the understanding even of mystical experience. What we want in religion, however, is not merely dry complexity of thought but warmth, adventure, and, as before, *vivified* ideas and experiences (*SMW* 190; *RM* 56).

The torpor of mere learning is a sign of civilizational decay, in contrast to the real belief that characterizes human community at its highest reaches. Perhaps the best state of affairs would be a balance of religious and aesthetic emotion, on the one hand, and logic and learning, on the other. When love is subordinated to mere learned accuracy, one likely result is hate. This is why making the conceptual world safe for a loving God is no small (neoclassical) achievement. Learning *about* the concept of God, important as this is, is not a substitute for *direct* experience. Further, a society that widely views mystical experience as foolish will, as a result, be somewhat sterile in that the idea that life has meaning in such a society may well be intellectually affirmed, but it might not be felt deeply in the bones, so to speak (*MT* 63).

Mystics are those who, with finite minds and hearts, come to grips with infinite possibilities somewhat better than the rest of us and who then try as best they can to communicate their experiences. It is not inappropriate at this point to compare mystical experience with the experience of the very greatest music: In both cases there is a sense of being in the presence of the sublime rather than the merely cute or pretty, a sense of being suspended in midair (although it would be a mistake to take this suspension metaphor literally). If mystics have a hard time finding the right words to describe their experiences, this is due in part to the fact that *any* experience of concrete singulars is at least partially ineffable, even when trying to describe the scent of a rose or the touch of a new basketball (*DANW* 191).

God is in the world or nowhere, just as creativity is everywhere and in process; by partaking in this creativity we vicariously partake in the divine. In this regard neoclassical theism as well as mystic literature keep alive the Platonic immanence of deity enshrined in the doctrine of the World Soul. Religion, in general, and mystical experience, in particular, translate abstract, general ideas into particular thoughts and emotions and symbols. Indeed, religious thinkers, in general, and mystics, in particular, *crave* to infuse generality into the particular. The pathology of mysticism was interpreted in indigenous, preliterate religions as demonic possession. Later incense became a symbol for religious emotion, even when it became easier to produce the former than the latter. But genuine religious experience is *integral* or *reticulative* experience that deals with ultimate, divine reality (*AI* 147, 161; *PR* 107).

There is no necessary opposition between philosophy and mysticism, as the present book is attempting to show. But one of the chief dangers in philosophy (not only in relation to mystical experience but also in philosophy itself) is narrowness in the selection of evidence. This narrowness may be due to the idiosyncrasies of particular authors, but it can also be exaggerated by particular schools of thought and in particular historical epochs. Balance between analytic acuity and synthetic expansiveness of vision is the ideal; and both analysis and synthesis are fallible tools that require constant critical attention. However, we need not fear if metaphysics passes over into religion or vice versa (*MT* 2; *PR* 15–16, 337).

Hartshorne's distinction between God's abstract aspect (especially God's necessary existence) and God's concrete experiences (*how* God exists and knows and loves from moment to moment) are strongly analogous to Whitehead's distinction between God's primordial and consequent aspects. What these distinctions signal is that there are also, as a result, two different aspects of mystical experience: experience of God's abstract (primordial) aspect and experience of God's concrete (consequent) aspect, the latter of which has been more prominent in what I have said thus far. But it is crucial to notice that God's primordial aspect acts as a *lure for feeling* that all of us prehend when we are drawn toward *ideals*. When such a lure is felt especially intensely, the experiencer is typically called a "mystic." As before, the mystic is not different in kind from the rest of us if all of us are capable of conceiving justice, goodness, and beauty as ideals; as a result, we can feel the conceptual feelings of the divine itself. Although the concept of God is an essential part of the religious life, the secularization of this concept in debates in politics, the arts, and the sciences is just as important as the effort to understand the concept of God itself. Strong religious emotion (as in a Jew meditating on the sayings of the prophets or a Christian meditating on the sayings of Jesus) is a result of the aforementioned lure for feeling, but the lure for feeling also pulls on many individuals who are not normally thought of as religious, as in a Rawlsian reading in detail *A Theory of Justice* because the topic of that book concerns the first virtue of social institutions. The primordial aspect of God is analogous to the remorseless nature of things in ancient Greek or Buddhist thought, but also to the Form of the Good or the Form of Beauty in Plato, which function as final causes or magnets, as it were (*PR* 185, 189; *DANW* 316; *WP* 116).

It is somewhat misleading to speak of the consequent aspect *of* God because the consequent aspect *is* God as God lives concretely from moment to moment. To be precise, the primordial aspect of God is an abstract feature *of* God, at least on Hartshorne's analysis of Whitehead. (If Hartshorne's analysis of Whitehead's theism is incorrect, then there is a danger that the concept of God as a single, eternal, actual entity, instead of as a society of actual occasions, will be too close for comfort to the static God of classical theism, as Nathaniel Lawrence [*Whitehead's Philosophical Development*] argues.) To cite an analogous example, what exists concretely is my experience at a particular moment, then a different experience at a later moment, and so on, with the abstract identity "Dan" applying to all of these experiences linked together in a personal sequence. This is related to the topic of mystical experience because the mystic experiences God both in the divine concreteness as well as in the abstract (primordial) aspect of God as the repository for, and lure toward, ideals of various sorts.

It must be admitted that Hartshorne finds Whitehead's primordial aspect of God too close for comfort to the idea that God is a single eternal (not temporally everlasting) entity, which flirts with classical theistic divine fixity. On Hartshorne's revision of Whitehead's view, the divine over time never reaches completion but is *always moving* on as it appropriates more prehensions of momentary states of the world. Mystics are those who can prehend both God's abstract aspect via *ideals* and God's concrete aspect via *feelings* of mutual relatedness.

Philosophy should exclude no experience but should try to gather together all types, including the Jamesian varieties of religious experience. Once this assemblage phase is reasonably complete, analysis and synthesis should run their course. Part of this assemblage should also obviously include evidence of the checkered history of religion, but this history should not prejudice us against the effort to understand mystical experience. In fact, there is something smug about putting aside mystical experience before it is adequately understood, especially when it is considered that politics, art, and science also have checkered histories. It would nonetheless be unjustifiable to put *these* aside. Our goal should be to try to advance the ideals of religion, politics, art, and science at their best.

Understanding of mystical experience is incomplete if its reference to process—both human and divine—is ignored. I have indicated that the goal of this book is not to *prove* the existence or veridical character of mystical experience. One reason for this is that mystical experience is not the conclusion to an argument that tries to establish proof but is rather more like self-evidence in the sense that encounter with the divine is *experienced* (or not). Of course, there are times when proof leads to experience or self-evidence, so there is no hard-and-fast difference between proof, on the one hand, and self-evidence or experience, on the other. If there is a God, we should expect both arguments indicating such existence as well as *disclosure* of such. This disclosure is unlikely if process is mere appearance and unconnected to ultimate reality. The assemblage of experiences and philosophic ideas is not a specialist's study. It shapes the type of civilization we are to live in by keeping *all* of the relevant experiences and ideas on the radar screens of reflective people. In this regard we should combat any effort to sterilize us with "good sense" so as to steer us away from even considering mystical experience as worthy of our attention (*MT* 48–50).

God as primordial is that factor of the universe whereby there can be Importance and Ideals beyond the importance and value that already exist in the world: It is these Ideals that lure us toward a better world. This view can be termed "intradeical" in that Ideals are the contents of the divine, omniscient Mind; and it is these ideals that are cognizable by human beings, too, when they direct their attention to what is best and most beautiful. As before, there is value for self, others, and for the Whole (the World Soul). Mystical experience of God thereby brings the *uni*verse within the ken of finite/fragmentary beings such as us (*MT* 28, 102).

It is certainly worthy of note that on the last page of Whitehead's last book, *Modes of Thought*, there is the striking claim that "philosophy is mystical" in the sense that mysticism consists in direct insight into depths yet unspoken. To be specific, philosophy's role is to *rationalize mysticism*, but not by explaining it away. Rather, philosophy can introduce novel verbal characterizations that coordinate concepts and experience regarding ultimate reality. In this sense the present book attempts to be philosophical (*MT* 174).

The criticisms of classical theism developed in this book are obviously not meant to apply as well to the history of mysticism. To the contrary. I am assuming that this history is rich and hence deserves a concept of God that does not contradict mystical experience. There is some evidence that the requisite changes needed in the classical concept of God are implicit in some features of popular culture, as is evidenced in the Netflix film *The Two Popes*, where the following exchange (partly fiction, partly nonfiction) occurs:

> POPE FRANCIS: Nothing is static in nature or the universe, not even God.
>
> POPE BENEDICT: God does not change.
>
> POPE FRANCIS: Yes, He [*sic*] does. He moves toward us.

The movement of God *toward* us is familiar to those who are experts in the history of mystical experience, such as Evelyn Underhill (*School of Charity*). She emphasizes the inner life of the mystic in *correspondence* with God. The mystic seeks God only to find that God has already been luring the mystic into the divine life. The correspondence that Underhill mentions is indeed a Whiteheadian situation where the two parties co-respond. God is unchangeable in *perseverance through* responsive changes. Mysticism involves engagement with a divine, ceaseless, creative process and hence involves a willingness to be transformed and to experience *metanoia*, a change of mind and/or heart.

A very helpful metaphor is developed by Underhill. Imagine a cathedral that, from the outside, is made of stone and apparently some indistinct glass. It is only when one goes inside the building that the splendor of the stained glass becomes apparent. Going from the outer to the inner makes possible an experience of radiant beauty that lies right at the fringe of what can be expressed in words. Those who remain on the outside might be incredulous regarding the alleged inner beauty of the cathedral, but one could say legitimately that these skeptics have never really seen the cathedral. By analogy, mystics are those who have worked hard to be passively receptive to divine beauty. They are sufficiently self-abandoned to let divine influence act through them. Because of the concept of God as the World Soul, the inner life mentioned above is not exactly "private" in the pejorative sense of the term connoting privation or lack. That is, the inner life in question is not part of any sort of metaphysical dualism or bifurcation of nature in that this "inner" life is nonetheless embodied, both individually and cosmically (*CN* 30–32; *SMW* 75, 103).

It must be admitted that there are differences of opinion regarding the relationship between God and human experience. One theory is that God can be known only through inference such that there really is no direct experience of God, only indirect experience via philosophical argumentation. A second theory is that there is a unique and remarkable type of knowledge found in direct experience of God when seen as a perfect, personal existent. A third theory views God as underlying being rather than as *a* personal being; on this view the underlying ground is experienced in and through ordinary experiences. As I see things, the first theory is acceptable in its endorsement of the possibility that there could be valid (indeed sound) inferences regarding the existence of God, but this theory oversteps its bounds when it precludes any experience of God beyond the inferential. That is, the second and third theories are correct to point us toward the possibility of mystical experience. But I am not convinced that the second and third theories are incompatible. In Whiteheadian terms, the category of the ultimate, *creativity*, is the process equivalent to classical theistic *being*, but creativity is not a rival to God so much as it is a universal characteristic of reality, including subatomic particles and God. Mystics sometimes experience a personal God, and sometimes they experience something about the cosmic body, as in the pervasiveness of self-motion or creative response to causal inheritances from the past. That is, Whiteheadian cosmology aids in the understanding of how mystical experience could be both *personal* and *natural* (WIG 548).

It should be emphasized that ordinary consciousness alerts us to dimensions of experience other than the sensory; and ordinary consciousness does this without escaping into supernaturalism. Consider memory, which is obviously an important type of experience, despite the fact that it is not a type of sensation, even if one can have a memory *of* a sensory experience. Memory gives us a powerful awareness of temporal passage. Present experience, including memory, arises out of experiences that are now past. Memory is a way that past experience affects present experience. Too much attention has been paid historically to the quality of mystical experience as ecstatic wherein the mystic lives *ek stasis*, outside of a human being's natural place. On the Whiteheadian view of mystical experience, by contrast, direct experience of God is nonetheless mediated by quite natural phenomena such as sensory experiences and memory and expectation and encounters with *persons*. Mystics not only are not always ecstatic, they need not be ecstatic at any time (although we ought not rule out religious ecstasy in principle). John Cobb (*Christ in a Pluralistic Age*) is astute to point us toward the view of the process theist Teilhard de Chardin to the effect that it is not only true that *my* matter is a part of the universe, it is also the case that the universe as a personal whole is prehended or grasped or intuited by me *partialiter*. There can be a progressive realization of sharing a common life, of the cosmos as organic. Cobb emphasizes the Whiteheadian/Teilhardian thesis that our bodies are not so much bits of matter that alienate us from each other as they are mini-unities through which we are drawn into realization of a higher unity (*AI* 163).

It is understandable if process thinkers sometimes exhibit skittishness regarding mysticism due to the long association of the term "mysticism" with the aforementioned pole-vault out of the natural world into an alleged supernatural one. It is not without reason that the long association of mysticism with classical theism has led to the charge of escapism. By contrast, process mysticism has to be compatible with the nature of *this* world. Roland Faber ("The Mystical Whitehead") is helpful in locating a distinctively processual contribution to the understanding of mysticism by pointing out that one prominent feature of a world in process is the unknowability in any detail of how future contingencies will be resolved. The "not yet" quality of the future is essential for the novelty that is crucial in a process worldview. In this sense there is something mysterious about the future, which philosophers should not resist but rationalize in terms of temporal asymmetry. The future has an apophatic character, which seems a small price to pay to avoid the cold death of the repetition of the same. Along with opposition to the bifurcation of nature and a defense of relationality, apophatic novelty is integral to a process worldview (*AI* 32–33).

However, I would like to differentiate my view from Faber's in four respects. First, I am not sure that the primordial nature of God is more characterized by the apophatic than the consequent nature. That is, it is not the abstract fact that God exists everlastingly or God's essence as the greatest conceivable that are the real ciphers but rather God's concrete actuality from moment to moment. It is the *particularities* of God's existence that are difficult for us to understand. For example, I can easily understand the *concept* of omnipresence, but to know concretely what it would be like to animate not this or that body but the whole body of the universe is quite an achievement and seems to require mystical intuition.

Second, I am not convinced that process mysticism is illuminated by positive comparisons with Nicholas of Cusa's coincidence of opposites wherein *all* of the opposites in the world can be reconciled. Much depends on what sorts of opposites one attempts to reconcile. For example, there is no good reason to abandon the history of logic that goes back at least as far as Aristotle in leaving *contradictories* unreconcilable. One ought not (indeed cannot) affirm X and not-X at the same time, in the same respect, in the same subject. Otherwise intelligible discourse itself collapses into nonsense. However, *contrasting* terms can be reconciled so long as they do not degenerate into contradictions. I have been at pains in the present book to argue that God is both permanent and changing, but *in different aspects* of the divine nature. God's permanent existence and essence are perfectly compatible with God's changing actuality, as in the quite intelligible aforementioned neoclassical motto that God *always changes*. I admit that Nicholas of Cusa's "coincidence of opposites" perhaps points toward a dipolar view of God, but it does not amount to a clear formulation of that idea or to a version of dual transcendence. Further, although Nicholas of Cusa is correct that the concept of divinity cannot be encapsulated by the simple-minded expedient of negating one side of polar contrasts (say by dropping divine becoming in favor of pure being), this does not amount to the *identity* of polar contrasts, as Nicholas of Cusa seems to think. This is due in part to the principle of polar inclusion: The abstract is included (as Aristotle correctly realized) in the concrete, being is an abstraction from becoming, just as permanence is an abstraction from a series of changes, etcetera (*IO* 108).

Third, I think that the concept of mutual immanence needs clarification. If what is meant is that God has an effect on the world and the world has an effect on God, with both effects being experienced by the mystic, then there is no problem. However, mutual immanence is sometimes temporalized. Here problems arise because, although earlier events are immanent in the later events that prehend them, the later events are *not* immanent in the earlier ones. To cite a simple example, the fact that I was born and grew up in Philadelphia has an effect on who I am today, but the fact that I now live in Seattle had no effect whatsoever on who I was as a child. My fear is that a misplaced emphasis on mutual immanence will return us to a Leibnizian version of classical theism wherein, because God already knows with absolute assurance and in minute detail the outcome to all future "contingencies," the future in a way would in fact be internally related to the past (and present), which would end process in all its forms.

And fourth, I would urge caution regarding the claim that nothingness is presupposed in the effort to understand Whiteheadian mysticism and that "nothingness" names the apophatic origin of becoming. From the time of Plato (*Sophist*, 237a–241e, 256a–258e) there has been a crucial distinction between two different sorts of nothingness or nonbeing. *Relative* nonbeing is intelligible and poses no serious problems. This sort of nonbeing is roughly synonymous with otherness or difference, as in the claim that a corkscrew is not a cat. But corkscrews and cats exist. *Absolute* nonbeing, however, as we have seen, is problematic in that any attempt to think about, or speak about, *it* turns absolute nothingness into a something and hence results in contradiction, which, given what I have said above regarding Nicholas of Cusa, is a serious shortcoming. Further, opening up the possibility of divine *creatio ex nihilo* (based as it is on the concept of absolute nothingness) also implicitly reintroduces the concept of divine omnipotence that is anathema to process thinkers for several reasons, as we have seen, not least of which is the fact that it leads to the nastiest version of the theodicy problem. Perhaps my view here is closer to Faber's than I realize. In any event, I have at least noted the care that I think is needed regarding an aggressive version of apophaticism, a topic to which I will return later. An energetic effort to say very little about God sometimes (ironically) leads to saying too much (*AD* 69; *DANW* 59; also see FO).

Faber is surely correct that Whitehead is onto something worthwhile at the end of *Modes of Thought* by pointing to mysticism as direct insight into "depths as yet unspoken," into God as the universal society of the world (even if Faber does not really view God as a temporally ordered society of occasions). He is also correct in emphasizing the fact that Whitehead insists on both the singularity of religious experience *and* the need for cosmological rationalization. The need for both of these is exemplified in Whitehead's idea that two key moments in the history of religion were Plato's discovery of the concept of God's power as persuasive rather than as coercive *and* the instantiation of this concept in the life of Jesus (*AI* 166–67). The present book is an attempt to understand both of these crucial moments in intellectual history. Such understanding leads Faber to see Whiteheadian spirituality in terms of a *process* of self-transcendence, a process that aims at a sense of peace, which should not be confused with world-negating anesthesia (*AI* 296). I agree with Faber that descent into violence constitutes a failure of (politically liberal) civilization. That is, Faber's approach to process mysticism has much in common with my own, despite the fact that there is a need for greater clarity in chapter 2 of Faber's *Depths as Yet Unspoken* regarding the principles in modal logic that bear on the distinction between God's *necessary* existence and *contingent* actuality, the latter of which especially illuminates religious experience. As Hartshorne emphasizes, God's necessary existence does not lead to classical theistic substantialism. Love among the creatures flows into divine love and then flows back again (*PR* 351). Further, as Faber (and Teilhard) agrees, divine unity is actually a process of unification, a becoming unified, thus enabling process theists to avoid the charge of "totalization."

It is certainly tempting to solicit support from the great mystics for aggressive apophaticism. But it is important to notice that the mystic does not worship God due to the defects God lacks but rather because of God's eminent love. I am not denying the importance of ineffability, but I think that this concept applies most appropriately to the effort to appreciate divine actuality, where *exhaustive* describability seems unobtainable. As George Shields and Donald Viney (*Mind of Charles Hartshorne*) insightfully argue, ineffability is concerned primarily with the mystic's experience of God, and with the mystic's struggle to understand divine actuality, *not* with the abstract existence of the God that mystics experience. In any event, most mystics *do* speak kataphatically (positively) in affirmative terms that are more basic than the apophatic (negative) ones. To have information *about* something is not the same as having firsthand awareness: One sort of knowledge is abstract and the other is concrete. Generally speaking, the more abstract the knowledge, the less it is characterized by emotional attachment. The direct *acquaintance* with God found in the mystics (in contrast to the knowledge by *description* found in philosophical arguments concerning the concept of, and possible existence of, God) is laced with affectivity and with *care*, as Shields and Viney also emphasize (see *RM* 76).

Whitehead is famous in *Science and the Modern World* for viewing God as "a principle of limitation," or as the source for potentiality in the universe. That is, there must be some persistent actuality in which resides the potency for things to occur. Finiteness as such is not evil in that whenever a literal decision is made, a de-cision or cutting off of some possibilities so that others can survive on the analogy of an artist choosing this color rather than that, such a decision presupposes a background of various possibilities. This ground of possibilities also provides the background for divine action in the world, or better, the background for interaction with the world. Process theists reject the God who forces natural things to submit to divine edicts and point us toward a God who allows meaning to be conveyed within the world and by persuasively limiting its direction. The mystics come into contact with this God (*PSG* 273–75, 279, 321).

Perhaps the greatest contribution a study of Whitehead could make to the understanding of mystical experience concerns his doctrine of prehension. The aforementioned analogy between our relations with the cells in our body and God's relations with creatures (i.e., the view of God as the World Soul) highlights the importance of prehension. On a dualist view of human nature or on a mechanist view, in the experience of pain, say, there is no participation in the sufferings that occur at a subhuman level in cells. But there is such participation in the panpsychist view of neoclassical theists, and this participation helps us to better understand mystical experience. One crucial difference is that we are not aware of each of our cells as a distinct individual (hence they remain somewhat "mysterious" to us), whereas the greatest feeler/knower *would* be aware of us as distinct individuals. Prehension is specifically meant to counteract the Humean belief that all events are ultimately disconnected from each other. Further, to doubt that we prehend our immediately past experiences is, in a way, to doubt *everything*. This is because prehension is a one-way relation of asymmetrical dependence in that it is past actualities that are prehended in the present, not the other way around.

Prehensive memory of the immediate past is a participation of present experience in past experience, just as present experience is a participation in bodily feelings in our immediate past. Analogously, we participate in actual divine feelings and the divine participates in *all* actual feelings. Not only theists but all thinkers have the difficulty of trying to know how it feels to be another subject of feeling. Prehensions of our cells indicate to us that the task is not impossible regarding subjects of feeling radically inferior to us; mystical prehensions of God indicate to us that the task is not impossible regarding a subject of feeling radically superior. Indeed, in a Whiteheadian view feeling (of pleasure and pain, in particular) is the paradigmatic form of what was traditionally called "perception," rather than sight or hearing, etcetera. Here we can see why Whitehead's neologism "prehension" is more helpful than "perception" because the former, unlike the latter, includes memory, and prehension, unlike perception, takes the temporal structure of our coming to grips with the world seriously. Our prehensions in part are abstractions from the prehended items that precede us, in contrast to divine prehensions, which do not involve this limitation, even if the temporal structure of prehension remains in the divine case (at least on

Hartshorne's interpretation of Whitehead) in that God prehends all events just after they occur. God is both the universally prehending and, at least implicitly, the universally prehended (if not universally known) reality. As before, our continued existence depends on a vague sense that we are parts of an intelligible Whole. This is in contrast to Humean solipsism of the present moment. The prehender feels *how* the prehended felt, even if the prehender does not feel *as* the prehended felt (*CE* 4; *IO* 355).

Despite the fact that Whitehead's view is not widely known among contemporary philosophers, the view is quite intelligible in the sense that anyone with memory is familiar with a link between earlier and later and is also familiar with the sense that later events do not create their antecedents. In this modified Leibnizian view, each event or monad consists in a complex act of prehending various other events or monads. The datum in prehension is not first grasped, then felt and thought about, but is rather grasped (i.e., prehended) feelingly and thinkingly. This is the case both with respect to quotidian prehensions as well as those found in mystical experience. In different terms, all sensation is a type of feeling even if not all feelings are sensations. Prehensive becoming is both creative and cumulative (in contrast to Hume's mutual independence view, which makes the experience of later events being dependent on the earlier unintelligible). For example, the rings of a tree enable us to learn about the tree's past but not about the details of its future. Likewise, to remember certain past experiences is to be partly constituted by them. Each prehension is a creative synthesis of previous instances of such; this creativity militates against the preordained (or at least foreknown) world of classical theism. Previous occasions of experience do not determine the present, even if it is true that they provide a range of possibilities for a present occasion's unique synthesis (*IO* 131).

A rough synonym for "prehension" is "sympathy," especially when it is noted that prehension is defined as feeling of feeling, the manner in which one subject feels the feelings of other subjects (or, in the divine case, Subject). Because of the temporalized nature of prehension, indeed of reality itself, apart from our knowledge of the past we know very little at all. Strictly speaking, the absolute present consists in what we have not yet had time to know. One advantage in believing in God, even more in experiencing God, is that our extremely partial retention of the past may in God be ideally vivid and adequate to the world. As it were, God ensures that there can be historical *knowledge* and not merely feeling of the past. Our prehensions are robust enough, however, to speak intelligibly of the immanence of one subject in another, including the immanence of God's actuality in us (i.e., mysticism) as well as the immanence of our actuality in God. Obviously, if we prehend God we are influenced by God and vice versa. There is dipolar activity and passivity on both sides of these prehensive relationships. This does not "reduce" God to a merely human level for several reasons, not least of which is the fact that God cannot fail but to prehend all that there is to be prehended, whereas our finite careers and limited scope of concern means that there is a vast sea of events that could be prehended that we do not positively prehend.

Of course, past events do not exist *in the same sense* as they did in the past, but in a very real manner they have efficacy in the present. Although the new cannot be in the old, old experiences can continue to exist in new ones. In memory, previous experience, including mystical experience, is given as datum in present experience; and sensation is an effect of the sensed. For Whitehead, experience is essentially aesthetic, as we will see in a later chapter; indeed, it is religious in a very broad sense, with poets providing important witness to this fact. One of the key problems with classical theism in relation to mystical experience is that God is seen as completeness immune from experience, as a completely abstract being. To see this being as perfect is to commit the fallacy of *misplaced* concreteness (WIG 516).

It is ironic that critics of neoclassical theism often worry that on the basis of this view there is not a robust theory of personhood in that, on the neoclassical view, personal identity is composed of moments of experience that are strung together in serial order, rather than existing permanently. The irony is that on the basis of classical theism there was no possibility of *interpersonal* relations between human beings and God. The complete identity of God and the world in pantheism precludes interpersonal relations; further, the impersonal nature of the absolute, unchanging, outside-of-time God of classical theism precludes divine personhood and *a fortiori* precludes interpersonal relations.

It is interesting to note that what might appear to be suprarational doctrine in other philosophies is what Whitehead and other process thinkers propose as the result of sober metaphysical reasoning. The mystic need not be seen as engaging in suprarational powers but instead could be seen as operating in ways consistent with rationality when directed to cosmological and/or metaphysical issues. One of the reasons why the traditional contrast between the God of the philosophers and the God of religious experience is now outdated is because of an escape from the equation of rationality with analysis; certainly rationality involves at least this, but also the ability to develop fallible systems that attempt to explain a wide array of human experiences, including those claimed by the mystics. Metaphysics is reason at its limits in that it deals with universal and the most abstract concepts; the particular and concrete can only be intuited or experienced and are perhaps amenable to poetic or artistic expression. Each human person has a unique awareness of the relationship between itself and the universal of universals: God. The most particular of divine, accidental attributes can only be felt, not reasoned. But this does not mean that these experiences of God are *beyond* reason in some supernatural realm in that reason can understand the framework within which such experiences occur (*RM* 84; *AD* 205; *CS* 55, 84; *WP* 145; *PR* 183).

The bare knowledge that God exists is of a different type from knowledge by acquaintance of God. Regarding the latter our knowledge may very well be infinitesimally small, but the former may at the same time be required as an organizing principle. God can be both cognized and encountered, hence there is a grain of truth in both rationalistic and empiricist approaches to religion; the rational approach need not lead to supernaturalism. Divine reality, to the extent that and in the ways that we can know it, is basically reality itself as more fully conscious of itself at a reticulative level. The importance of the theistic question, and the ways in which we can experience God both cognitively and by acquaintance, means that it is not just one additional question that human beings can entertain but the key question in the effort to understand the real. On this Whiteheadian view, religion can be seen as the cultivation of both intellectual knowledge by description and knowledge by acquaintance approaches to God. Logical clarity has a role to play in the effort to understand these acquaintances. That is, the philosophical task in religion is to combine theoretical balance with experiential definiteness (*LP* 131–32).

The informal argumentation in favor of God's existence in Whitehead is multifaceted. His rational categories *require* a supreme example in several ways: Possibility implies a primordial ground, actuality implies an all-inclusive actual entity, the transition from possibility to actuality requires a supreme creative agent, memory presupposes a highest type of retention of elapsed events, purpose and love presuppose a highest type of purpose and love, and order implies a supreme example of order or limitation. In each of these theoretical issues there is a corresponding experience evidenced in mystic literature of individuals who have *felt* a divine lure functioning as a principle of order, possibility, value, etcetera. In no way should we assume that mystics have to distrust concepts in disciplines such as cosmology and metaphysics. In this regard a Whiteheadian mysticism is quite different from a Heideggerian one, although the latter's denigration of the "forgetfulness of being" can be translated into Whiteheadian terms in the realization that all nondivine intuitions are indistinct and complex in ways that language can depict only partially. This concession is not at odds with the aforementioned emphasis on prehension in Whitehead where there is a grasping or retention of the past, albeit indistinctly (*IO* 323–25, 330).

Process thinkers in general are committed to the idea that if the concept of God has been historically and still is vague, it is our conceptual task to help to clarify the concept, both for the intrinsic value of doing so and for the help such clarification could give to the understanding of mystical experience. Even if there are internecine disputes within process thought regarding whether Whitehead was correct in viewing God as a single actual entity (as opposed to a society of temporally linked actual occasions), the common task of clarification of how "God" functions in religion, but also in language, science, morality, etcetera, is what is most readily apparent. Once again, the paradigm in Whiteheadian perception is not vision but intense feeling, as in throbbing pain; likewise, those who have *felt* divine presence provide religious evidence in need of conceptual clarification (*PR* 207).

Chapter 6

Asceticism and Apophaticism

I would like to build on the previous chapter in the effort to rescue mysticism from the allegation that it is tied to a dangerous world-denying tendency that is fueled by both ascetical and apophatic negativities. Starting with asceticism, there is no doubt that the Abrahamic religions, heavily influenced by classical theism, have failed to genuinely synthesize "spiritual" and "physical" values, especially by denigrating the latter. It is precisely this failure that plays into the hands of religious skeptics like Friedrich Nietzsche, who see in asceticism something body-hating and world-denying.

It should be noted, however, that the ancient Greek *askesis* started out as something positive. The word referred to *training* for an athletic contest so that the body in question would be in the best shape possible at the time of the big event. In this context, training and exercise and bodily discipline are good, life-enhancing things. Any contemporary effort to revitalize asceticism would have to preserve this positive characteristic and place such training in a full, embodied life, analogous to the divine body affirmed in the doctrine of the World Soul. Asceticism in the negative sense, however, has had a broad influence that encouraged not only the "spiritual" over the "bodily" but also mathematics over historical truth, science over friendship, intellect over emotion, and celibacy over sexual activity. I would like to forestall all of these invidious contrasts in defense of ascetical training (almost a redundancy) as a positive contribution to a life that might facilitate mystical experience. That is, the religious life need not be, as Nietzsche assumed, a type of self-torture typified by twisted motives. In no way, however, am I denying that Nietzsche is correct regarding many types of religiosity informed by the monopolar prejudice, which *does* denigrate the body and exalt a bodiless (as if this were possible) spirituality. As before, classical theism is not to be identified with theism. We should also remember Saint Paul's implication that emphatic denial of the world is actually a type of weakness; to be self-disciplined is to be dedicated to the training needed to run the race, indeed to win the race (1 Corinthians 9:27) (*CE* 136; *DR* 149; *IO* 61–62; *LP* 306; *PCH* 621; *PSG* 44, 166, 219, 467–68; *WP* 103; *ZF* 202).

Any accurate self-knowledge seems to require at least *some* awareness of one's limitations and hence a need for repentance. This is as true in athletics as it is in one's moral life. It also makes sense that in many human projects that require cooperation, it is necessary to remind people to forget self so as to remember others. As the sports cliché has it, there is no "I" in "TEAM." The equanimity of the sage is one possible and quite admirable result of ascetical training, which need not include depreciation of the body. It is a commonplace in mystic literature that *some* sort of detachment from *pleonexia* is the first step toward wisdom, with *pleonexia* referring, variously, to compulsive consumption of goods, commodity fetishism, unbridled passion, egoistic mania, etcetera. Penitence might be good even if self-flagellation or fear before an angry, omnipotent God is not. Or again, the need at times to be alone, to be in solitude, is not to be equated with loneliness or alleged metaphysical separation from others. Neither the ascetic nor the monastic ideals are necessarily irrelevant due to previous tarnishing of these concepts as a result of association with classical theism.

It is important to notice that asceticism can mean different things. Consider the matter initially from an Aristotelian point of view (without necessarily adopting Aristotle's own terminology or his metaphysics), where moderation is seen as a virtue between two extremes, which are vices. One extreme is exhibited by someone who is excessive in the pursuit of pleasure, and the other is exhibited by someone who eschews pleasure as much as possible. It is too easy to accuse the latter person of exhibiting the vice of asceticism. For example, if one lived in a commodity fetishist culture, it would be easy to develop the habit of compulsive consumption of goods, such that (at least intermittent) ascetical discipline would be needed to pull the person toward moderation. In this case, asceticism would be part of a virtuous life, rather than something that was morally harmful.

Or again, even if it is admitted that moderation consists in denying ourselves what is superfluous, whereas penance consists in denying ourselves what is essential and hence proper for us to have, it is not *necessarily* the case that a close association between penance and asceticism is a problem. Granted, the *habit* of penance may very well play into the hands of a

Nietzschean critic, but, once again, intermittent or temporary penance/asceticism might be needed to help us calibrate our way to a life of moderation and away from hedonism. Presumably this is what Yom Kippur, Lent, and Ramadan at their best are all about, although I am willing to admit that it is also possible that these phenomena might also be perverted into a view that really *is* life-negating and body-denying. The recent birth of some new sorts of asceticism (due to either increased concern for bodily health or to concern regarding the effects of overconsumption on the environment and on future generations of sentient beings) is evidence in favor of the idea that we ought not to trash asceticism *simpliciter*. Not even the "mystical death" discussed by several mystics, including Teresa of Ávila, should be seen as overly negative in that it seems to refer not so much to utter negation but to transformation of self as hubris "dies" and a more loving self is born and matures.

The question to which I am responding in the present chapter concerns what sort of, and how much, negativity is involved in mystical experience. I have claimed above that asceticism does not necessarily involve the sort of negativity, nor is there as much negativity, as its critics allege. But there is also the issue of the *via negativa* or apophatic discourse regarding mystical experience. Contingent facts are not the sorts of things that can be known through concepts alone, but require intuition or direct experience. Here is the place for negative theology in that we cannot know with any finality how the contingent world feels to God. However, it would be a mistake, I think, to suggest that God is utterly indescribable, if only because this suggestion itself is kataphatic (or positive) in the sense that the person who offers the suggestion *claims to know something* about God, that is, that God is utterly indescribable. Likewise, the claim that there is no relationship whatsoever between God and creatures is contradicted by this very association in that God would thereby be related to creatures by way of otherness. When classical theists claim that God is strictly independent and in no way dependent, they fall victim to the monopolar prejudice that has been criticized throughout the present book. It makes more sense to see God as independent of creatures in the divine necessary existence and in the divine essence itself, but nonetheless dependent on creatures in the divine actuality. As a result, we *can* say positively that God and the creatures are mutually related to each other. To say that God is strictly absolute in the sense of not at all being related to the creatures is actually to engage in a sort of idol worship, in contrast to worship of the living God (*ZF* 16; *PSG* 13, 77, 111, 113–15, 117–20, 176, 215, 288, 419, 434).

The program of exclusively negative attributes of God cannot be carried through consistently. To say that God is above and beyond all of our descriptions involves relatedness in that "above" and "beyond" are relative terms. Or again, if divine knowing is in no way whatsoever like human knowing, why claim that it is a sort of knowing? My critique of runaway apophaticism, in contrast to a more judicious sort of apophaticism, is connected to my dipolar theism. This is because the runaway apophaticist nonetheless has a classical theistic tendency to defend divine unity at the expense of diversity, absoluteness at the expense of relatedness, eternality at the expense of temporality, etcetera. To force the question, *either* one has to settle for a rigid ineffabilism wherein one should refuse to talk about God altogether (not even saying that God is one, active, changeless, etc.), which is a severe ascetic discipline seldom exhibited by aggressive apophaticists themselves, *or* one chooses between a monopolar and a dipolar doctrine. It should be clear at this point which choice, in my view, leads to the fewest conceptual problems (*OO* 31; *PCH* 570–71).

I understand why aggressive apophaticists recoil when theists speak univocally and/or dogmatically about God; the latter sort of discourse can indeed feel like a prison house. No concept of God can avoid the problem that analogy is meant to resolve: Either the divine nature is totally incomparable or totally other, in which case nothing whatsoever can be said about God, or we could speak univocally about God, thereby trivializing the divine attributes, say if God's goodness is alleged to be the same as our own goodness. Some sort of mediation between these two extremes is needed, say by restraining univocal urges by making sure that discourse about God is analogically tempered. The first option as defended by aggressive apophaticists is hard to distinguish from religious skepticism (or atheism), as Hume realized. It is for this reason that it is crucial not to assume that the God question has only two interlocutors: classical theism and religious skepticism (*MVG* 22, 68, 76, 88; *NT* 6).

The tendency of aggressive apophatic versions of classical theism to coincide with atheism, by depriving the concept of God of definite content, is no small defect. It is crucial that mysticism not be identified with overly ambitious versions of apophaticism. Such an identification is in part what has given mysticism a bad name in the modern world. However, such denigration is understandable *if* mysticism is identified with what we know when we claim to know nothing; this identification is frighteningly close to the atheist definition of "God" as what is left when we deny all that we know. Nonetheless, I agree with apophatic theology in noting that insight into the sense in which God is absolute is not in itself an absolute insight. Description by analogy, tempered by a fallibilist epistemology, works against dogmatism. For example, if we conclude that God's existence is necessary, this discovery itself is contingent on our part (*AD* 31, 69; *CE* 28; *CS* 108, 151–55, 228).

The defects found in the monopolar prejudice reinforce the defects found in overly ambitious apophaticism. Notice how thoroughly classical theism is laced with negativity, as when God is claimed to be *in*finite, *im*mutable, bodi*less*, *in*dependent, *a*temporal, and *im*passible. Of course, it must be admitted that every affirmation implies negation (as in omniscience implying *lack of* ignorance), so the goal here is obviously not to avoid apophaticism altogether. As I see things, it is vagueness regarding divine actuality with which we must contend, not sheer ignorance. The relation of God to the world is to be understood by way of (somewhat vague) analogies to human experience: knowledge, will, and love prominent among these (*MVG* 122, 127, 174).

Another consideration that should lead us away from an extreme version of apophaticism is that in neoclassical theism divine transcendence does *not* refer to God existing outside of the temporal world but to God having cosmic, rather than parochial, influence (both active and passive) throughout all of time. However, not all of *our* difficulties are due to human limitation per se, but rather to premature closure regarding the concept of God, by the assumption that classical theism just *is* theism. Our problems are largely due to inattention to nuances of meaning in the logic of perfection and to a failure to take accounts of mystical experience seriously enough, rather than to taking them too seriously. Extreme apophaticism quite ironically exhibits both undue deference to tradition and a false humility encouraged by the idea that by speaking apophatically one is being demur in the face of deity. The humility is false because we do not really honor God through lazy thinking. Further, the apparently soft words associated with paradox and the *via negativa* often conceal the harsher words apophaticists use regarding intellectual systems they oppose. The neoclassical view involves both discursive thought regarding the concept of God and the existence of God as well as nondiscursive mutual relations to deity that involve two-way prehensions between God and creatures, as George Shields and Donald Viney emphasize; at least some of these are consciously acknowledged by some of the creatures (*DR* 4–6, 26, 30, 35, 37, 77–80, 82).

Indeed, there is much that we do not know, and cannot know, about the relationship between God and the rest of the world, but the *conceptual* problems regarding the permanent and the changing, the infinite and the finite, existence and actuality, need not in principle be insoluble. "Impenetrable theological mystery" is often not that at all. To be something referred to at all is to be, in a sense, temporal, finite, and actual; it is to be in relation. To speak of the "mysteriousness" of God is not to say that God escapes the resources of *all* of our language and analytical abilities. It is quite odd to think otherwise, especially if one also insists that God *is* absolute, infinite, and immutable *simpliciter*.

Divine perfection is not compromised in neoclassical theism but is affirmed. Dual transcendence, after all, is richer than monopolar transcendence. It is *our* decision, not God's, to exclude relativity, temporality, and internal relations to God. The evidence from mystical experience replaces the predicates removed by apophatically aggressive versions of classical theism. The fact that classical theists often welcome the religious testimony from mystics indicates the insufficiency, at best, or the contradictory character, at worst, of classical theism itself. The way of negation in classical theism plays favorites among the divine predicates, say by denying God as effect and exalting God as supercause. Yet eminent passivity is just as easily defined as eminent activity. It is true that God is unique as cosmic cause, but God is also unique as cosmic effect and as the cosmic sufferer who understands. Our very dependence is ironically very dependent, whereas God's dependence is in a way unfettered in divine actuality (*IO* 328; *LP* 45–46, 104).

The fact that we (including religious skeptics) can identify God as the greatest conceivable indicates that we are not totally in the dark regarding what to say about God. One cannot think everything away and still be thinking. Three different levels of discourse about God can be distinguished. What is crucial is that two extremes be avoided: that we can capture deity in some verbal formula devoid of any doubt or obscurity, on the one hand, and that we are totally in the dark in the effort to describe God, on the other. The latter extreme leads not only to aggressive apophaticism but also to atheism, or at least to agnosticism or fideism; whereas the former extreme leads either to intolerance or idolatry.

First, *literal* terms applied to God are not matters of degree but must be matters of all or none. That is, literal terms express a purely *formal* status by classifying propositions as of a certain logical type. For example, the categorical terms "absolute" and "relative" have a literal meaning when applied to God as an individual: Either God is independent of creatures for divine existence or not, and either God is internally related to creatures in the divine actuality or not. Second, *analogical* terms applied to God, by way of contrast, admit of matters of degree as they apply to different entities *within* the same logical type. For example, concrete individuals feel in different degrees of intensity and with different levels of adequacy, with God being the supreme example of feeling. And third, *symbolic* terms applied to God are used to apply locally and not cosmically to a particular kind of individual in a particular culture, and so on, with an even greater degree of specificity than analogical terms, as when God is referred to as a shepherd or king (*CS* 157; *EA* 38–39; *LP* 134–42; *MVG* 194, 221, 295; *OO* 11).

There is an obvious distinction at work between formal and material predication. To compare God with a rock, a king, a shepherd, or a parent is a material description that cannot be literal. Formal or nonmaterial predication is illustrated when one refers to God as noncorporeal or nonrelative *or* (and this point is often missed) when one refers to God as corporeal or relative. That is, when the abstraction "concreteness" or "corporeality" is applied to God one is not identifying God with any particular concrete thing but is rather contrasting the abstraction "materiality" with the abstraction "immateriality." The formal (literal) predicates of deity are not exclusively negative, however. If God's very existence cannot be contingent, the question arises: Is God's necessary existence to be conceived as having the ability to be internally related to creatures or simply as the absence of relativity? These are two categorically or formally opposite ways of interpreting the necessary truth of the proposition "God exists." On either interpretation something literal is being said of God. In between the formal, literal terms (absolute-relative, being-becoming, etc.) and the most material, particular, symbolic ones (shepherd, monarch, etc.) there are analogical terms (love, knowledge, personality, etc.). To the extent that analogical terms involve qualitative distinctions of degree they are removed from the all-or-nothing character of literal terms: Who can say literally how divine love differs *qualitatively* from ours?

Neither abstractness nor concreteness have been properly understood by classical theists, overly influenced as they are by aggressive apophaticism. It makes sense to say that God is not literally a shepherd or a ruler but is these things only symbolically, because shepherds and rulers are quite specific sorts of things; to "forbid" God to literally be a shepherd does not really restrict God. Something quite different occurs when we treat abstract terms such as "becoming" and "relative" in this manner. There are not many different types of reality alternative to being relative; there is only being nonrelative or absolute. It may well be the case that if God is not a shepherd God could be a supershepherd, whatever that means, but "super-relative" can be thought of as an eminent form of relativity only if "relative" implies in some way or other being constituted in one's actuality by contingent relations.

Regarding abstractions we can speak literally about God; and regarding the most specific, concrete predicates we can speak (indeed, we must only speak) symbolically. But in between there are terms related to psyche such as "knowledge," "will," and "love." These denote states of functions like the human ones; however, as is well known, there is the issue regarding how far these psyche terms can be broadened beyond human application. In some abstract way, God's knowledge is like human knowledge in that merely absolute, wholly nonrelative "knowledge" is an impossibility for anyone. In the strongest possible terms, to veto all internal relatedness in God is a sort of blasphemy. My thesis here regarding religious language is that mystical experiences *can* be described in analogical and/or symbolic terms, if not literal ones, hence we need not succumb to aggressive versions of apophaticism.

To say that God is literally relative because God knows is not to deny that we should be sensitive regarding the *levels* of knowledge and relativity that different beings possess. That is, in one *abstract* aspect of the divine nature God is relative and this can be stated literally, but what it is like to be *concretely* related to the entire world through knowledge, as God is, can be talked about only in outline, analogically or symbolically, with the full details of concrete occurrences left out of the picture. We cannot speak literally about what it is like to *be* God. But if there is no sense whatsoever in which univocal meaning or literal terms can be used regarding the concept of God, then talk about the concept of God is not of much use. Maximal conceptual flexibility is perhaps needed regarding analogical and especially symbolic terms, but there is a real impediment to progress in the effort to understand mystical experience when vague or flabby analogies or symbols are used regarding philosophical abstractions. As discussed in an earlier chapter, there is a need to consider *both* the abstract and the concrete in the religious life.

Before leaving the issue of literal terms or univocal meaning connected to the concept of God, it is crucial that we treat a second sense of the term "literal" to refer to those abstract terms that can be used to describe God as exhibiting a certain logical type or not. This second sense of the term (hereafter "literal-2") refers quite ironically to a certain distinction within the use of analogical terms. It is a commonplace to start with human experience or psyche and then analogize regarding God. In learning the meaning of words, we necessarily follow the us-to-God path, but once we reach some understanding of the concept of God the reverse path is also crucial. As Ludwig Feuerbach (*Essence of Christianity*) and others have (over)emphasized, God has always somewhat resembled human beings, but theists have also always been convinced that there is something deimorphic about human beings.

There is a sense in which analogical terms apply literally-2 to God and only analogically to us. We are said to "know" certain things, but we are always liable to make mistakes. Our having "knowledge" means that we have evidence, which falls short of indubitable proof, that certain beliefs are true. The indefiniteness of our "knowing" is in contrast to the divine case. God, as infallible, has conclusive evidence regarding all truths: God simply knows! God literally-2 knows. In a sense, what is needed is not only negative theology but also a negative anthropology. We could say the same regarding love in that human love is intermittent and mixed with apathy, vanity, and fear. Human love enables us to analogize so as to talk about divine love, but once one has mystically experienced divine love one realizes that God loves, period, whereas we love in an attenuated way. If we allocate to ourselves properties like knowing or loving in a literal way, there is little left to characterize deity. This is precisely the error made by aggressive apophaticists. Consider memory: We remember only tiny scraps of the past, and these indistinctly. By way of contrast, God remembers literally-2. God remembers, period.

It is true both that we form the idea of divine knowledge, love, and so on, by analogical extension of our own knowledge and love *and* that we know what knowledge and love are partly by knowing God. It is precisely the amphibious nature of analogical terms that makes them problematic, but they are problematic in neoclassical theism for a different reason than in classical theism. On the classical theistic view, human knowledge is a mere symbol for an otherwise inaccessible divine reality (hence the connection between classical theism and aggressive apophaticism). On the neoclassical view, human "knowledge" is, in a sense, derivative, and this derivativeness helps us to appreciate the importance of mysticism. Those who have experienced or perceived or intuited God make it possible for us to use literal-2 terms regarding God. Once again, the real problem is less the exaggeration of literalness as the defense of monopolarity.

God is the literal-2 instance of analogical terms because God is the preeminent instance of them. It is by self-flattery that we think of ourselves as loving beings when we notice the limitations of our social awareness. This is in contrast to God, the Soul of the World, who really *is* social. Aggressive apophaticists in classical theism have atoned for their paucity of discourse by an orgy of symbols and metaphors. Religious symbols and metaphors *do* have a crucial role to play in moving the emotions toward God. But description must be based on *some* literal terms (whether literal-1, those of metaphysicians, or literal-2, those of the mystics). This is because analogy is a comparison between things that are somewhat similar and somewhat different, and *some* univocity is needed so as to secure the similarities. It is true, however, that the contingent or concrete (as opposed to the abstractions "contingency" or "concreteness") transcend reason in the sense that these realities must ultimately be felt as sheer facts. Regarding God's actuality as contingent or concrete we can talk analogically or symbolically, but when God is symbolized as judge or monarch there is always the danger of distorting what the best available arguments indicate is the case metaphysically (*PSG* 11, 406; PUK 88–89; *PCH* 706, 724; *DR* 119–20; *AW* 45, 47; *CA* 241).

Neoclassical theists are very much like classical theists (especially in Catholicism) in thinking that any worship worth the effort must be coherently conceived in philosophy. This coherence is complex, however. On the one hand, coherent thinking should shape our emotions, but we should also be open to experiencing surprising facts that will alter the way we think. That is, I am arguing for at least the *partial* autonomy of mystical experiences against the possible hegemony of the intellect. In fact, I am arguing that the experiences of the mystics should help to shape how we think. The possible hegemony of the intellect I am criticizing comes from several different directions. One is the thought-provoking view found in two carefully written books by Steven Katz that the phenomenological content of all experience, including mystical experience, is shaped by (indeed, it is caused by) a complex, culturally acquired, sociopsychological mold consisting of concepts and beliefs that the experiencing subject brings to the mystical experience. I will attempt to limit both this hegemony of intellect as well as a different sort of hegemony of intellect through a consideration of the dipolar contrast between divine immutability and divine mutability, relying in a significant way on the work of Nelson Pike (*God and Timelessness*).

Those who defend the hegemony of intellect think that experience is always preformed or preconditioned. On this view, mystical experiences largely have the content they have because mystics come to their experiences with traditional religious concepts as a background. Hindus have experiences that phenomenologically are of Brahman, and Christians have experiences that phenomenologically are of Christ. It is alleged that there are as many kinds of mystical experience as there are significant religious contexts. This view is often articulated as a sociopsychological version of Kant's mind-construction theory of human experience applied to the special case of mysticism.

Katz focuses on Jewish mysticism, wherein the conceptual background of a God who is ontologically distinct from humans defines in advance what the experience is that the Jewish mystic wants to have. The ultimate goal of Jewish mystics is *devekuth*, a loving intimacy with God but not identity with God or absorption into God. By way of contrast, in Christian mysticism there are reported experiences of both a nonabsorptive type that are reminiscent of *devekuth*, and of an absorptive or unitive type in which the self is absorbed into God in an all-embracing unity. The latter seem to be due to Christianity's incarnational theology wherein it is more difficult than in Judaism to think of God as *totaliter aliter* (*PCH* 677).

In order to criticize this view one does not have to move to the other extreme, as exhibited by Walter Stace, where something like a presuppositionless experience occurs that is later interpreted and described and expanded in terms of a subject-object structure and in terms of the traditional attributes given to God by Christian thinkers. That is, a Kantian approach to the problem may be the best one *if* what it means to be a Kantian is to insist that in any experience something is contributed by the experiencing subject and something contributed by something or someone outside the experiencing subject. Katz overemphasizes the subject's contribution to the mystical experience, but this does not justify Stace's claim that the mystic does not really experience a personal God in that this descriptive content (of God as personal) of the experience is added at a later interpretive moment. Stace's view is not supported by an analysis of the writings of John of the Cross and other famous Christian mystics.

On Stace's view (*Mysticism and Philosophy*) the (Christian) theistic interpretation of mystical experience as union with *God* is like John Stuart Mill's example of someone seeing a colored surface of a certain shape and concluding that he was seeing his brother. Regarding the question as to how we can determine where the report of the mystic is accurate and where it includes a later interpretive element, Ninian Smart ("Interpretation and Mystical Experience") offers the following (Stacean) response: A mystic's writing is interpretive rather than descriptive to the extent that it contains doctrinal ramifications or propositions that are presupposed as true by the description in question. In sum, Katz is on the right track in his "Kantianism" until he overemphasizes the role of the experiencing subject; and Stace and Smart are on the right track in claiming that we should not accept at face value the ex post facto interpretations mystics give of their experiences, but there are good reasons not to go so far as to rule out, as Stace does, the possibility that mystics experience a personal, loving God.

Pike (*Mystic Union*) emphasizes a part of the conceptual inheritance of classical theism that is alleged to either precondition mystical experience (Katz) or be read into mystical experience after the fact (Stace): the belief that God is immutable. But if the mystic were to experience God, then something would have been added to God's actuality. Even if mystical union refers to a phenomenological reality rather than a metaphysical one, it is nonetheless undeniable that the pervasive use of the bridegroom metaphor in the literature of mysticism, and especially its use in John of the Cross, indicates that in mystical experience God is the receiver of a definite benefit. That is, mystics attest to *mutual* embrace in their extraordinary, yet natural, experiences of God. Of course, there are other metaphors used to describe God in mystical literature, say the view of God as parent, in which the relationship between God and creatures is an asymmetrical one. But to the extent that the bridegroom metaphor is to be taken seriously we must also take divine mutability seriously.

In general, the evidence from mystical experience conflicts with what we should expect on a classical theistic basis. John of the Cross's mysticism, in particular, provides a locus for both divine steadfastness and constancy of love, on the one hand, and passionate-sensuous mutability, on the other. God is unique in being *always* mutable, whereas we mortal beings can be changed by those whom we love for only a short while. Further, as we have seen, on the evidence of divine mutability provided by the mystics, we can say that God is literally related to us.

Pike rightly remains unconvinced by Stace's claim that pressure from ecclesial authorities is a major factor in determining what the mystic eventually says about the mystical experience itself. If Stace were correct, then we would not find as many interpersonal metaphors as we do (metaphors that make sense only against the background of abstract divine relativity taken literally), wherein divine mutability is a prime component of the mystic's experience and of the mystic's description of the experience. As before, Katz and Stace are each somewhat correct in their interpretations of mystical experience, even if they are also somewhat hyperbolic. For example, Stace is correct that when interpreting their experiences Christian mystics sometimes refer to God as "immutable," and this is perhaps due to the weight of theological (not biblical) tradition and perhaps due to the fear that a partially mutable God could be misinterpreted as a fickle God. It might also be due to divine necessary existence, which *is* immutable. And Katz is correct that what is "given" in mystical perception is difficult to separate from the preconditions that make the given possible.

But Pike is more instructive than Katz because of a distinction he makes that Katz does not make between two sorts of givenness. The *theoretical* given is what is taken for granted in a theory and hence functions as an epistemological category only indirectly applicable to mystical experience, whereas the *discernable* given is that which can be discerned in an act of reflection as having been given not in a theory but in some particular perception or experience. For example, if one sees a white patch outside one's house on a dark night it could be variously interpreted as a ghost, a sheet, or a painted rock. But on a clear morning when one sees a white teapot in the kitchen, the fact is that "it's a teapot" expresses a presentational element in consciousness that is part of the discernable given. Or again, when a mystic experiences a loving relation with God, the fact that God is changed by the loving embrace is part of the discernable given, it just *is* what is experienced and hence is reported by the mystic even if the mystic's preconditioning and ex post facto interpretation both militate against the existence of divine mutability.

The doctrine of divine immutability has been taken as the orthodox standard when determining theological or metaphysical truth, but not when determining the phenomenological truth in mystical experience. Some thinkers may, even after considering the evidence of Christian mystics like John of the Cross, continue to insist on divine immutability when the metaphysical status of mystical experience is *assessed* (but even here, as we have seen, there are problems), but one cannot insist on divine immutability when the phenomenological content of the experience is being *described*. It is true that phenomenological *context* in part determines phenomenological *content*, as when the silence before the last measure of the *Hallelujah* chorus is part of the auditory experience, or as when Teresa of Ávila compares Christ as present near her to the awareness one might have of someone present in the dark when one cannot see. But even if context in part determines content, there is an insistency to the phenomenological content of mystical experience that neither Katz's Promethean forethought nor Stace's Epimethean hindsight can explain away.

Even given the possible differences between Jewish and Christian mysticism, we should not on Katzian or Stacean grounds expect (due to the influence of classical theism) to find Christian mystics sometimes using interpersonal metaphors and indicating that God literally changes in mystical union. But we do find them often using such metaphors and talking about literal divine change. On independent (neoclassical) metaphysical grounds there are good reasons for believing that there are problems with seeing divine permanence and divine change as contradictories. Rather, as before, they are mutually reinforcing correlatives. God is immutably mutable, the one who is *always* affected by the creatures loved. The mystics come to realize this.

We cannot explain away the mystic's experience of divine mutability. My hope is that such experience can gain intellectual respectability when illuminated by a better concept of God than that found in classical theism. We should guard against both hegemony of religious experience and hegemony of intellect. Religious truth is developed when *both* our attentiveness to experience and our intellectual operations are at their highest pitch of discipline. Religions die when they find their inspiration in their dogmas, say in the dogma regarding divine immutability. The bases of religious belief lie in the experiences of *and* in the thoughts of the finest types of religious lives. These bases are always growing, even though some highly admirable expressions lie in the past. Records of these sources are not mere formulae but spurs to elicit in us affective and intellectual responses that pierce beyond dogma, in this case the dogma that God is immutable *simpliciter*.

If the Anselmian formula "God is whatever it is better to be than not to be" had conformed to aggressive apophaticism, it would have been "God is not what it is worse to be than not to be." I am arguing that this would not have been an improvement over Anselm in that we do not worship God primarily because of the defects that God does not possess, even if that is part of the story. Negation presupposes something to negate. The apparent modesty of aggressive apophaticism is exposed when it is realized that the aggressive apophaticist has the audacity to prohibit God from being internally related to creatures and from accepting the definiteness that comes from having internal relations with some finite being. It is unclear if we really have veto power over God in this regard. Not to sustain internal relations with others and not to respond sensitively to others is to be wooden or to be an empty abstraction. We do not really honor God by offering only vacuity to the divine by putting a human veto on the wealth of the divine life.

We have seen that traditional identification of deity with infinity was a half-truth: God is infinite in what could be, not with respect to what is the case concretely. That is, possibility and infinity go together, just as actuality and finitude go together; an infinite actuality does not make sense in that the actual consists in some determination among what were previously determinables. In dipolar fashion, there is both good and bad infinity, just as there is both good and bad finitude. A term that better gets at the huge difference between a human life and the divine one is "fragmentariness." The fact that we are finite does not enable us to plot accurately the distance between us and God if, in some respects, God is also commendably finite. But only we are fragments of infinite space and time (*CS* 234–35; *NT* 21).

The exaggeration of literalness in description of God *is* a problem, but monopolar idolatry of permanence, activity, and infinity at the expense of change, passivity, and finitude, with the latter set of attributes completely denied of deity, is also problematic. Presences imply absences due to the fact that the positive is the key to the negative. "Something exists," it will be remembered, is a metaphysical truth incapable of falsification. That is, it is a mistake (albeit a popular one) to assume that the question "Why is there something rather than absolutely nothing?" makes sense. The being of total nonbeing is a contradiction, and no one has yet indicated intelligibly what it could mean, even if relative nonbeing is not only intelligible but necessary in the effort to understand the differences among various existents. Even aggressive apophaticism, however, is at least partly kataphatic. Like monopolarity itself, the apophatic gives us half-truths that, though valuable in themselves, cause problems when they are assumed to give us the whole story (*WP* 153).

Since there must be something, the proper metaphysical question is: What is the necessary content of that which is, in contrast to the contingent entities that may or may not be? Vacua, in the sense that, and to the extent that, they exist, have positive characteristics. Once a proper understanding is achieved of the roles of asceticism and the apophatic in the life of the mystic, one is in a better position to appreciate the potential of mystical experience to transubstantiate, as it were, a human life from a quotidian one characterized by quiet desperation (to use Thoreauvian terms) to a sacramental one characterized by both *élan* and a sense that one is contributing to an everlasting Whole wherein achieved value will be preserved by an omnibenevolent being with perfect memory.

We cannot dispense with analogies when talking about God, but we must work hard to ensure that we are playing fair with the analogies that we use, which are easily distorted by monopolar prejudice. Of course there are intellectual dangers involved when we analogize, but it is not often noticed that there are other and greater dangers involved when we do not analogize, say in a downward direction when we do not see the cells in our very bodies as microorganisms, rather as machines. (Even without analogy it is a datum of experience that the microscopic parts of our bodies can feel, as is once again obvious in the cases of localized pleasure and pain.) We can also err by failing to analogize in an upward direction by not appreciating divine action and passion, divine thought and feeling. It is the *failure* to analogize intelligently that leads to monopolar theism and to the inability to make any sense whatsoever of divine knowledge and love. Granted, Feuerbach and others have understandably chastised us for profligate analogizing from the human to the divine, say by describing God as vengeful, but we should also be chastised for insufficiently analogizing from our highest levels of experience, say in our nuanced knowledge, both abstract and concrete; our love and sympathy for the sufferings of others; and in our memory of the past in its rich detail. It is to our advantage that our analogies regarding God can be supplemented by direct intuition, by sheer experience of divine actuality. But such mystical experience is hard to understand without generalized analogies surrounding the very basic realities of thought and especially feeling (ZF 32, 103, 116).

It should not surprise us that in *some* sense the experience of God is ineffable (in the most concrete features of the experience) in that in some sense *any* experience is ineffable (or, to use roughly synonymous terms, unanalyzable, indescribable, indefinable, inexplicable). But this is not equivalent to saying that experience is ineffable *simpliciter*. For example, to say that an orange is both red-like and yellow-like does not quite capture our experience of the particular piece of fruit in question, but it does not leave us totally in the dark, either, in that such a description is better than saying that the (rather normal) orange is both grey-like and blue-like. Or again, to cite an example from intersensory awareness, even a blind person could come to know *something* about the color scarlet by suggesting to this person that it is more like the sound of a trumpet than that of a flute. Helen Keller–like examples abound in this regard as part of what she called "the spirituality of the universe" (SQFT 168–69; TIS 221; IS 161–68).

Likewise, to say that God is ineffable *simpliciter* is a mistake in that we can speak quite intelligibly about the definition of God as that than which no greater can be conceived, of the nature of God as dipolar, of the existence-actuality distinction, etcetera. It is the concrete actuality of God that is to a certain degree ineffable and knowable only experientially or by intuition. Only God can adequately know God as concrete actuality. Language is especially adept at abstraction such that we can more easily define joy than we can describe what it is actually like to *feel* it. In this regard we should thank the mystics in the Abrahamic religions for saving us from the conceptual mistakes of classical theists, including insights from the Jewish Kabbalah indicative of divine influence on the human *and vice versa*. The real problem conceptually is not ineffability but the temptation to content oneself with striking half-truths. More rewarding is a grasp, however inadequate, of the balanced whole truth found in dipolarity. It is not without reason that John of the Cross speaks oxymoronically of silent music (*musica callada*) *and* sounding solitude (*soledad sonora*) (*DR* 114; *IO* 79–80; *CS* 40).

What has been said in this chapter regarding asceticism and apophaticism is very much in the tradition of Platonic mysticism, properly conceived and purged of the monopolar prejudice (a prejudice that is partly the work of Plato himself). We are drawn toward the good, on the Platonic view, and all of our abstractions and experiences of longing for something important in life are expressions of this divine lure. Any so-called war between the head and the heart indicates an imperfect development or internal disharmony existing within each. Intellectual and affective meaning are gradually deepened, reinforced, and enriched by forces at work in the history of ideas, especially in neoclassical theism. I have previously indicated support for the idea found in Plato's *Sophist* (247e) that anything that is real has the dynamic power to make a difference somehow, either to affect or to be affected by something else, in however slight a way. These real powers in the world are arranged in light of the dipolar, correlative tension and cooperative work between unity and diversity. The mystics are those who catch glimpses of the ubiquity of these and other dipolar correlatives as they are experienced as features of the divine life. The symbolism of the sun in the *Republic* (book 7)—also found in ancient Egyptian and Hindu and Persian thought—is Plato's attempt to characterize these glimpses, which involve a blend of both kataphatic and apophatic elements (*AD* 55, 59, 139–40; *AW* 4–5; *CS* 69; *HB* 93; *IO* 23, 26, 70; *NT* 14, 28, 107).

The sadness is that Plato sometimes gives the impression that regarding two key principles in his work—the pure being of the forms and the dynamism of psyche—the former has hegemony over the latter. I do not think that Plato's mature metaphysics supports this dominance in that in several of the later dialogues dipolarity is affirmed, both with respect to creatures and with respect to God. As noted above, it is also sad that Aristotle and Plotinus picked up on the worst aspects of Plato's view and bequeathed to classical theism its monopolarity. On Plato's own view, as I interpret it, dipolar divine power is exercised persuasively with respect to all of the other beings in the universe who have their own powers, however miniscule. That is, Plato seems to waver between classical and neoclassical theism, or between the view that deity is pure absoluteness or necessary existence and the view that deity is indeed necessarily existent but actualized from moment to moment contingently. Aggressive apophaticists, however, very often retain monopolarity and hence inherit all of the problems with this prejudice. Intellectual history in its assessment of mystical experience would have been quite different if it had not been saddled for so long with pseudo-Platonic oversimplifications (OD 11, 15, 84–85, 90–91, 102, 160, 179, 239; *OO* 52–53, 77; *PCH* 643; *PSG* 38–39, 47, 51, 54–57, 276, 309, 436; *WP* 54).

It should now be clear that I think that classical theism is not so much wrong as one-sided. Plato's concept of the World Soul (in addition to Plato's use of the more abstract Demiurge in the *Timaeus*) can help to introduce dipolarity into a contemporary concept of God, an introduction that would ironically change significantly discourse regarding the apophatic. The forms or abstract objects in general can have an influence in the world only through soul (including divine soul), as Plato's dialogue style makes clear in that reified concepts can neither speak nor listen; only living organisms can do these things. Only an extreme and unbelievable "Platonism" would see abstract objects as having agency. Here the contrast between Aristotle's unmoved deity (and its influence on classical theism) and Plato's besouled self-moving deity (and its influence on neoclassical theism) is quite sharp. The *via negativa* is almost inevitable if we are saddled with the task of showing how an unmoved God nonetheless could be supremely loving (*DL* 388; *WM* 16).

In two key passages in Plato (*Theaetetus* 176b–c and *Timaeus* 90a–d) it becomes clear that our goal in life should be to become as much like God or the gods as possible (*homoiosis theoi kata to dynaton*). Here Plato sets in motion the philosophical project of trying to intellectually understand mysticism, a project that continues in the present book. Although there are debates regarding what Socrates' or Plato's own mystical experiences might have been, and regarding the role of mysticism in Plato's entire philosophy, it seems safe to say that for Plato it is not so much that mystical experience cannot be expressed in words at all (in which case Plato's dialogues, myths, and symbols would be useless), but rather that it cannot be expressed *adequately* by any formulae or oral/written language. The mystical way that proceeds by stages from the darkness of the cave to the light of the sun, wherein the chains of the everyday world must be broken in order to experience the sudden awareness of the desired goal, the value of which can be expressed, albeit only partially, requires reason to lead the way. Dialectic is not betrayed but fulfilled in mystical experience. Further, especially in the *Symposium* in the quest for ideal beauty, Platonic *askesis* does not involve any sort of body hatred; to the contrary, it involves the effort not to escape from the world but to transform it (*CS* 160; *DR* 40).

Another way to put the theses defended in this chapter is to say that the goal is not *apotheosis*, where the mystic allegedly ceases to be a human being and becomes a god, but rather *deification* (we have seen that there are related terms such as John of the Cross's *endiosamiento* and Eastern Orthodoxy's *theosis*). Deification occurs when the human being remains such but is more infused with the divine. This process of deification is compatible with very defensible versions of both asceticism and apophaticism, in contrast to the perverted versions of these positions that I have treated above. Platonic *homoiosis* can also be usefully translated as "assimilation." Assimilation to God (seen as the World Soul) prevents us from becoming enslaved to any one part of the universe, even our own asceticism. The effort to assimilate to God as much as possible, however, is futile if God is lifeless and unchanging. The tendency to view the Platonic God as static is counteracted by an interpretation, defended by Ulrich von Wilamowitz-Moellendorff (*Platon*), wherein *theos* is primarily a predicative notion. Rather than saying that God is love or an orderer, it might be better to say that love and a just order are divine. Theism is a personal*izing* process. Or again, perhaps we should view the divine attributes that are to be imitated adverbially: God exists lovingly or justly. Becoming like God is not so much a self-abnegating way to virtue and happiness, it just *is* virtue and happiness.

Chapter 7

Visions and Voices

I have indicated in the introduction that the purpose of the present book is not to establish "the truth" of mystical experience, but at different points in the book I have talked about the factors that would have to be considered *if* one were to try to establish that the sorts of experiences reported by mystics were veridical, that such experiences had their source in the sort of reality reported by the authors of the classics in the genre called "mystical theology." (I have also spent a considerable amount of time arguing for the concept of God that could help us to make sense of such experiences, in contrast to a concept of God that is at odds with them.) The present chapter is intended to focus on questions related to those factors that would have to be considered in the effort to establish mystical experience as veridical.

Critics of mystical experience, some of whom are religious skeptics and some of whom are theists, are likely to say that mystical intuition *might* intuit nothing. An initial response to this criticism is to say that mystical intuition (indeed, intuition in general) is a sort of having and as such it cannot be a having of absolutely nothing. That is, no intuition as such is completely illusory. The question is, when one *has* a mystical intuition, what is had? By analogy, although some intuitions in the desert turn out to be mirages, those who are thirsty in the desert do experience *something* out of the ordinary. If the intuited qualities of the mirage are not really in the desert, they may very well be in the bodily processes of the experiencer. Further, the intuited qualities of the mirage may *in part* be the result of interpretation, but an act of interpretation involves interpretation of *something*. "Intuition" is the word for our having of this something that is open to interpretation.

Religious intuition is what occurs when this having of something is claimed to be of ultimate concern or of the greatest conceivable (see AB).

If there is no independent content of mystical intuition, none whatsoever, then there would be no mystical intuition, only interpretation. However, once again, interpretation of what? It is at this point where a signal contribution from neoclassical theism can be offered because its concept of God *centers* on the idea that God is love, whereas classical theism is at odds with this idea, as we have seen. When the mystic experiences God as loving, as is very often the case, even if divine love is a mirage, such that the mystic is really experiencing human love, this love would nonetheless be independent of the intuition, as in a type of immediate memory of a preceding act of love. In a sense, even this intuition would be true if love really occurs; it would be false only if there were no love in the world, say if the psychological egoist thesis is correct that love is actually a disguised version of egoism. The *experience* of love is in a sense true if only because whenever there is intuition, there is truth regarding *something*.

At a minimum we can say that mystical experience establishes the truth that there is love in the world, which is no small accomplishment. Ascetical detachment, as discussed in the previous chapter, is not an end in itself but a way to protect ourselves from insistent attachments to things that get in the way of our intuition or prehension of there being love in the world. The ideal is participation in this love rather than distance from it. The mystic thinks that such participation includes us in divine love. The God of love experienced in mystical intuition, I have argued, could hardly be unmoved, with no unactualized potential, and with no ability to passively receive influence from others. The Unity experienced by the mystic may very well have an abstract aspect that is underivative (divine essence and existence), but there also has to be a derivative aspect (divine actuality) in order for there to be *mutual* love. Neither the underivative nor the derivative aspect of God is completely ineffable, even if experience of God's derivative (consequent) actuality requires analogical discourse, at best, or symbolic language, at the very least (see GR).

On a neoclassical view, one can claim abstractly, on the basis of God's essence as omnibenevolent and existence as necessary, that God will always exhibit love, but this love is expressed concretely in contingent ways depending on the idiosyncratic lives of creatures. Divine loving*ness* is one thing, particular loving acts are another sort of thing. The mystic alerts us to how the latter *feels*. We *can* experience the creative power of love, even ordinary love, and it seems premature to close off altogether the option that this love is connected to Someone Greater, and this on the evidence from the mystics that such a connection can be experienced. God *is* love, in the Johannine biblical tradition. There is no reality, especially not love, that is not knowable to some degree in a sufficiently adequate form of participation.

One way to classify mystical experiences is in terms of a distinction between infused contemplation, on the one hand, and divine apprehensions, on the other. The latter category can be seen as composed of divine visions and voices. One controversial issue within mystical theology itself concerns how seriously we are to take divine visions and voices. Some people might put a great deal of emphasis on divine visions and voices in that they could be seen as providing information regarding God and propositions of importance to religious belief. (These same people often erroneously *equate* divine visions and voices with mystical experience in general.) John of the Cross and other monumental figures in the history of mystical theology, however, are rather skeptical of the value of divine visions and voices and emphasize instead mysticism as infused contemplation. In his classic *The Ascent of Mount Carmel* (book 2, especially chapter 11, *Collected Works*), he indicates an ironic sympathy with religious skeptics and rejects the idea that mystical experience should be identified with divine visions and voices. In fact, these latter experiences ought not be viewed as providing information that is religiously useful.

I will argue in a John of the Cross–like way that mystical experiences are misunderstood by way of trivialization if they are equated with divine apprehensions (visions and voices). To treat divine visions and voices as information is risky because the "information" obtained from them may very well be false and destructive of the spiritual life. The "discernment of spirits" is, of course, a traditional problem in the Abrahamic religions: One must determine if an apprehension is really from God or from an unreliable source (or is the result of indigestion or the side effects of an allergy medicine). The recipient of divine visions and voices should be anxious due to the possibility of making a mistake in this discernment effort. The claim here is that we ought not to bother ourselves with the "discernment of spirits" *in the sense that* we should not seek out divine visions and voices, and if they do come, the best thing to do is to reject them *as sources of information*.

What are the reasons in favor of this claim? In order to initially respond to this question, a further distinction should be made between understanding a proposition and knowing whether a proposition is true. It is common to understand a proposition and not know whether it is true, but it is also important to notice that it is possible to know that a proposition is true but not understand it. Nelson Pike (*Mystic Union*) gives us the helpful example in which Paul Revere receives a signal from his trusted friend, but he forgets whether the signal was to have been "one if by land, two if by sea," or perhaps the reverse. He would know that the information given by his trusted friend would be true, but he would not know what the propositional content of the message was supposed to be. Divine visions and voices are very much like the case of Paul Revere.

Consider the biblical case of Abraham being told by Yahweh that Canaan was to be given to him, yet he found himself old and enfeebled without ever having ruled in Canaan. What went wrong? Even if Abraham's apprehension were from God, and hence contained truth, it is not assured that Abraham would understand the apprehension. Perhaps what was being revealed to Abraham was not that he, but his descendants, would rule in Canaan, or perhaps "Canaan" stands not for a piece of land but for peace of soul, etcetera. Similar hermeneutic difficulties can be seen when Jacob was told by Yahweh that he would be led out of Egypt, but Jacob died there; or when Jeremiah was told by Yahweh that peace would come to him, but only trials and wars befell him; or when David was told that the Messiah would reign, but the Messiah (at least on a Christian interpretation) was born in a humble estate and was eventually persecuted and slain; or when a devout person (to take a nonbiblical example) is told by God that she will be freed from her enemies, yet she remains the object of envy and is told lies by those who oppose her.

Spiritual progress is hampered by what is usually called scriptural "literalism." Rather, one needs to advance to a symbolic or spiritual interpretation of scripture, as Origen realized long ago, in order to prepare for infused contemplation. In the above examples, it appears that when God communicates verbally with human beings, the words employed are not to be understood in their ordinary senses. Although God may use the words found in everyday speech, they are nonetheless part of a symbolic or spiritual code that is not easy for us to decipher. The message contained in a given locution must be true if it comes from God, but an ordinary understanding of this locution can lead to egregious distortion. It might be asked why God might use words in such a way that they can be so easily misunderstood. Perhaps the difficulty lies in the nature of the messages themselves. Or perhaps the difficulty lies in the fact that the spiritual meaning of words is richer than ordinary meaning, such that something eludes us if we use the latter so as to get at the former. However, it is important not to overemphasize this last point. Almost all of the great figures in the history of mysticism are relatively clear writers. The point is not that it is not possible to describe divine locutions or revelations, but rather that they can easily be misunderstood.

My comments regarding locutions or voices apply to images or visions as well. Although the distinction between ordinary and symbolic (or spiritual) meanings of words does not automatically apply to visions, a similar set of problems faces the person who tries to interpret religious visions. Consider the following example from Teresa of Ávila: A small, beautiful angel appears holding a spear with a hot iron tip, which is then plunged into Teresa's heart and causes pain. Let us assume that this apprehension is from God and that it contains a message with propositional content. What exactly is the message? There is no fully adequate way to respond to this question. The various elements of the vision (the size of the angel, the hot tip of the spear), it can be assumed, are symbols that together indicate some propositional message. But there does not seem to be any way to be sure that whatever meaning we assign to the message is the intended one.

At the very least, there is nothing *transparent* about divine visions and voices; they are not polished windows through which we can see God. Nor are they strictly *opaque*, like looking through a brick wall. Rather, they are *translucent*, like the glass bricks often used in 1950s architecture, where some light passes through, but not quite enough of it so that one can easily decipher the details on the other side. Or better, divine visions and voices are like the cloudy mirror (*aisoptros* in Greek, *speculo* in Latin) through which one can see God, but darkly, as described by Saint Paul (I Corinthians 13:12).

To be convinced, as I am, by the case against taking divine visions and voices seriously *as sources of information* is not necessarily to be convinced that we should not take them seriously in other ways or that we should not take mystical experiences in general seriously—for example, those that involve infused contemplation in the process of *theosis*. But before examining infused contemplation, I would like to consider three possible criticisms of what I have said thus far about divine visions and voices.

First, it might be alleged that skepticism regarding divine visions and voices is due to a lack of firsthand experience and an exclusive reliance on biblical examples held at arm's length. It should be noted, however, that such skepticism might be the result of, and in John of the Cross's case was in fact the result of, personal experience. He claims to have received divine visions and voices himself, and as a confessor brought to the Carmelite order by Teresa of Ávila he had countless conversations with those who claimed to have received divine visions and voices. That is, this ad hominem criticism is defused when one willingly admits that there are such things as visions and voices that come from God but thinks, based on one's own experience and that of others, that these visions and voices are best ignored as sources of propositional content.

A second criticism comes to light when the Abraham example is examined. When one claims that the real message to Abraham when he heard the words "I will give you this land" is either that his descendants would receive the land or that "land" here referred to peace of soul, one is admitting that we can, in fact, correct Abraham's mistake in interpreting these words literally. If divine visions and voices are as opaque as skeptics claim, it might be argued, then we should not have confidence that we could correct Abraham's (or the biblical literalist's) mistake. The appropriate response to this criticism, however, is to readily admit that divine visions and voices are not opaque but translucent: some light does shine through, but not quite enough of it to make the message found in a divine vision or voice transparently clear.

A third criticism of the position I am defending comes not from the point of view of someone who is optimistic regarding the ability of human beings to understand the meaning of divine visions and voices, but rather from someone who is utterly pessimistic in this regard. My own skepticism is a moderate one in that I do admit the existence of divine visions and voices, and I do admit their translucency, if not their transparency. The severe skeptic, by way of contrast, is one who either denies altogether the existence of divine visions and voices or who insists on their opacity, perhaps due to human depravity (as in Emil Brunner). On this view, as it were, the message is being beamed from the tower, and receiving equipment has been provided (as in rationality), but the equipment has for a long time been in disrepair (the Fall).

There is perhaps something to be said in favor of this objection. God attempts to communicate something to intelligent creatures through visions and voices that is, for one reason or another, not understood. But we need not, I think, be so pessimistic. Really bad interpretations of divine visions and voices can be rejected and better ones can be identified, but none is so good that we can allege that we have received accurate information or precise propositional content from God. Consider the following range of interpretations of words spoken to Abraham ("I will give you this land") arranged in order, starting with the least defensible: (a) "this land" refers to the square meter or so of earth that Abraham himself was standing on; (b) "this land" refers to Canaan, and "you" refers to Abraham; (c) "this land" refers to Canaan, but "you" refers to Abraham's descendants; and (d) "this land" refers to Abraham's soul when it achieves *theosis* or true peace or infused contemplation, etcetera. The "et cetera" at the end of the previous sentence is as crucial as the ascending order in the sentence.

Thus far I have argued in favor of the claim that divine visions and voices should not be seen as valuable sources of information, hence they do not give knowledge. But, like dreams, they may very well be valuable in another sense. If one were asked to give the reasons why he knows that he was loved by his father, it would make sense to say that his father was his Little League baseball coach and that his father always worked hard to pay the family bills, etcetera. But in addition to these reasons one cannot in a public way verify the proposition that he was loved by his father by citing a dream in which his father reached out and hugged him (something that had never happened in waking life).

It is important to notice that in everyday discourse one cannot support a proposition as true by pointing to a dream. Dreams are not accepted as legitimate sources of knowledge because they are not communications subject to public interpretation. The issue here is not what is believed but what is to count as a legitimate ground for believing it. Both dreams, on the one hand, and divine visions and voices, on the other, may literally in-spire us—breathe new life into us—but they cannot be cited in either ordinary or more formal philosophic discourse as reasons for thinking that what one believes is true. To determine what a dream—or a divine vision or voice—means requires a great deal of energy that might better be used elsewhere because of the aforementioned absence of rules to break the code. Further, if one tries to break the code, one might make a mistake and thus be led into a false belief.

Even if one is profoundly moved by a dream or by a divine vision or voice, it is not necessarily the case that the propositional content of the dream/vision/voice was crucial. For example, it is not necessary that the father hug the son in the dream mentioned above in that a pat on the head, a gesture, etcetera, could have had the same effect. The point I am trying to make, however, is that, despite the fact that dreams/visions/voices should not be seen as sources of propositional content/information/ knowledge, they are, and should be seen as, especially intense and vivid reiterations or reminders of things that we should know from other sources, say that we are loved. The intensity and vividness of dreams/visions/voices enables us to "really get it," but "it" here has to be some propositional content/

information/knowledge that can be secured by some means other than by dreams/visions/voices. It can be said that dreams, on the one hand, and divine visions and voices, on the other, can have a powerful effect on the *manner*, rather than on the *content*, of the knowledge state. Like dreams, divine visions and voices should not be allowed to shape the content of knowledge claims because they are untrustworthy information bearers.

If God were omnipotent in the classical theistic sense, then we should wonder why God could not just make it possible to communicate quantum mechanics to a severely mentally disabled person. That is, if God were omnipotent, then anything that God tried to communicate would, in fact, be communicated. Two points can be made here that indicate why we need not inherit the classical theistic worry about how God could possibly be misunderstood due to belief in divine omnipotence. First, if "omnipotence" is to be a useful term at all, it has to refer to power to bring about logical possibilities only, and it is by no means clear that it is logically possible for a severely mentally disabled human being to understand quantum mechanics. A severely mentally disabled person by definition cannot gain such knowledge. Likewise, *human* understanding is—by its very nature—the sort of understanding that finds it difficult to comprehend divine meanings.

Second, it is by no means clear that the power possessed by the greatest conceivable being would have to be coercive power to *make* creatures understand divine visions and voices. It seems the greatest conceivable being could have power over others only if these others had *some* power of their own to affect others and to be affected by others, in however slight a way. We have seen that a monopoly of divine power over the utterly powerless would lead one to wonder if the utterly powerless existed at all. God could have only as much power as is compatible with the greatest conceivable goodness: It would be persuasive rather than coercive power over others, who would retain some freedom and power of their own. A cosmic tyrant would not really be God, the greatest conceivable being. The (albeit limited) power of creatures, it seems, may very well get in the way of their understanding of divine visions and voices.

An analogous difficulty arises with respect to divine omniscience *as understood by* classical theism. If God is omniscient in the classical theistic sense, such that God already knows with total assurance and in minute detail what will happen in the future, then one can legitimately wonder why God would communicate with human beings through visions and voices if it were already known that such communications would be misunderstood.

Once again, however, this concern hinges on what may very well be a defective view of the concept of God. For example, perhaps what it means to be the greatest conceivable knower is to know everything that is logically knowable: past actualities as already actualized, present realities in their presentness (limited, perhaps, by laws of physics), and future contingencies *as contingent*. To claim to know a future contingency as already actualized is not necessarily an example of supreme knowledge, but may very well be a defective grasp of possibilities or probabilities *as* possibilities or probabilities. That is, God is not "ignorant" if God does not know exactly how adequately or inadequately human knowers will respond to divine communications. It may very well be the case that God gives us all sorts of evidence regarding the existence and nature of divinity, including visions and voices, and then awaits our at least partially free responses. This waiting is what one would expect in the view of God as an eminently loving being, as opposed to the classical theistic view of God (as strictly active).

On the neoclassical view, God can persuade, hope for, invite, or cajole us through visions and voices, but not even God can utterly force partially free beings like us, with our own intellectual/aesthetic equipment, to fully understand them. It should now be clear why it makes sense to claim that John of the Cross's view of divine visions and voices is more compatible with the neoclassical concept of God than with the classical theistic concept, despite his own training in the works of Thomas Aquinas. His own way of putting the point, given his unfamiliarity with twentieth-century neoclassical (process) theism, is to complain about the deficiencies of the God of the (classical theistic) philosophers.

Divine visions and voices, even if they are not legitimate sources of propositional content, are nonetheless possibly productive of beneficial effects for the spiritual lives of individuals in a way analogous to the effects of vitamins for their bodily lives. They are causally efficacious regarding a range of attitudes, feeling tones, and behavioral dispositions conducive to infused contemplation; they are means to an end. From the point of view of mystical theology, what one wants from a philosophical concept of God is a conceptual scheme that enhances our ability to understand the place of divine visions and voices in what Eastern Orthodox mystics call the process of deification or *theosis*. Divine visions and voices do have an important place in the spiritual life, but this value is more conative than epistemic.

Thus far I have not said much about infused contemplation or *theosis* or what in Islam is called *ifran* or *marifa*. In order to say more, I would like to point out one more problem with divine visions and voices: They necessarily involve us with "physical" or "exterior" images of God. They appeal to us precisely because of their physicality or exteriority. It is the sensual nature of these visions and voices that encourages us to take them literally as our senses present them to us. But there is another sort of mystical experience, a more spiritual sort, that appeals to us in a more interior way, even if mystical experiencers obviously retain their bodily existences. That is, "physical" and "exterior," in contrast to "spiritual" and "interior," are not meant to play into the hands of the metaphysical dualism that has characterized much of classical theism. In fact, neoclassical theism does a better job of following through consistently the logic of hylomorphism than nominally hylomorphist thinkers like Thomas Aquinas. "Hylomorphism" comes from the Greek words for matter—*hyle*—and structure—*morphe*—a structure that is given to a human person by mind or soul. To say that human beings are hylomorphs is to say, to coin some terms, that they are mindbodies or soulbodies. These are designations meant to emphasize the composite character of human existence, in contrast to the dualist view that human beings are essentially minds or souls accidentally inside of, or imprisoned in, bodies. In dipolar fashion, soul/mind and body mutually reinforce each other; they are correlatives rather than contradictories. The sort of mystical experience I am examining here is found in hylomorphs. This experience can be called infused contemplation or mystic union or *theosis* or, to use John of the Cross's designation, *endiosamiento*.

Once one is disciplined or habituated into a certain spiritual practice, to an *askesis*, and once one is sufficiently detached from trivial concerns, one waits. There is a great deal of waiting in the spiritual life, much of advent no matter what the liturgical season. One actively works hard, say through various *meditative* efforts, in order to put oneself in a position to passively receive God, to literally be in-spired or in-fused in a *contemplative* life with God. Hence one should also notice the dipolar complementarity between activity and passivity, with meditation admittedly involving more activity than passivity, and contemplation involving more passivity than activity, with both meditation and contemplation to some extent containing both (*DL* 38).

Divine visions and voices are indeed instances of mystic apprehensions, but they are also consolation prizes for those who need blatant physical or exterior or sensual evidence, as opposed to more intellectual or interior or spiritual evidence of God's living, loving presence. An analogy to overreliance on visions and voices would be married partners whose love for each other is felt intensely only when one buys a flashy gift for the other. One suspects that the two are not really held together by love. I am claiming that even a symbolic or spiritual interpretation of divine visions and voices is inferior to the presence of the divine detected by the mystic in infused contemplation. Here God is experienced in a fashion analogous to the aforementioned way Teresa of Ávila says we can detect the presence of someone in a quiet, completely dark room (i.e., without visions and voices). John of the Cross and Charles Hartshorne also affirm the intelligibility of hearing silence just as we can see darkness. Divine visions and voices are not so much to be interpreted as savored as preparatory events on the way to mystic union with God, on the way to Eastern Orthodox *theosis* or John of the Cross–like *endiosamiento* (*PPS* 64).

What primarily makes John of the Cross's "dark night of the soul" so dark (and quiet) is precisely the temporary departure of images (and sounds). Visions and voices postpone the departure. To be a theist entails, I assume, the belief that God sustains or dwells with every person in any event. But by traversing the dark night of the soul one might be better able to appreciate, indeed to experience, this inspiration or infusion. John of the Cross puts the matter this way in book 2 of *The Ascent of Mount Carmel*:

> A ray of sunlight shining upon a smudgy window is unable to illumine that window completely and transform it into its own light. It could do this if the window were cleaned and polished. The less the film and stain are wiped away, the less the window will be illumined; and the cleaner the window is, the brighter will be its illumination. The extent of illumination is not dependent upon the ray of sunlight but upon the window. If the window is totally clean and pure, the sunlight will so transform and illumine it that to all appearances the window will be identical with the ray of sunlight and shine just as the sun's ray. Although obviously the nature of the window is distinct from that of the sun's ray (even if the two seem identical), we can assert that the window is the ray or light of the sun by participation. The soul upon which the divine light of God's being is ever shining, or better, in which it is always dwelling by nature, is like this window. . . . A [person] makes room for God by wiping away all the smudges and smears. (John of the Cross, *Collected Works*)

The whole idea of mystical experience, an idea that strikes religious skeptics as incredible, is that human beings can have experiences that are out of the ordinary, but this does not necessarily mean that they are "supernatural." Divine visions and voices (and, according to John of the Cross, divine smells, tastes, and touches) bridge the gap between the ordinary and the mystically extraordinary wherein there is mystical union (by participation).

On a practical level, it should be noted that divine visions and voices can be ready occasions for vanity: How special we will think ourselves to be, and perhaps others will think us to be, if we have actually seen or heard God! But this is largely beside the point. The mesmerizing character of divine visions and voices will tend to make the recipient desire more of them, such that they, rather than God, may very well become the objects of our attention. Once again, there is a clear analogy here to married couples who stick together solely or primarily due to the bright and shiny objects they give to each other, rather than to quiet yet deep love. The religious life at its best is a type of self-reflection that involves the joy of knowing that one's life is enjoyed. In addition to encouraging a dangerous supernaturalism, overemphasis and/or misunderstanding of visions and voices also tends to trivialize charitable actions that should count for more than these showy phenomena.

What is crucial in process mysticism is that deity be viewed as analogous to a human person. Without this analogy, Abrahamic religion, at least, loses its essential trait, but so does Zoroastrianism, Hinduism, and some forms of Buddhism, among others. In fact, we might go so far as to claim that it is blasphemous to assert that there is anything more real or more worthy of respect than a personal God. This is not to claim, however, that God is *the* absolute or is an unmoved mover. These doctrines actually work against the view of God as personal, even if absoluteness in existence and essence is an abstract *part* of what it would mean to be God. The classical theistic version of the God of philosophy is very much at odds with the God of religion, whereas neoclassical theism tries to develop a concept of God that is compatible with religion and with religious experience, wherein God is, in some respects, not absolute but relative, albeit supremely relative. "Absoluteness" is not only abstract but extremely abstract, like the laws of long division in mathematics. God can be seen as absolute (in existence) without being *the* absolute if absoluteness involves only one pole of God's overall nature. In addition to necessary existence, it is also necessary that there be a supreme example of relativity or of being lovingly related to others. Sheer independence is not a positive characteristic at all but instead indicates a privation.

It is one of the signal achievements of process thought that it is one of the first philosophies to have an intellectual right to speak of divine personality. This is because to be a person involves a sequence of experiences and a cluster of habits and purposes, otherwise known as personality traits. The mystics in the Abrahamic religions, and perhaps in other religions as well, speak of person-to-Person experiences, rather than person-to-inertness experiences. On the view I am defending, God would be even more personal than we are in that the sequence of God's experiences would be endless, the habits and purposes of God much grander and purer than our own, and the divine personality traits extraordinarily more admirable than our own. To reach this abstract conclusion, however, is somewhat different from actually *feeling* it in the concrete (*DR* x; *PSG* 274, 374–75).

To love God is to love a person, in contrast, say, to the sort of love a mathematician might have for a beautiful piece of reasoning or a philosopher might have for an elegant argument. And God's love for us, as experienced by the great mystics, involves a *concern* for our happiness. This is in contrast to the classical theistic concept of an impassible God as pure spirit who externally imposes order on the world. If we understand the relationship between the sentient members of our own bodies (especially cells) and their effect on us, and vice versa, we would come closer to analogously understanding the creative power of deity, both active and passive. We have seen that this requires of us that we develop a concept of the world body. After all, our own experiences involve bodily influences, both active and passive. We contribute our experiences to a being whose body is everlasting, in partial contrast to our bodies, whose shelf life is finite in duration. To emphasize, as I have, our embodied existence is also to suggest that the doctrine of the personal immortality of the soul is hubristic in that this doctrine seems to suggest that God could not endure any longer than we do in that one cannot endure any longer than forever. There is, however, already a kind of immortality involved in being taken up into divine prehensions through perfect memory, a social immortality that can give us the solace that comes from the realization that our accomplishments and regrets will not be forgotten (*DR* 141).

A personal God is one who has social relations, *really* has them, in the divine actuality. In fact, God's actuality is *constituted by* real relations with creatures. God's absoluteness consists in the ideally comprehensive way that the divine relativizes evaluations of all creatures and is relativized by all creatures. God is Ideal Relativity, hence is Ideal Personality. If the primary reality *is* relation (i.e., the power to affect others and the power to be affected by them), it is crucial to notice that those who experience God would need to avoid both self-alienation and alienation from others, as perhaps is the case in the life and writings of Søren Kierkegaard (*DR* 129).

If one's overall religious duty is to serve God, rather than to receive visions and voices, it would be nice to have a concept of God wherein God *could* be served, rather than a concept wherein God would be impervious to such service. The need for a two-way street in religion receives magisterial expression in Martin Buber's classic *I and Thou*. Unfortunately, classical theism is a one-way street where God is active, not passive. The classical theists who defend this one-way view, it should be noted, do so as theorists, but not as worshippers or as mystical experiencers, where the two-way view is the norm. Religion involves *inter*action because sorrowful love is more befitting than indifference for both admirable human beings and the Most Admirable being. Here there is a family resemblance among Yahweh, God, and Allah in the Abrahamic religions, and Ishvara in Sanskrit and in many other languages used to describe God. It is philosophy's and theology's jobs to find the appropriate conceptual apparatus needed to express the intuitive idea that God is love. It is easy to make mistakes in this regard, and even easier to continue those mistakes once they have become entrenched and dogmatized. However, to say that God is supreme cause does *not* preclude the possibility that God is also supreme effect. To say that in one sense God is immutable does *not* preclude the possibility that in another sense there are perfect changes (*PSG* 302, 304–5).

If the religious idea that God is love makes sense, it is the central human conception. This is why the effort to understand this idea as best we can is not in vain. The standard terms of religious philosophy—absolute, infinite, immutable, eternality, self-sufficiency, necessity, cause—are the results of commendable efforts on the part of classical theists and their predecessors, especially Aristotle. But more effort is needed so as to incorporate the correlative terms that are required so as to explicate well divine love: relativity, finitude, mutability, temporality, dependence, contingency, and effect. Divine love is sufficiently well grounded so as to carry the load of neoclassical dual transcendence, in contrast to the more lightweight cargo of monopolar transcendence. We perpetually create content not only for our own lives but also for the divine life. *If* divine visions and voices help us to better understand the neoclassical view, so much the better (*HB* 89, 91).

Because neoclassical theism is a type of religious naturalism, rather than supernaturalism, it would be useful to examine a few expressions of a contemporary discipline called "neurotheology," which locates mystical experience not only in embodied human beings in general but in brains in particular. Two noteworthy authors in this discipline are Eugene d'Aquili and Andrew Newberg, but I will be relying heavily on the process philosopher John Gilroy in the effort to understand neurotheology's implications for the debate between classical and neoclassical theism.

The study of mystical experience can be enhanced by showing how mysticism has been shaped by neurological factors. However, Gilroy's thesis is that, despite the cutting-edge novelty of neurotheology, d'Aquili and Newberg rely on certain classical theistic assumptions such that they are, to use Gilroy's helpful metaphor, pouring neuro wine into some very old bottles. The neurotheologians in question have written books with tantalizing titles such as *The Mystical Mind: Probing the Biology of Religious Experience* and *Why God Won't Go Away: Brain Science and the Biology of Belief*. However, the authors often assume a version of dualism or epiphenomenalism in philosophy of mind that is conducive to (classical theistic) cosmological dualism in theology. Although I will not examine in detail the neurotheologians' views in philosophy of mind and philosophy of science, I will concentrate on the implications of their views for the understanding of mystical experience. Further, d'Aquili and Newberg problematically affirm what many mystics say when they *interpret* their own experiences in classical theistic terms.

On the epiphenomenalist view, the human mind is an inert byproduct of the body, especially the brain. The effort to localize mystical experience in certain parts of the brain is admittedly problematic because every area of the brain is interconnected with every other area of the brain and with other parts of the body. However, the key neurological process involved in the issues under consideration here is *deafferentation*, wherein there is a blockage of neural input to certain brain areas from both other brain areas and other parts of the body. The process of deafferentation sometimes occurs as a result of illness, as when a brain tumor blocks transmission of impulses. Deafferentation can occur outside of illness in either bottom-up fashion, starting with the automatic nervous system and then moving up to higher functional areas of the brain, or top-down fashion, starting with human intentions in the higher brain areas and then moving down to the automatic nervous system. The rhythmic and/or repetitive character of some religious rituals can provide examples of the bottom-up approach, and intentional meditative practices can provide examples of the top-down approach. Ritual-based deafferentation can be sustained for relatively long periods of time, although formal meditative practices can produce especially intense deafferentation experiences that are characterized by hyperlucidity. Given the present book's concentration on dipolarity, meditation practices can develop a sort of *passivity*, wherein the volitional area of the brain tries to clear the mind of thoughts or other distractions, or a sort of *activity*, wherein the mind sustains attention on a single object, say a religious icon.

Mystical experience is characterized by d'Aquili and Newberg as absorption of the self into "absolute unity being" (AUB), where there is extreme deafferentation of relevant brain areas. Please note that all three words in this designation indicate monopolarity. In any event, studies of both Franciscan nuns praying and Buddhist monks meditating are claimed to confirm such extreme deafferentation. This is what leads some analysts of mystical states, and some mystics themselves, to refer to mystical experience as beyond space and time, as supernatural. Loss of a sense of having an independent self is a primary characteristic of AUB, it is claimed, whether the experience involves the personal God of theistic religions or the void of nontheistic ones.

In addition to deafferentation, there is another, more cognitive, sort of brain function that is relevant in the present context. In baseline conditions, human beings are driven by a cognitive imperative or an irresistible urge to know the world, which d'Aquili and Newberg think is crucial for human spirituality and that leads to philosophical belief in an uncaused cause for the world. The hope of the neurotheologians in question is that we would be able to develop both a metatheology and a megatheology. The former consists in a view that has no theological content of its own but that lays out the principles regarding how a theology should be structured. The latter tries to isolate the universal features of the religious views held by people around the globe, once the idiosyncratic features of particular religions are purged. That is, deafferentation-based AUB could provide the template for an understanding of the most intense spiritual experiences, both theistic and nontheistic.

A basic question arises at this point: Does the human brain produce God or does it make us aware of a divine reality independent of itself? Either way, mystical experiences are real. If one subscribes to a reductionistic version of materialism, then it would be easy to conclude that AUB and other mystical experiences are produced by the brain. However, if one subscribes to panpsychism or some other view wherein subjective awareness is primary, then mystical experiences might be more readily seen as pointing toward some reality other than the brain. Even without a surefire way to resolve this question, it is interesting to note one way to distinguish between mystical experiences, including divine visions and voices, and insanity. Those who suffer from delusions and hallucinations might think that those states are more real than everyday experience while they are occurring, but once they return to baseline experience, they discover the error of their ways. By way of contrast, when mystics return to baseline experience, they continue to believe not only that their mystical experiences were more real than baseline experience, but they also provide tranquility and direction to their baseline lives. This is in contrast to the regret or shame or fear that is felt by those in baseline experience who were previously delusional.

Perhaps it can be said that both options regarding AUB—that in one sense God is created by the brain and in another qualified sense the world is created by God—are defensible, so long as these two senses are distinguished and carefully analyzed. Or better, perhaps the horns of the dilemma posed by these two options can be softened, as Gilroy insightfully argues. Theists need not feel threatened by neurotheology, especially if they are naturalists committed to the essential embodiment of human beings, indeed to the essential embodiment of deity via the doctrine of the World Soul for the cosmic body. However, this does not mean that we need to adhere to the epiphenomenalist view that any attribution of spontaneity or ability to grasp divine influence is *merely* brain activity. Experience, including mystical experience, is real. What can be learned from neurotheology is that historically rich meditation practices in various religious traditions involve not only the intention to clear the mind of irrelevant perceptions, thoughts, and emotions; also involved is intelligible brain activity. The association area of the brain—the source of willed actions—via the thalamus, causes the limbic structure known as the hippocampus to dampen the flow of neural input. Deafferentation involves the direction of neural-chemical traffic in such a way that there is an altered state of mind.

In a panpsychist or panexperientialist worldview, feeling is a cosmic variable (as in chapter 8, titled "The Cosmic Variables," in Hartshorne's *Beyond Humanism*) of an extremely wide range, from microscopic to mesoscopic to macroscopic (cosmic or divine) levels. Each center of feeling is conceived as a diachronic society of occasions that contributes something, however small, to cosmic history. On this panexperientialist view, the brain is a well-organized aggregate of neuronal individuals, not a separate kind of stuff from all of the other centers of feeling in the universe. This is why, in principle, those interested in mystical theology need not be threatened by neurotheology; and mystics need not be led into a mysterious (in the pejorative sense of the term) supernaturalism or epiphenomenalism wherein the mystic floats above the natural world of the brain. But we need not view the brain as a machine or a computer, as is common. Perhaps it is the legitimate fear of mechanism that leads some to fear neurotheology. However, it is possible to bring neurotheology into a thoroughly processual view of the world as *organic*, as evidenced in three different sorts of studies: *activation* studies can show that performance of a certain task involves neuronal firing in certain brain structures; *dysfunction* studies can show that damage to a brain structure yields a certain loss of function; and *stimulation* studies can show how electrical stimulation of a brain structure can induce a certain behavior.

However, none of these studies supports the case for determinism. A central feature of process philosophy is that the *exact* character of each experience requires an element of creativity in response to causal inheritances from the past. Neuronal impulses *are* relevant, but as necessary rather than as sufficient conditions for present experiences. If the right amygdala is stimulated, a hallucination might result, but this exact hallucination at this precise time and place is at least partially indeterminate. Even divine actuality, we have seen, involves particularity and partial indeterminacy.

The "old bottles" mentioned above are nowhere more apparent than when d'Aquili and Newberg conclude that AUB is the creator of matter, despite the fact that they think AUB is utterly unknowable. The combination of classical theistic omnipotence and aggressive apophaticism preserves the worst in the traditional concept of God. Likewise, there are problems with their accepting at face value the claims of some mystics that AUB is timeless and unchanging. Perhaps a better way of interpreting AUB is to say that deafferentation involves a registering of temporal relations that is out of the ordinary and that God is unchanging in existence and essence but not in actuality. These philosophical nuances are nowhere to be found in d'Aquili and Newberg's forays into neurotheology. Divine "pulses of feeling," to use Gilroy's helpful label, might be so extraordinarily quick that they register to the person in mystical experience as "timeless." The historical figures in the history of mysticism can be excused for such language if they were only familiar with classical theism's concept of God, but contemporary thinkers have no excuse for not being aware of the neoclassical alternative. However, mystics might trend in the future in a process-friendly way, especially if theistic processuality has a two-thousand-year run like classical theism.

An altered sense of self, time, and space is not to be equated with a complete loss of these three. The fact that those who have AUB experiences later identify them as theirs, then, and there, is evidence of the fact that mystical experience is not literally selfless, timeless, or spaceless. Reduced self-awareness is not selflessness. Regarding the neurotheology in question, Gilroy says at the very end of his article that it "requires great clinical wisdom so that cutting-edge medical technology is not used to sustain ailing theoretical patients with inoperable conditions" (Gilroy, "Neuro Wine in Old Vessels").

Chapter 8

Bergsonian Contributions

Like chapter 5 regarding Whitehead, the present chapter will deal with the distinct contributions to an understanding of mystical experience and the concept of God that are made possible by considering the thought of Henri Bergson, another magisterial figure in the history of process metaphysics.

Bergson helps us to realize that mysticism and the concept of God are rooted in social life, broadly conceived. But there are two sorts of social life, each of which is connected to a particular view of God. In "closed society," as Bergson uses the term, the concept of God is likely to have an imperative character that is supposedly inscribed from all eternity, as it were, on the transcendent tablets Moses acquired on Mount Sinai. A breach of this social order appears as an antinatural act. That is, closed society maintains tight bonds among three elements: alleged natural order, social order, and religious command. Nature, society, and religion live together as if they were cellular members of a living organism. To adopt a metaphor from Bergson himself in his great work *The Two Sources of Morality and Religion*, just as in an aquatic plant whose leaves on the surface of the water are deeply rooted in what cannot be seen beneath the surface, so also the visible manifestations of natural and social order and religion (including mystical experience) are rooted in a concept of God that lies far beneath what is normally seen (*TS* 1–26).

The two sorts of society in Bergson, as well as the two concepts of God that are connected to them, are also related to the two main lines of the evolution of animal life. The arthropods are typified by the instinct of insects, whereas the vertebrates culminate in human intelligence. Although the two interpenetrate (there is nascent intelligence in insects, and human life is still largely influenced by instinct), the inventiveness of human intelligence has as its consequence the ability to partially transcend the reified characteristics of insect life. Human community is more variable in form and is much more open to progress than the rigidly communal lives of insects. What is natural in human beings is in great measure overlaid with what is acquired. Our societies, too, can be closed in the sense of being dominated by custom, habit, and instinct, but there is always at least the possibility of openness, intelligent choice, and progress. To be precise, human societies need instinct—surviving without it would be impossible—but this claim is nonetheless compatible with the idea that the difference between a closed society and an open one can be significant (*TS* 27–32).

Human beings have come to respect each other in degrees, gradually including those outside of one's clan, one's ethnic background, one's gender, and indeed outside of one's own species. These developments are often aided (or hindered) as a result of the concept of God dominant in a particular society. To the extent that this concept concentrates on a God of love, to this extent a society is able to progressively open itself. Great moral personalities and great mystics are very often those who open us up to a more dynamic and defensible concept of God. And herein lies Bergson's contribution to a sound relationship between the concept of God and feminist as well as environmental concern: It is an ethics of love, integrally connected to a God of love, that facilitates an ever-expanding scope of concern to include not only all human beings but also all sentient life (*TS* 33–41).

Of course, the issue of whether society is primary and the concept of God derivative, or whether the concept of God is primary and society derivative, is a complicated one. But Bergson cautions us against a facile acceptance of the idea that the concept of God (and mystical experience) is pushed around by societal organization, especially in its material or economic aspects. For example, claiming that romantic love plagiarizes mysticism rather than the other way around is plausible, and hence those who criticize mystics for describing God in terms of passionate love are wrongheaded in their assumption that the mystics are borrowing from the raptures of two lovers. They may very well be reclaiming for mystic love of Preeminent Love what was originally its own. Romantic love has a definite history that started in the Middle Ages under the inspiration of the Song of Songs from Hebrew scriptures. In this regard, that Bergson himself was a Jew who converted to Catholicism is noteworthy; he was, therefore, familiar with both of these great religions in both their closed and open varieties, making him something of an expert in four religions (*TS* 42; also see Levi, *Philosophy and the Modern World*, chapter 3).

Emotion drives intelligence, despite all obstacles, in Bergson; it vivifies or vitalizes it. Hence there is the following sort of dynamism in his thought: Initially instinct drives things in closed religion; but as the intellectual abilities of human beings become enhanced, a concept of God develops that, in turn, affects moral discourse and the societal lives of human beings; yet despite the efficacy of the concept of God, in reality the morality of a group of religious people "wins souls" more than the concept of God or any other intellectual aspect of religion. The present book has inserted into religious discourse an account of the concept of God that is partially at odds with the classical theistic concept, but it has not questioned either the importance of instinct/intuition in the lives of religious believers/mystics or the importance of moral beliefs and structures in the concrete lives of individuals, whether or not they are religious believers. To take a now familiar test case, the importance of love in the Abrahamic religions has not been sufficiently supported (if supported at all) by the metaphysics of belief classical theism fosters; this lack of support has very practical (indeed negative) consequences (*TS* 43–50).

Neither closed nor open morality/religion can be found in a pure state, although a completely closed morality/religion can be closely approximated in some cases. An attitude of aspiration or the hope that there can be progress is one of the preconditions, it seems, for open religion to flourish. All of the great mystics in the Abrahamic (and other) religions aid the cause of open religion, albeit unwittingly in some cases, by saying, in effect, that by loving God we love all those made in the divine image (as qualified, however, by a prohibition of images in Islam). These mystics have a sense of a loving current passing from them to God and then back again through them to the rest of humanity and to the rest of nature. Between the first morality/religion and the second lies the distance between repose and movement. The first is alleged to be immutable. The second morality/religion is more complicated than the first because it does not have amnesia in this regard; it is both "neo" and "classical." Both Socratic reason and the morality of the gospels implicitly point the way toward openness in that both Socrates and Jesus were open to divine influence in terms of either a mysterious *daemon* or a caring, parental force at work in the world, respectively (*TS* 51–64).

To note the failure of strictly intellectualist systems of morality/religion is perfectly compatible with noting the crucial role that rationality plays in the development of the open. Reason itself has a divine character, once again as indicated by Socrates' *daemon* and Jesus when seen as the *logos*. Just as great political reforms at first seem impractical, so also great intellectual reforms, as in reform of the concept of God. But an overflowing of love and rationality together is almost irresistible. Almost. Pure aspiration is a limit concept or an ideal in that there is always some closed or instinctual element in morality/religion, some formula or structure that endures and tends to resist change (*TS* 65–89).

But there is also the possibility of religious "mysticism," as Bergson uses this term, which consists in opening up to the oncoming wave of divine influence in the world. These mystics, who are at the forefront of open morality/religion, are not to be equated with those who have extraordinary visions and voices (although these are not unheard of), as we have seen, in that those who are open to divine influence, and who, in turn, influence the divine, are very often those who are efficacious actors in the world, such as Teresa of Ávila, to take just one example, who was in effect responsible for the reform of the Catholic Church in Spain in the early modern period in the absence of any significant Protestant Reformation in that country. Bergson insightfully notices that those of us who are not mystics nonetheless often find an echo of what mystics say about their experiences in our own lives, which perhaps indicates that the capacity for religious experience at a high and nuanced level is dormant in each one of us (*TS* 90–101).

For neoclassical or process theists, thinking that the concept of God would be polished at an early stage of its articulation is implausible. Seen in this light, by the time of Philo in the first century and Thomas Aquinas in the thirteenth century, half of the concept of God had been carefully examined and illuminated (i.e., God's permanence, if not God's change; God's activity, if not God's passivity; etc.). This is amazing in that 50 percent can be seen as a very high percentage. But by leaving the other half of the concept of God not carefully examined and not illuminated, classical theists have facilitated numerous theoretical and practical problems. The spectacle of what religions have been historically and still are today is a source of humiliation for reflective religious believers. For example, it is not unreasonable to think that the classical concept of God as active and not passive is not unrelated to the dismal history of religious intolerance and persecution. The proper response to this problem, however, is not to give up on religion (no more than we should give up on politics when political leaders make grave mistakes, and no more than we should give up on art when talented people give themselves over to overly commercialized or exploitative creative projects) but to improve it by putting it on a more defensible abstract basis, including the effort to articulate a comprehensive yet consistent concept of God (*TS* 102).

Despite all of the historical problems with the concept of God in particular and with religion in general, Bergson thinks it remarkable that neither the concept of God nor religion itself have died out. (Likewise, neither politics nor art have died out, despite the long history of political corruption and artistic "license" in the pejorative sense of the term.) There is a demand for forward movement, a vital impetus to improve the concept of God and religion. This impulse to improve means that in principle predicting what will happen in the future in any sort of detail regarding either the concept of God or mystical experience is impossible. As we have seen, the classical theistic version of omniscience would lead us to think otherwise (*TS* 115, 204–5).

Bergson defends the commonplace in process thought that an animal individual, including a human animal, is itself a society composed of cellular members, which are themselves microorganisms. Although he is not explicit regarding the question of whether God is a World Soul whose divine society includes us as cellular members, such a view seems to be implied in his stance regarding the primacy of the social in nature. Indeed, he thinks that what it means to be a religious believer is to think that some sort of divine force is diffused throughout all of nature. But it need not be assumed that this diffused divine force is omnipotent; this is due in part to the very real role that chance plays in both nature and human culture (*TS* 117–19, 134, 147–48, 158).

Just as the neoclassical critique of omnipotence makes it possible to better understand the chance elements in nature as detailed in evolutionary biology, so also neoclassical theism makes it possible to establish a significant difference between mystical experience and magic. The latter involves a certain degree of selfishness, a desire to alter the laws of nature to conform to one's own wishes. Overconcentration on petitionary prayer to an omnipotent God who can at will alter any natural law, who can at will supernaturally contravene nature, can be seen as a glorified form of magic. By contrast, in neoclassical theism we are encouraged to see ourselves not as central to the cosmos but nonetheless as significant parts of a mighty (but not omnipotent) Whole. The goal of spiritual life on this basis is to understand and appreciate one's worth, but always within a larger Whole that involves tragedy for both us and God. It is to return to the best aspects of Platonic theism and to the insights of the Greek tragedians, as Nancy

Arnison rightly argues in a comparison of Aeschylus and Whitehead (also see *TS* 175, 201).

Although the dynamism of open religion might at times need the static and structured character of closed religion for its expression and diffusion, this is notably different from the idea that closed religion in itself is consistent and intelligible. The chief problem with closed religion in its classical theistic version is that it cannot come to terms with the concept of God as personal. Admittedly, static religion lives on in open religion to the extent that in neoclassical theism there is both a "neo" aspect as well as a "classical" aspect, with the latter indicating the importance, but not hegemony, of divine permanence. That is, equating God *simpliciter* with immutability is a huge mistake. Ancient Greek polytheists anticipated this point in their stories about Zeus and Dionysus, say, whose characters were never set in stone and exhibited significant changes. In this regard Bergson notes the poverty of Roman mythology relative to the Greek. The Roman gods tend to coincide with certain functions and tend to be immobilized by these functions; by partial contrast the Greek gods had more dynamic characters and histories. Or more precisely, to the extent that one can detect dynamism in the Roman gods it is with respect to those gods who are most derived from the Greeks (*TS* 178–79, 187–88, 194).

Furthermore, ancient polytheism anticipates in large measure the crucial Hartshornian distinction between existence and actuality. Whereas any particular god was contingent and could come or go, the gods as a whole had to exist, as Bergson argues in his analysis of ancient religion. Here we have a link between closed and open theism in that God's actual experiences from moment to moment are contingent and can come and go, but God's everlasting existence is necessary (*TS* 200).

Thinking that a current of creative energy is at work in the world, a restless advance into the future at each moment, is characteristic of a process worldview, which has profound implications for the concept of God. One of these implications is that if we talk about divine foreknowledge, then we have to qualify such talk by saying that such "foreknowledge" involves only possibilities or at best probabilities, even for the preeminent knower. The confidence that closed religion encourages needs to be transfigured in that there should also be a degree of inquietude regarding the future. It is true that at present—both Bergson's present in 1932 and our present in the twenty-first century—people tend to turn to closed or static religion for support in time of trouble, but with mixed results. One is familiar with a ceremony wherein the participants go through the motions without really meaning them. But the situation is not hopeless. Even a listless and mechanical science teacher can occasionally awaken in a pupil the vocation to pursue research; likewise, even in closed, static religion, finding people who have been seized by the inwardness of a religious tradition and who start to wonder about how to articulate a concept of God of love is not uncommon. Many of these despair of classical theism in this effort. In a strange way closed, static religion and open, dynamic religion are both antagonistic to each other and come together in a common pursuit. This is because neoclassical theism is, in part, inclusive of the best insights found in classical theism (*TS* 209–17).

The sedimentation of the concept of God is in large measure the easily visible result of classical theism. But this sedimentation is due to seismic forces that are not on the surface easily seen. Primary among these is the dialectic among Plato, Aristotle, and Plotinus on the concept of God. Whereas there is a prominent place for mysticism in Plotinus's philosophy, and hence for the possibility for open religion in his thought, there is much more Aristotle than Plato in his concept of God, which counteracts the tendency toward openness. The ultimate end of mysticism is contact with God, as various giants in the history of religious experience in various traditions, including Plato's *homoiosis theoi* (becoming as much like God[s] as possible), reported. To establish such contact is to act in such a way to be able to passively receive divine influence, such as working hard to pay attention to someone who says, "You have not been listening to me!" Once such contact with God occurs, it creates a wellspring of energy in the mystic, much like a lake filled to the brim with water that is held back by a dam; when the dam bursts, this energy flows back into the current of life and creates the open possibility for a richer understanding of both creaturely and divine dynamism (*TS* 219–20, 226–27).

It can be a shock to pass from the static to the dynamic, from the closed to the open, from everyday life to a mystic life. One can overcome this shock when one realizes that we all have the potential for mystic experience. Mystic (temporary) repose is the source of a sort of agitation to creatively change things, such as in a steam engine fully powered and ready to move forward. At the far side of the mystic dark night of the soul John of the Cross made famous is found an energetic movement into the light. As a result of *inter*action with God, the mystic comes out of contemplative repose ready to hurl himself or herself into vast enterprises. We can easily misunderstand the cliché in mystic literature regarding contemplative repose that Plotinus made famous: alone with The Alone. Such aloneness (not loneliness) is but a moment in the systole/diastole movement of the spiritual life that both mystics and process theists extol. Granted, many of the great figures in the history of religious experience *claim* that they are orthodox (or classical) theists, but these mystics are always the first to point out the uneasy alliance between the religious experiences they report and what I have called the classical concept of God. They often complain of "the God of the philosophers," without realizing that only some philosophers defend the concept of God that they see at odds with their personal experiences (*TS* 229–32).

Human beings are, along with God, cocreators of the evolving universe. Such cocreation is especially dramatic when mystic open religion erupts within the confines of a particular closed religion; then all of the pieces of the closed religion have to be rethought. What personal religious experience pours red hot into human existence is then cooled under the rational analysis of philosophers and theologians, who engage in an abstract metadiscipline that tries to understand what happens at the more concrete level. Religious institutions are also the result of the cooling process, but not at an abstract level; rather, religious institutions serve the function of popularizing the insights and experiences of the great mystics, including Moses, Jesus, and Mohammed, among many others. The influence of the God of Aristotle (which itself relies on one facet only of Plato's more complex concept of God) on the Abrahamic religions has had a distorting effect on the cool rational analysis of philosophers and theologians over the centuries. Distortion resulted because of an overly aggressive version of divine omniscience with respect to future contingencies, which runs afoul of a belief in human freedom, and an overly aggressive version of divine omnipotence, which runs afoul of the theodicy problem (*TS* 234–41).

One might legitimately wonder why Aristotle chose as his first principle a mover that remains motionless and a thought that can think only itself. One might also wonder why Aristotle identified this first principle with God, given the fact that the phenomenology of religious experience in various traditions indicates that God is a being who can hold communication with human beings. That is, Aristotle's immutable deity (or deities) has very little in common with either the ancient Greek gods or with the God of the Abrahamic religions. On the contrasting process account, the real is mobile, or is rather movement itself. It would be a mistake, Bergson thinks, to slow down the movement of life, even divine life, to the point where a particular frame was confused with the whole, such as when a motion picture is gradually slowed to a halt and all that can be viewed is an individual, static picture, as if in a frame. This is what occurs in the Aristotelian view of God. Immutability need not be seen as superior to mutability, as Aristotle thinks, nor should we assume that mutability itself indicates a deficiency. Rather than seeing time as a deprivation of eternity, we would be better served by viewing the everlasting as derivative from an endless series of temporal moments, which are primary (*TS* 241–44).

We do not find dynamic creativity unintelligible when we consider that the movement of life itself, activity, and freedom are commonplace. When we think of God, we should think of preeminent movement rather than of the complete absence of it. Philosophers need to intervene when thinkers distort the living world that we live in as a result of habits that tend to go unexamined. The Aristotelian tendency to view God as an unmoved, permanent, immutable being is one of the habits that deserves to be examined in detail, contra the classical theistic reflex (*CEV* 196, 248, 322–25, 349, 351–52).

The indignant protests of those who see in mystic experience nothing but quackery and folly are contradicted by Bergson's (and William James's) observation that even those who have never had religious experiences nonetheless often resonate positively when they hear them described by others. The religious experiences find an echo in the hearts of those who are not nominally religious. In different terms, the feeling that we are each parts of a mighty (if not omnipotent), meaningful, beneficent Whole is widespread if not universal. The chief contribution of mysticism is to attest to the claim that God is pervasive love. In fact, it is the inheritance of the mystical tradition that love is the essential feature of God (a view that is not handled well, if at all, in the monopolar terms of classical theism). Claims such as these lead to the conclusion that the mystic tradition is somewhat anti-intellectual. A more felicitous way to put the point is to say that those who have had religious experiences tend to tire easily of systems, including religious ones, that lose sight of these insights/experiences. The mystics bear witness that God needs us, just as we need God. Why should God need us unless it be to love us? The Hartshornian distinction between divine existence and divine actuality is much needed here. To claim (legitimately) that divine existence is necessary and does not require any particular others is not to claim that there could be no others at all in that preeminent love requires some others to love. *How* God exists does partially depend on us if divine love is even remotely analogous to human love, which even the classical theist is willing to admit, albeit perhaps grudgingly (*TS* 246, 251–55, 311; *CS* 92).

One of the faults with classical theistic theodicy is that by relying so heavily on divine omnipotence, divine omnibenevolence is threatened. Why is there so much evil in the world, or any evil at all, if God is omnipotent and could eliminate the evil? One standard response to this is that evil is the result of misused freedom on the part of human beings, but this leaves unexplained why nonhuman animals who do not have free will suffer intense pain. Even if one is not an animal rightist, as long as one's view is not the Cartesian one wherein nonhuman animals are machines and are hence incapable of suffering, one must account for how there could be nonhuman animal suffering. Classical theists are inevitably led to something like Leibniz's theodicy wherein this is either the best of all possible worlds or the best way to reach it. But on this basis what are we to say to a parent who has just buried a child who died of an intensely painful illness? If evil is not merely a lesser good, then the Leibnizian view involves unwarranted optimism. Optimism of some sort may receive justificatory warrant on the Bergsonian view that is conducive to mysticism in open religion, but not the hyperbolic Leibnizian kind of optimism that is the result of the classical theistic concept of God, especially the overly robust versions of omnipotence and omniscience with respect to future contingencies that are the hallmarks of classical theistic theodicy (*TS* 260–61).

Bergson is at his best, I think, when he criticizes the "a priorism" of classical theistic theodicy in general, and its Leibnizian version in particular. It is taken for granted that God must be omnipotent, on this view, and from there certain characteristics of the world are deduced, notably either that ultimately there is nothing that is evil or that what appears to be evil is instrumental in bringing about a greater good. Not surprisingly, then, as a result of this problematic approach, atheism and agnosticism look attractive. The process view needs to correct this triumphalist approach, which is almost the reverse. *Start* with the experience of pain and evil in the world and then see what this experience can tell us about the concept of God. What we are told is that it is not merely us but God, too, who experiences tragic suffering, if not death (*TS* 261–62).

The very substance of closed society/religion is its static nature. The fact that its obligatory character is embedded in many institutions accounts for its pervasive and long-lasting influence. But movement need not be seen as the diminution of the static in the manner that women were seen traditionally as lesser men. The metaphysical issue of finding the proper balance between permanence and change, between being and becoming, is not unrelated to the major problems in political philosophy. Closed societies tend to be undemocratic in the extreme in that they rely on the assumption that political authority is embedded in an immobile hierarchy. By contrast, the democratic virtues are dialogical rather than monological in character and involve hearing as well as speaking. As a result, the impassive classical theistic God is ill-suited to people who defend democratic political ideals; many classical theists opposed to democracy themselves have defended over the centuries the claim that I am making here (*TS* 270–71, 281–83).

It is becoming *and* being, change *and* permanence that must be accounted for in the concept of God. If two contrasting (not contradictory) ideas that are part of the same overall reality are severed and pursued separately, disastrous consequences will follow. Unbridled worship of being, say, would dry up the obvious indeterminacy of the future. The process thinker is calling for a thoroughgoing philosophical and spiritual reform concerning the concept of God, but, as the word literally implies, "re-form" does not mean that one has to start from scratch in an ahistorical manner. The idea that the future will be detailed is not equivalent to the idea that it is already detailed in any mind, even a divine one. It is time (albeit everlasting time) that leads us to experience God, not the fiction that there really is no time in the eternal divine mind. Although the present can influence the future, especially the near future, it cannot precisely necessitate it in that the world grows in determinations and concreteness. Earlier moments, even in the divine life, are abstract in the sense that they contain their futures only in outline (*TS* 296–99, 313, 317; *MVG* 14, 140, 269, 286–87).

When process is seen as the ultimate mode of reality, being does not vanish but is rather seen as an abstract aspect of that which becomes. The present contains within itself the necessity that some future will follow it, but how it will be superseded can be understood only within certain limits of variation, rather than in terms of precise details. Never again should thinkers take it for granted that God must be conceived as motionless in static perfection and self-sufficiency, incapable of receiving influence from humans—especially from mystics—and incapable of anything that has ever been understood as love (*RSP* 159).

Thinking that the progressiveness of open religion is primarily due to naïve optimism would be a mistake. It is, rather, primarily due to a reasonable tenet of process thinking that reality is cumulative in character. Reality is enriched at each moment as new events come into existence, but there is no necessity that previous phases have to pass out of existence. The more comes from the less. That is, reality is creative rather than destructive in character if memory is at base psychological in that in memory there is direct possession or grasping of past events by present ones (what Whitehead calls "prehension"). God as omniscient (properly conceived) and omnibenevolent ensures that no achieved value is lost in that such would be preserved in the ideal Memory. In this regard, we can even say that the past is immortal. Human freedom, in particular, exhibits a sort of creativity that has a very real effect on the divine actuality (*PSG* 85, 95, 228, 469, 501, 509; *LP* 174, 185).

The very existence of time indicates that there is indetermination in things; time *is* that indetermination. This enables many people to come to terms with both their finitude and their orientation toward infinitude, whatever their religious beliefs or lack thereof. After all, once we die, we will be dead all the time. Furthermore, at least some events endure in later events, and if there is a God then all of them so endure. But the fact that events endure in the memory of those who live on is not to be confused with the idea that the future was mapped out in detail beforehand in that inexorable purpose would be at odds with individuality, self-activity, and temporal reality itself. But these things do exist, which is good because it is in our free creations, our deciding of the otherwise undecided, the forming of the previously inchoate, that our dignity lies (*CM* 109–25; *LP* 15, 18, 206, 232, 236).

If reality, even divine reality, is essentially creative process, with an aspect of futurity or partial indeterminacy built into it, then objective necessity is what all possibilities have in common, their "no matter what" aspect. Experience, both human and nonhuman, is necessarily preservative *and* creative in that it inherits causal influence from its past and is thrust into new moments that require some sort of decision, whether conscious or not, some cutting off of some possibilities so that others are enacted. In a sense, "to be is to create," and what it means to be creative is to be incompletely determined in advance by causal conditions and laws; to be creative is to make additions to the definiteness of reality. Hence, reality, even divine reality, is predictable, but only to the extent that it is not creative and is habitual. Becoming is reality itself. Determinism attempts to abstract away from the creativity of experience, and reductionistic materialism tries to abstract away from experience itself (*AD* 43; *CS* xv, 1, 3–4, 13, 26, 29).

Process theists commonly think that modal distinctions in logic are ultimately coincident with temporal ones. The actual is the past and the possible is the future; the present consists in the process by which what is possible becomes actual. On this view, a future actuality is a contradiction in terms, despite what classical theists might claim in their defense of divine omniscience with respect to future contingencies (or, to be true to classical theism, "contingencies"). From a slightly different angle, the distinction between time and (classical theistic) eternity is itself a temporal one because eternity is a negation of temporality; temporality is not a negation of eternity. Time is a positive aspect of the real with which we are all, in a way, familiar, as Bergson famously holds. The centrality of time is in evidence when we notice that possibilities are determinables, rather than determinates, contra classical theism and pantheism (*CS* 61–65).

The endurance of the past through causal influence, memory, or perception (of the immediate past) need not be as strange as it may initially sound. Past events may not exist in the same sense as they once did. But they may nonetheless still exist in the present in a different sense. The new cannot exist in the old, but the old *can* exist in the new. Novelty is inclusive in the sense that it is a combination of the old and the new, but such combination is always in the present. That is, becoming is the creation of novel wholes with old elements. Process is cumulative; or better, it involves creative synthesis. On the basis of this view, there is room for *some* prediction of the future, but such prediction has to be abstract and incomplete if the details regarding the future are not here yet to be known. This hiddenness is not necessarily due to any defect on our part but to the asymmetrical nature of time itself (*CS* 105, 109, 118, 192, 211).

The Bergsonian phrase that captures the prime difficulty with the classical theistic version of omniscience is the "spatialization of time." According to the classical theistic view, God already knows our future actions. We have seen that the problem with this view is that it assumes that our future actions are already in existence for God to know. The classical theist, however, thinks that God can see these actions as a spectator from a great height. This involves the effort to slow down the flux of history, which can be analogized to a film, to a single frame, which can be analogized to a photograph. This is precisely the spatialization of time wherein the new "totality" that comes into existence at each moment is fixed in a single, all-encompassing view. But there just is no fixed totality in the dynamic world within which we live. That is, the cliché that "truth is timeless" is a piece of baseless dogmatism; we can make sense of it only in terms of the constant features of an ever-changing reality. Reality is more filmlike than it is photograph-like (*CS* 135).

The temporal structure of the real is evidenced in experience itself, where what is present epistemically is later than the datum experienced, given the time lag due to the speed of light or auditory waves. One of the reasons why classical theists might be skittish about attributing this temporal structure to the experience of God is the assumption that temporal succession involves loss or perishing of that which happened before. But God as the ideal knower would not allow the fading of immediacy as events cease to be present events. The order of succession involves not perishing but rather a distinct difference between retrospection and prospection. Later events grasp earlier ones, but the converse is not true. In fact, all of our experience of concrete actuality is retrospective, like the view from the back of a train whose objects are already past when seen (*WP* 5, 83–85; *IO* 342).

Except perhaps for truths in mathematics, logic, and the most abstract claims in metaphysics, truths come into existence at a certain time, but they exist everlastingly due to divine memory. As before, becoming is creative, not destructive. Preservation-plus-creation characterizes all concrete singulars, from subatomic particles/waves to God, who is the preeminent example of preservation-creation. The creative advance that is reality itself finds its ideal in God. In one sense the past creates the present by supplying its necessary conditions, but in another sense the present occasion makes itself, even in the divine case. The former claim warrants saying that memory is the key to the temporal structure of the universe, but we have seen that even "present" perception is, in a peculiar way, a type of impersonal memory (*EA* 68, 76, 102; *CA* 56, 107, 149, 178, 201).

There are some positive things that can be said about closed religion. For example, it is something of a biological necessity even for members of a species who exist with a sufficiently high level of intelligence. Religious sanctions partially take the place of instinct as an antidote against destructive behavior, some of which is actually driven by intelligence. Hence creative advance is not the whole story in that religion itself can be seen as a natural defensive reaction against the dissolvent and destructive uses of intelligence. Many societies have existed without science and philosophy, but none have flourished without religion. The creativity that characterizes open religion grows out of the best in closed religion. The best of religion in the past is embraced within the present without being determined by it; the past provides necessary but not sufficient conditions for the present, even in the divine case. Bergson more than makes up for what is sometimes claimed to be the paucity of logical rigor in his thought with original insight, such as in his subtle treatment of the relationship between closed and open religion and between closed and open concepts of God, with the latter concept especially illuminating the nature of mystical experience (*TS* 122, 131, 140, 205; *OO* 85, 105; *DL* 120, 393; *CE* 121).

Hartshorne is like Bergson in being a critic of static Platonic forms, including Whitehead's eternal objects. The problem here is to avoid a return to old-style metaphysics based on an idea of substance and the primacy of being over becoming. The new-style metaphysics all three thinkers (Bergson, Hartshorne, and Whitehead) want to defend emphasizes self-motion, dynamism, freedom, and creativity (assuming that there is a family resemblance among these terms) at all levels of nature. A prime example of such self-motion is memory, which consists in one's present prehending or feeling of one's own previous prehending or feeling. What is clearly and distinctly remembered at a given moment is much less than what is effectively remembered in that our brains filter out irrelevant (or seemingly irrelevant) factors from our past experiences. If such filtering did not occur, we would be overwhelmed by mnemonic material. In this regard it makes sense to say that our implicit awareness of God (of our being parts of a meaningful Whole) as well as the mystics' explicit awareness of God are both important topics for the present book. The points made above about memory also apply to divine memory. However, the aforementioned filtering process does not apply in the divine case, where even the fall of a sparrow is remembered, as we have seen (*PCH* 662; *CE* 3, 15; *CS* 89).

Bergson's snowball metaphor is also instructive. The rolling ball acquires new layers while retaining old ones. Or again, an adult can remember his or her childhood, but no child has a comparable awareness of the adult life that individual might lead. This processual, asymmetrical, and cumulative set of circumstances typifies all of reality, including the divine case. Every actual occasion in this processual, asymmetrical, and cumulative scheme has a certain degree of power, which means that if God is aware of all actual occasions, each of these has a certain minimal power over God's actuality if not God's existence. This partial power of the creatures over God, however, does not play into the hands of classical theists who think that any concept of God that omits omnipotence leaves God in an utterly power*less* state. Here it makes sense to reference a version of the design argument that does not avail itself of the concept of omnipotence. Either the agents of creative action throughout the cosmos just happen to fit together so as to maintain a viable cosmic system or there is a supreme form of creative decision making that has influence over all lesser forms of decision making so as to set limits to the conflicts and frustrations that characterize the disorder inherent in a multiplicity of self-determining occasions. That is, order is either due to each occasion adapting to the numerous others or it involves each occasion adapting not only to the others but also to a supreme entity that can give guidance to all (*CE* 71, 116, 135).

One of the most important tasks in the effort to find a defensible concept of God is to calibrate an idea of divine power that can be seen in equilibrium with all of the relevant factors that must be balanced: the order of nature, creaturely power, the presence of evil, and so on. None of the nuanced problems involved here is solved by appeal to divine omnipotence. One wonders what this word could mean if every concrete singular has some power of its own. It is a pseudoconcept in that we can vocalize the word "omnipotence," but we cannot understand what it could possibly mean, given the multitude of dynamic centers of power in the universe. Furthermore, because belief in divine omnipotence has historically gone hand in glove with belief in creation ex nihilo, it is noteworthy that Bergson has offered one of the most detailed and insightful analyses of this concept, the conclusion of which is that the very idea of absolute nothingness makes no more sense than a square circle (*TS* 229, 251, 261).

Bergson is very much compatible with the comparable idea in Plato's *Sophist* that whereas relative nonbeing makes sense, absolute nonbeing does not. A basketball does not have the sort of existence that a baseball has and hence can be said to be "nothing like" a baseball. But each of these exists in some manner. Or again, when a creative action is taken one is bringing something into existence that did not exist before, but this is hardly creation out of absolutely nothing in that each of these absences is built on a certain presence. The root of the difficulty lies in imagining the nonexistence of this or that thing, which leads to imagining the nonexistence of a whole class of things, which in turn leads to the erroneous conclusion that this imaginative process could go on indefinitely and that one could really imagine the nonexistence of everything. But to say that "it" (i.e., everything) does not exist is, once again, to engage a sort of absence that is really a presence because the "absolute nothingness" in question would actually be something. To talk about "it" is to talk about somethingness rather than supposed absolute nothingness. The admirable classical theistic attempt to exalt God, which in itself is understandable, is not aided by attributing omnipotence to God in that such an effort both leads to logical contradictions and creates the most troublesome version of the theodicy problem. However, given the general order of the world, the overall problem is not easily solved by running to the other extreme by claiming that God is utterly powerless, or, what amounts to the same, claiming that there is no God. By contrast, Hartshorne goes so far as to claim that Bergson's analysis of open religion, which is fueled by mystical experience, is nothing less than profound (*CEV* 273–98; *ZF* 14).

Neoclassical theism is obviously wedded to a different view of time from that found in classical theism. Temporal process is seen as the creation of new events whose totality is itself new each time we consider it. That is, God's relationship with the world *requires* temporality. Both the classical theistic denial of temporality to God and the denial of potentiality to God make divine personality impossible. To impute responsiveness or love to a nontemporal God is to develop a misleading ideal. Time can indeed be seen as a moving image of God, but perhaps not as a moving image of "eternity" if this term refers to a strictly nontemporal being. Temporality, as Bergson realized, and as Augustine almost came to realize, has a psychological aspect that should not be ignored. This is due to the fact that memory involves the retention of definite actuality from the past, while anticipation involves present delineation of an outline regarding what might happen in the future. Due to our and especially the divine memory, what has become actual can never be destroyed; reality is, as Bergson well knew, creation and not destruction. Strictly speaking, not even death is sheer destruction, but only the nonprolongation of a personal series of events. Death is the boundary of the last item in the series, but what happened to each event in the series can be (and in the divine case, is) remembered (*AD* 51, 193; *CS* 53, 115, 291; *DR* 84; *PSG* 11, 19, 23–24, 54).

By seeing God in a Bergsonian way as the categorically supreme example of temporality, we are able to counter Kantian objections not only to theism but also to mystical experience (due to Kant's own assumption that God would have to be outside of time altogether). The Kantian claim that all of our positive conceptions must be in terms of time no longer has negative implications for religious experience, just as new divine knowledge does not imply any defect in divine omniscience, as the Socinians and Gersonides, among others, realized in opposition to classical theism centuries ago. (Thus, in a peculiar way Kant can be turned into a process philosopher.) As God sees things change, there is also change in the very beholding of these changes. Every kind of life involves succession such that "being" is still a useful term, but only in terms of abstraction away from "becoming"; being denotes the continuity among a series of events in process. *Absolute* rest would be, if it were possible, the complete negation of the inherent activity of the real. Growth (if not progress) is a primordial element of the cosmos, hence, to understand experience adequately, including mystical experience and relations with a personal deity, one must come to terms with the processual and evolutionary character of the real (*PSG* 75, 146; *IO* 171, 176, 181; *FVRS* 236–37).

We have seen that the process theism found in Bergson and other thinkers is nonetheless compatible with those aspects of divine permanence that are accurately described in mystical literature. Loving divine dependability is in itself unalterable through all earthly and divine alterations in their fluency. Further, it would be a mistake to equate transiency with insignificance if the transient is preserved in our (somewhat adequate) memory as well as in divine (supremely adequate) Memory. Time involves not so much loss as accretion, even for divine time, especially for divine time. Classical theists, tied to substantialist thinking, will likely continue to talk of temporal change in terms of new adjectival states added to the same substance, rather than in terms of new entities themselves. Process thinkers, in general, prefer the latter way of speaking because it enables them to understand better the crucial idea of time as objective modality: The past is the region of conditional necessity in that it must be the way it is given the actual present; and the future is the region of mixed modality in that it involves conditional necessity given the actual present *and* real possibilities yet unrealized. Mystics, along with the rest of us, have always acted as if there is a difference between the settled past and a partially open future (*CS* 182, 253; *PSG* 88, 94–96, 225–29, 237, 242–43, 252, 261–62, 270, 282, 382).

Terms like "the universe" and "the whole of time" are demonstrative pronouns in the sense that they get their meaning from context, with a partly new meaning at each moment. This is due to the fact that time involves genuine creation, rather than the classical theistic view that what is "new" is in some way the instantiation of what has always been in the (divine) cards from eternity. Of course, this does not mean that our experience of enduring individuals is mistaken, only that such experience should be understood differently from the way it is understood in classical theism. Enduring individuals, including the divine individual, is an abstractly conceived version of a sequence of events, each one of which individually is unique, a uniqueness that is given ample testimony in the history of mystical experience. If all events are real together, as classical theists think, then there just could be no becoming; but there is obviously becoming, hence the defects of the classical theistic view. The unforeseeable character of the future is not a defect; it is incurable, contra the timeless God of classical theism that is at odds with the God of religion (*RSP* 91, 200–2; *WP* 35).

The divine present, as experienced by mystics, is not a mathematical instant or a theoretical abstraction but an "epochal" affair that is temporally thick in its own way, in conformity with Bergson's view of temporal thickness. That is, the divine present experienced by the mystics includes human and divine memory of the past (albeit with obvious differences in degree and quality of adequacy), as well as human and divine anticipations and plastic control over the future (once again, as analogically predicated in the human and divine cases).

Chapter 9

The Aesthetics of Mystical Experience

We have seen that if mysticism is direct (albeit mediated) experience of God, then neoclassical metaphysics not only permits such experience but *requires* that all of us have it, although only implicitly or without bringing such experience into conscious awareness. But if mysticism includes the requirement that the experience of God is consciously recognized as such, that not only is God given, but given *as* God, then there are relatively few mystics, even if they are not exactly rare, either. In this latter sense of the term "mysticism," there is agreement among mystics (at least in the Abrahamic religions) that God is not only personal but engages in interaction with other (human) persons. The purpose of the present chapter is to explore the aesthetic dimensions of mysticism, both in its generic and specific senses.

The Greek word *aesthesis* originally meant nothing other than feeling or what we today might call "experience." Only later did the word refer to a disciplined feeling for beauty, in particular. To explore the aesthetic dimensions of mysticism is to avail ourselves of both senses of *aesthesis*, as we will see (*MVG* 217, 220, 224, 227; *WM* 51–54, 84–85, 94, 107; *ZF* 47).

Aristotle is rightly famous for the view that virtue consists in a mean between extremes, the latter being vices. But the principle of moderation applies much more generally than Aristotle supposed, as Hartshorne sees things, in that it applies not only in ethics but in aesthetics as well. Beauty can be seen as a mean between two sets of extremes, as figure 9.1 indicates (*CS* 303–13; *IO* 62; *RE* 9–13; *SSH* 86; *WM* 1–4; *ZF* 203–06):

It is a mistake to *identify* beauty with order in that too much order creates an aesthetic problem, that of monotony. Mechanical order that is too strict or unrelenting is not beautiful, nor is chaos or a sheer lack of order, in

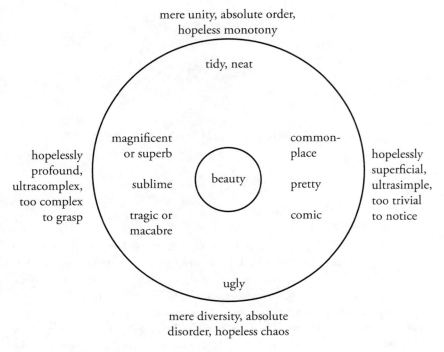

Figure 9.1.

that with mechanism we are bored and with chaos we are confused. Beauty, it seems, is ordered diversity, as is symbolized by the imagined vertical axis that runs through figure 9.1.

It should also be noted that there is an imaginary horizontal axis. A musical chord or a little flower is a superficial harmony, in contrast to a Mahler symphony or an old-growth forest. Deviations from beauty, however, when seen as the central aesthetic value and as a double-mean between vertical and horizontal extremes, can obviously be of great aesthetic value themselves. The simplicity of a Willa Cather novel is part of its appeal. And the profound discords in, say, Frédéric Chopin's funeral march disrupt expected harmony in a way that is tragic and that challenges us to the depths. It is only those realities outside of the outer circle (if there are such) that are utterly devoid of aesthetic value. The horizontal axis should also make it clear that the beautiful and the pretty should not be seen as synonymous, as they often are in popular culture. That is, the vertical axis illustrates that beauty consists in harmony or unity-in-variety, whereas the horizontal axis illustrates that beauty requires an appropriate intensity of experience (*IO* 326).

The point to this diagram is to help us appreciate the aesthetic dimensions of mystical experience, which, if it is experience of an omnipresent God, would involve aesthetic values around the diagram in all four directions, even if the vast extent of divine existence, knowledge, and love impresses us as sublime beauty rather than as pretty beauty. Once again, the core aesthetic value is beauty, with the adjectival uses of sublimity and prettiness intended to highlight this centrality (OD 235; *MVG* 213; *NT* 15; *LP* 127).

A musical chord has both unity and variety, but superficially so. One can imagine a symphony with the same proportionate balance of unity and variety as the chord, but vastly more diversity is unified in the symphony. It does not seem an exaggeration to speak symbolically at this point of the divine symphony. However, experiences all around the diagram, but nonetheless within the larger circle, can be seen as religious experiences, as intrinsically (i.e., aesthetically) valuable, in contrast to whatever instrumental value they may have in leading to happiness or unhappiness, to joy or sadness.

Values, in general, may be seen as connected to three activities: thinking logically (truth), acting morally (goodness), and experiencing satisfyingly (beauty). It makes sense to consider the hypothesis that the last is primary. This is because if we knew what experience at its best or most beautiful consisted in (as in mystical experience), we would then perhaps know how to act. And if thinking is a type of acting, as Charles Sanders Peirce insisted, then logic as a normative science would be a branch of ethics. This line of reasoning indicates why an understanding of the aesthetic dimensions of mystical experience is so important.

Process thinkers in general tend to see beauty as the mutual adaptation of the elements of an experience, but mutual adaptation or harmony, although a necessary condition for beauty, is not yet sufficient in that some *intensity* of experience also seems to be needed, even in the case of the pretty, as illustrated by the horizontal axis. Thus, aesthetic value, including the supreme aesthetic value found in mystical experience, is diversified, intense harmonization of experience. Beauty involves not only variety of contrast but also *depth* of contrast that affects the perceiver (the mystic) in an intense way.

Perhaps it will be objected that if beauty is at least partially defined by unity-in-variety, then *all* experiences would have aesthetic value in that each would have unity as one experience and each would have variety in terms of the parts of the experience itself and in terms of its differences from other experiences. However, we need not be any more frightened away by the possibility that minimal aesthetic value is ubiquitous than we are by the claim that divine presence and influence are ubiquitous. In effect, sheer aesthetic failure (outside the larger circle) can quite legitimately be equated with the sheer absence of experience. To see beauty as a mean is to make an effort to understand aesthetic value somewhere above the bare minimum (*PPS* 103, 119, 133, 187; *PSG* 324, 327; *RSP* 48, 82, 103; *ZF* 80).

Deviations from the mean need not leave us aesthetically dead, at least if they are not too far from the mean. Beauty is the ideal aesthetic value, but not the only one. Some of the other aesthetic values are found in the diagram. Further, the aesthetic value of deviations along the imaginary horizontal axis varies according to the sensibilities of the perceiver: A musical chord may, in fact, be profound to a child just as a birdsong that may seem superficial to us may very well be beautiful to a bird. This perhaps helps us to better understand the aesthetic sensibilities of the mystic, who is better able than most of us to appreciate divinity in its sublimity.

The larger circle could move to the right or left depending on various capacities to assimilate complexity, as when a bird would (probably) find a piece of chamber music hopelessly profound, the way we might be bewildered by the ability of the mystic to appreciate divine sublimity. The diameter of the larger circle may also vary, depending on the experiencing organism's scope of sensibility. Some, for example, may have a hard time appreciating a macabre story by Edgar Allen Poe. The diagram should also make clear that ugliness is not, strictly speaking, the opposite of beauty, but rather refers to the aesthetic value characterized by a mixture of order and discord/deformity, with the latter dominating. Not even ugliness is *pure* discord or de-formity, however, since pure discord would lie outside the larger circle and hence could not be experienced as *a* case of disorder.

I think it is very important to notice the aesthetic deficiencies of classical theism in that the version of divine omniscience found in classical theism—where God knows with absolute assurance and in minute detail *everything* that will happen in the future—leads to a determinism that in turn leads to a cosmic monotony, not beauty. That is, diversity in time requires unforeseen novelty, including unpredictability regarding future scientific discoveries. If the specifics of future theories were predictable (I write during the COVID-19 crisis), we would have them already and there would be no need to discover them. Predictability is to a certain extent a good thing because it enables us to see the world as orderly, as a cosmos. But strict predictability without remainder is a negative aesthetic value, hence from an aesthetic point of view we should be glad that we are temporal beings who enact a creative advance into the future (*DL* 206–7).

This creative advance should not be assumed to be the special prerogative of human beings. Beauty as integrated diversity and intensity of experience, far from being anthropocentric, is metaphysical: It is present to some extent in any state of concrete reality, from microorganisms to God. The latter, as omnibenevolent and omnipresent, enjoys harmonized contrasts on a cosmic scale. The more sophisticated one's abilities to perceive and think, the greater one's ability to order and to diversify and to appreciate order and diversity in others, with mystics exhibiting these abilities to a greater extent than the rest of us.

In addition to the principle that beauty is a mean between two sets of extremes, which includes the intensity principle, we also need a principle of positive incompatibility. Aesthetic discord does not so much involve a clash of positive and negative as one between incompossible positives. Being a first-rate philosopher is a good thing, as is being a first-rate pianist and a first-rate second baseman, but it is seemingly impossible to be all three. The conflict of positive values is at the root of tragedy, the profound aesthetic value that tends toward discord in neoclassical theism. (In classical theism, where God is omnipotent, there should be no tragedy, even if such obviously exists.) So as to minimize the tragedy of life, some goods must be renounced, hence we are all ascetics who must do without many good things, with the more rigorous ascetics (often mystics) being those who *deliberately* choose their renunciations and who choose them to a greater extent than the rest of us.

The beauty of friendship can also be explicated by the view of beauty as unity-in-difference. Friends harmonize in a concrete way felt by both parties both the commonality of interest between the two as well as the deep contrasts that are inevitable among any human beings, who are more highly individuated than members of other species. This unity-in-difference also helps us to understand better the friendly relationship between a mystic and God. To try to explain friendship strictly in terms of the similarities between the friends fails to do justice to the friends' own intimate awareness of each other's differences; in fact, it is the latter that make the bond of friendship all the more remarkable and beautiful.

Strict causal necessity, as implied in classical theism, would be monotonous, whereas sheer chance would lack unity and hence coherence. Luckily for us, the world in which we live is something of a beautiful compromise between the two. Both scenes in nature and great works of art, in whatever medium, are characterized by the unity-in-variety principle. Further, art critics and aestheticians have been in agreement on this for over two millennia. That is, we are not so much imposing a view of beauty as a dual mean on the subject matter in question but starting from how all of us, along with art critics and aestheticians, *experience* natural beauty and works of art (AAP 65–66; *CS* 128–29, 143, 155–56, 300; *HB* 84; *IO* 159, 173; MMEJ 107).

It is clear that some ordered complexities are experienced as superficial and some are experienced as deep. This leads us to consider the oft noticed analogy between some aesthetic experiences and some religious ones, as in the exaltation found in someone listening to George Frederick Handel's *Messiah* when compared to the exaltation found in a worshipper in a magnificent cathedral. Additionally, some aesthetic experiences, along with some religious ones, possess a high degree of value without having much diversity at all, as in a Henryk Górecki song on a religious theme that consists of only a few tones. Great aesthetic (and religious) value can be achieved in a "northerly" direction from core beauty so long as it is not outside of the larger circle in the above diagram. Likewise, great aesthetic value can be achieved as a deviation in a "southerly" direction from core beauty—as in *A Love Supreme* by the jazz musician John Coltrane—as long as it is not outside the larger circle.

Of course, the symmetries of the above diagram do not help us to feel the *intensity* of aesthetic/religious experiences. Although beauty is the ideal aesthetic value, it is not the only one, such that aesthetic values all around the diagram can be experienced with various levels of intensity. It is such intensity that keeps interest alive in the concept of beauty, despite the fact that this concept might seem to be fading in contemporary aesthetics. This alleged fading may very well be due to the classical theistic assumption that beauty is something that descends from a supernatural God and then irradiates the objects of the senses. But the neoclassical concept of a God who is not supernatural does not encourage this view. In fact, the very concerns that educated viewers and listeners have today when viewing and hearing art are *precisely those* that lie behind the theory of beauty as a dual mean: unity, diversity, balance, incongruity, dynamic contrast, complexity, insipidity, etcetera. That is, despite the "revolt against beauty" in aesthetics (to use Arthur Danto's phrase), there is ample room in contemporary thought for the approach to beauty developed here and to how this approach illumines mystical experience (*DR* 123; *PPS* 271–72; RGW 140–41).

It can be said that for the religious believer the goal in life is the generation of beauty, which is then contributed to the divine life. This view is compatible with descriptions of the God of the Hebrew bible in aesthetic terms such as sweetness (*no am*), splendor or majesty (*hah-dahr*), and glory (*tiphahrah*), as Patrick Sherry (*Spirit and Beauty*) notices. Such terms are instructive in the effort to rethink the logic of perfection in the transition from classical to neoclassical theism. Such a transition involves the effort to rescue religious aesthetics from the tameness of outdated perfection in that the tragic and the overwhelming sublime are also aesthetic values. Even the ugly and the horrible are aesthetic values, as in Shakespeare's *Richard III* or Pieter Breugel's painting *The Blind Leading the Blind*.

Maintaining an aesthetically satisfactory unity-in-diversity is no easy task. For example, we can fatigue easily with life or with art when things get too unified and predictable. We can also experience fatigue with life or religious ritual or art through constant exposure. This is one reason to be concerned with the commercialization of great art and religious symbols, where Giuseppe Verdi is played in elevators and the *Mona Lisa* is used to sell candy bars. It is always a danger that Christmas will be trivialized through both overexposure and commercialization. But it is not wise to specify in advance the boundaries of art in a strict way, say by stipulating a priori how much unity or diversity is allowable. Maurice Ravel's *Bolero* stretched the concept of repetition more than we might have supposed allowable before the fact, just as bebop stretched, at the other end, the already wide range of diverse possibilities given to jazz musicians, including religious musicians like Coltrane.

What can be said with confidence, again on the evidence of judgments made by artists themselves and art critics and religious aestheticians for centuries, is that there is something basic about the aesthetic tension of unity within contrast. Beauty is to be located in the aesthetic prehender and in the aesthetic object. Aesthetic objects exhibit mutual adaptation of several factors, and aesthetic experiences are prehensions of this harmony. This applies even when the aesthetic prehender in question is the mystic and the object prehended is the supreme example of beauty, God. Such prehensions can be explicit, say if the experiencer is reflecting on the beauty (or Beauty) prehended, or implicit, say if the prehender is only remotely aware of the dim, massive pattern of beauty throbbing microscopically in the cosmos as a whole. Regarding those aesthetic experiences that are explicitly appreciated as such, if the depth of contrast that is the object of such experiences is great, then the depth of satisfaction in the aesthetic experiences themselves is also likely to be great (STF 87, 90; WP 114; PSG 3; PUK 81; RSP 34, 44; OO 5, 37, 40; PCH 580, 684).

The importance of aesthetic considerations for an understanding of mystical experience is put into sharp relief in an aesthetic argument for the existence of God, which supplements consideration of the ontological argument in a previous chapter. This Hartshornian argument consists in laying out the logically possible options when certain variables are considered: (a) either there is a beauty of the world as a whole or there is no such beauty; and (b) if there is such a beauty, then either (i) either no one enjoys it; or (ii) only nondivine beings enjoy it; or (iii) God also (and only God adequately) enjoys it. Thus, four options are possible:

1. There is no beauty of the world as a whole.

2. There is a beauty of the world as a whole, but no one enjoys it.

3. There is a beauty of the world as a whole, but only nondivine beings enjoy it.

4. There is a beauty of the world as a whole, and God alone adequately enjoys it (*CS* 287–90).

If (1) were true, the world would be either a chaos or a mere monotony. Neither is really possible. It cannot be a chaos because a merely chaotic world is unknowable, for no knowledge could exist in it. But the world *is* knowable, hence the impossibility of (1). It cannot be a monotony because order implies a contrasting (dipolar) element of disorder; the two terms are correlative, and neither can be understood without the other. On classical theistic assumptions, however, a completely determined world *would* be monotonous. Further, the testimony of the great mystics confirms the beauty of the world.

And (2) is unconvincing because by thinking and feeling the world as a whole, we enjoy at least a glimpse of its beauty. Not only every experience but also every thought yields *some* sort of aesthetic result.

The problem with (3) is that our enjoyment of the beauty in question (or the enjoyment of the whole by any localized, nondivine being), although real, especially for the mystic, is disproportionate to the cosmic, sublime beauty in question. If this disproportion obtained, then there would be a basic flaw in reality that could never be eliminated. Because God cannot exist contingently, for such an existence would be inconsistent with God's status as the greatest conceivable being, God's existence is either impossible or necessary. Therefore (3) would signal the impossibility of God's existence. Thus, (3) involves a permanent ugliness or flaw to the world as a whole. This thought does not console us, but quite apart from its psychological effect, its pragmatic value seems to bring us to the realization that *if* the world as a whole is *really* beautiful, it could not fail to have an adequate appreciator.

Although (4) is the view of theists, the hypothetical character of the argument highlights the fact that this argument cannot stand alone as a convincing argument for the existence of God, although it can supplement the ontological argument like mutually reinforcing strands in a cable that results in something quite strong. The beauty of the world is dynamic in a processual universe; it is less like a statue and more like a theatrical performance that exhibits a balance of unity and variety. The mystic especially, but all of us at least implicitly, cannot remain indifferent to the beauty of the cosmos. Although the only being who could *adequately* appreciate the beauty of the world as a whole is God, the mystic more closely approximates this august standard than the rest of us in that we are likely to be overwhelmed by the sublimity of the project.

We tend to think that it is a good thing if beauty is appreciated, and we tend to regret it if beauty is not appreciated. It is the mystic who comes closest to appreciating such beauty, which can be seen as excessive. *Some of the beauty in the world serves a biological or evolutionary function*, as when the bright colors of flowers are explained in terms of the selection of bees; if bees are attracted to these colors, these flowers will be pollinated and thus have a better chance at surviving. The attractiveness to females of the otherwise dysfunctional tail of the male peacock can be explained in a similar fashion. But when all such explanations have been exhausted, there is still much beauty that remains. From a strictly utilitarian point of view, the beauty of the world is, in part and as a whole, excessive. We are fortunate that there are some people, the mystics among them, who are sensitized to such excess and are not scared off by the obvious tragedy in the world.

It might be objected that there is also excessive ugliness and evil in the world, but we should remember that the nastiest version of the theodicy problem is found within classical theism due to an attachment or fetish for divine omnipotence. This type of God could eliminate all birth defects, but for some strange reason chooses not to do so. That is, the objection is not fatal to neoclassical, process theism. The fundamental order of the world is aesthetic, including sublime and tragic beauty. The mystic knows that, if the many instances of suffering are taken as evidence against the beauty of the world, it looks as if there is an insufficient unity in the universe. It should be noted, however, that it is, in fact, a *uni*verse, as Donald Viney emphasizes in a book devoted to the complementary nature of arguments for the existence of God in Hartshorne, including the ontological and aesthetic arguments.

The complex theory of beauty that I am defending is integrally connected to neoclassical theism when the sublimity of religious belief is considered and when such sublime beauty is experienced by the mystic. Astronomy shows the cosmos to be vast *almost* beyond comprehension, with perhaps billions of planets. This should convince us, at the very least, that the universe is not here only for *us*. Replacing anthropocentrism with theocentrism is one possible way to do justice to the mystic's (and our own) experience of the sublime. A theistic metaphysics that enables us to appreciate the sublime beauty of the cosmos, as well as its pretty and comic features, makes it easier to articulate the appropriateness of the mystic's religious faith.

If life is essentially aesthetic creation, the ongoing achievement of harmonious experiences, and if we are fragments of the whole of things, then religion consists in what we do with this fragmentariness as an aesthetic problem. An elephant is also a fragment, but presumably the elephant does not know this. We are able to consciously accept the fact of our fragmentariness in that we are aware of our status as partially self-creative fragments of the actuality of divine Creativity. Our efforts in this regard face two dangers along the vertical axis in the above diagram: At one extreme we have aesthetic incoherence or disorder, and at the other extreme we have a lifeless, tedious orderliness or regularity. We have seen, however, that mutual adaptation or harmony is not a sufficient condition of great value in that there is also a need for intensity of experience appropriate for the experiencer in question, with mystics capable of a level of intensity that is somewhat greater than that found in most of us. Integrated diversity and intensity of experience in one sense is metaphysical as it is exhibited in any possible state of reality, whereas in a more specific sense it is exhibited in high degree in those who are especially able to appreciate highly unified yet highly diversified reality in an especially intense way.

Aesthetic value is intrinsic rather than instrumental. In this regard God can be seen as both the greatest intrinsic (aesthetic) value and the greatest aesthetic Valuer of other intrinsic values. To be God would be to aesthetically appreciate *all* intrinsic values, in contrast to our rather meagre ability to appreciate only some of them and in our somewhat defective, biased way. Aesthetic value, in general, and the aesthetic value of mystical experience, in particular, involve the delight of beholding just to behold; both of these types of experience involve knowledge by acquaintance. The doctrine that there is something spiritual in the experiences of the mystics can in attenuated fashion apply to the experiences of all of us when we encounter intrinsic value. These latter experiences involve a maximum of attention paid to the emotional qualities of the experiences themselves, rather than to the instrumental value to which they can be put (economic, practical, teleological, etc.). This view is related to the familiar distinction between a sign, where instrumentality is foremost (as in a road sign that says "Seattle 38 miles"), and a symbol, where instrumentality is diminished and we are asked to pay attention to the meaning found *in* the colors, shapes, etcetera, that are experienced. Symbols (especially religious symbols) call us up short, in contrast to the looking beyond that characterizes signs.

The unqualified simplicity of the classical theistic God would not constitute very much in the way of intrinsic value; experience of such a God would quickly lead to monotony. Metaphysics, which deals with abstractions, and aesthetics, which deals with concrete experience, dovetail in the effort to avoid simplistic solutions to complex problems. Likewise, a God who knows, but who does not feel, would be an aesthetically empty being and not the greatest conceivable. Because God is the supreme artist who deals with lesser artists (including us), the symbol of a chorus director or a director of a theatrical performance is a better model for God than a painter or a poet, who does not have to deal with free beings other than the artist in question. It is for this reason that the outcome of the human drama cannot be predicted in any detail in that the actors have their own aesthetic sensibilities and freedoms. Mystical experience involves the joint assertion of unity (or some sort of contact) with God and the mystic's own individuality. It involves the crucial dipolar aesthetic principle of unity-in-diversity. As before, the mystic is not lost or obliterated in this unification but transfigured or transformed.

Aesthetic experience is intuitive or concrete prehension of the real in a direct (albeit mediated) manner. The unity-in-diversity that characterizes "aesthetic experience" (which, in one sense, is something of a redundancy, but the phrase in this context is meant to contrast with experience of instrumental value) necessarily involves complementarity of elements. One shares in the life of the aesthetic object so as to enrich one's own. This is true in all aesthetic experience, especially so in the mystic's aesthetic experience of

God. In this regard it should be noted that theism itself is an attempt to account for the beauty of the world. But theism need not involve a belief in personal immortality in that, on aesthetic grounds, a temporally infinite lifespan would lead to monotony if the immortal being in question was not infinitely wise and good. The good life is one where monotony is avoided such that each day should be treated as a creative adventure. Granted, life also requires regularity, and some surprises are unpleasant. But the tedium of the block universe found within classical theism can be avoided, indeed must be avoided, if life is to be beautiful in some way.

To serve God is to make one's contribution to the beauty of the world as something of a spectacle for divine enjoyment in that God is the supreme example of life interested in other life. Aesthetic value is intrinsic, immediately felt value, whereas instrumental value is extrinsic and indirect. On this account, instrumental value is good only if it eventuates in intrinsic value. Further, intrinsic value is found in experience and nowhere else. The best experience, that with the greatest intrinsic value, consists in a dynamic equilibrium of the contrasting features illustrated in the above diagram. It is incorrect to say that pure unity or pure simplicity is the supreme aesthetic ideal, whether in art, politics (where sheer uniformity is the goal of totalitarian states), or religion. What makes life worthwhile is the depth and variety of harmonious experiences we can have and can enable others to have, including the divine Other.

Many of the great figures in the history of mystical experience were also closely tied to the lives of nonhuman animals, John of the Cross and Francis of Assisi among them. Presumably this is due to the close connection between a critique of anthropocentrism and a defense of theocentrism. That is, the distinction between God and the rest of creation is wider than the distinction between human beings and animals. However, while animals have always been objects of aesthetic interest to human beings (as in the song of birds), it is also important to notice that they can be subjects of aesthetic experiences themselves. Granted, birds often sing due to evolutionary reasons, as in the protection of territory or the attraction of a mate. But one wonders why they sing when territory is not threatened and out of mating season. Just as members of a military band can both inspire the troops and also enjoy the music that they play, so also birds can sing for biological reasons as well as aesthetic ones. The notion that aesthetic emotions are fifth wheels or epiphenomena is surely a suspect one. In fact, when bird singing becomes sharply functional, say when territorial rivalry transitions into actual combat, bird singing deteriorates. Birds, too, experience in their own ways aesthetic value in the sense of felt harmonies, unities-in-variety. This is evidenced in Hartshorne's book titled *Born to Sing* in a tendency in singing birds (Oscines) to exhibit a "monotony threshold," where birds with many songs in their repertoire vary their songs and where birds with only a few songs in their repertoire vary the pauses between songs. In Sanjuanistic or Franciscan fashion, even the birds try to avoid the monotony that would characterize a world dominated by "the God of the philosophers," the God of classical theism (*BS* 3, 53, 253–54).

Because mystical experience is indeed experience, it would serve us well to understand what experience is. Neoclassical theism takes a momentary experience as the model or paradigm case of concrete reality. What resembles no aspect of experience is, in Whiteheadian terms: nothing, nothing, bare nothing! This panpsychism is implicit in theism because if God is Supreme Experience, and if God is omnipresent, then mere matter or the sheer absence of experience would mean the utter nonexistence of God. We have seen that, in one sense, it is our general everyday experiences that provide a springboard for the understanding of religious experience, in particular. However, in another sense, we come to understand quotidian experience by way of experience at the greatest degree of intensity, by way of mystical experience. Previously I referred to this as a type of negative anthropology, in contrast to the more familiar negative theology. There is no simple or unqualified inaccessibility of God in that our inchoate experience of God's Knowledge (the truth) and Experience helps us to understand our more familiar efforts at knowledge or experience (*AD* 194, 197, 200–201, 203; *CA* 128, 169, 221; *EA* 14; *ZF* 31, 152).

The primary data of experience are both physiological and emotional; they have a temporal structure and a feeling tone. If our idea of God is in some sense derived from our experience, then it would not be surprising that there are privileged experiences that facilitate the development of this idea, whether or not the idea corresponds to a divine reality. One need not commit to the idea that religious experiences are the only or chief reasons for believing that God exists in order to realize that these experiences play an important role in the assessment of religious belief. For example, we have seen that experience is crucial in the development of dipolarity in that we just do not experience change as always being inferior to permanence, or passivity as always inferior to activity, etcetera. The minimum of experience is a type of feeling or *aesthesis* or *psyche*, with the combination of experiences at the root of social reality. The mystic, at a higher-level, experiences perfect reality, but this is not exactly to "observe" it as would an empirical biologist observing a frog. It makes sense to suggest that it is possible for X to experience, however inchoately, that Y is in pain without making the extravagant claim that X could experience it exactly as Y feels it. I think that this sort of thing occurs all the time.

    I take it that all feeling is participatory in some fashion. Experience is our constant companion as we encounter all that happens in the world. Even our cells have experiences on the panpsychist view, and we participate in their experiences, as we have seen, when we have localized pleasures and pains. Artists, in particular, have alerted us to the concreteness of experience at various levels, as in Wordsworth's directing us to "see into the life of things." Those who are skeptical of panpsychism often fail to distinguish between the indistinctness of the experiential given, whether mnemonic or perceptual, and the clarity of the interpretation of what is given. That is, they often overemphasize the latter at the expense of the former. The clearest cases of human experience involve data that are themselves experiences, as in memories of previous experiences or experiences of bodily pain, where cells are themselves agitated. But no matter how directly given, these data are never given with complete distinctness and are in some respects blurred. This helps to close the gap between ordinary experiences and mystical ones.

    One way to know God is via encounter, by religious experience. This idea is reasonable even if it is not infallible. In almost all other areas human beings differ in levels of skill or insight, as we have seen. Some people hear the counterpoint in difficult pieces of music better than others, and some people can hear what is said in a foreign tongue better than others, etcetera. Why not also regarding experience of God? It is not very plausible to claim that no one can have insight that is any clearer or deeper than others regarding religious matters. As Hartshorne notes in *Omnipotence and Other Theological Mistakes*, these "experts" include a group as diverse as the Buddha, Lao Tse, Confucius, Moses, Zoroaster, Sankara, Jesus, Dorothy Day, Mohammed, Mary Baker Eddy, and new examples that might happen at any time. Of course, we must be critical regarding what we accept from these figures so as to avoid the false testimony of, say, Jim Jones, who led many uncritical souls to their deaths. As usual, we must negotiate our way between the extremes of strict certainty and utter skepticism. That is, there are no more complete certainties in religion than there are in engineering. We have to remain content with gradations of confidence and tendencies toward belief.

    One important reason for this caution is that the contingent is much richer than the necessary. Even regarding the ontological argument there is something more involved than mere deductive reasoning; there are also inchoate prior sources and antecedent experiences. Our subjectivity is basically composed of feelings in social relationship with other feelings; these relationships follow us wherever we go, even when our analytical skills are at their highest pitch of discipline.

I am not convinced that this highest pitch of discipline is in evidence in the received view of perception. The familiar account of perception involves an acceptance of dualism whereby a mechanical operation outside the body acts upon the mechanical operation of the sense organs to produce a mechanical operation in the nerve fibers, which in turn cause a mechanical operation in the brain, which (somehow!) leads to subjective experience. It strikes me that this account is as magical as anything found in the history of religion. A quite different account, and one that I accept, is that the cells of our body are themselves primitive examples of psyche in their own manner and degree. Even single-celled organisms exhibit active responses (not merely reactions) to their environment, as well as digestion, oxygenation, and locomotion. There is no mystery here as there is in the gap between mechanical bodily operations and the spontaneous appearance of psyche. By contrast, the less problematic "gap" in panpsychism is actually between primitive psyche and more advanced forms of the same. Cells stimulated by light, say, are raised to a higher level of self-enjoyed activity. Our world, too, is first of all enjoyed or suffered before it is cognized in that our access to the world is through our cells. There is no need to enlist the support of telepathy to find examples of psyche-to-psyche communication. All of this is instructive in the effort to understand mystical experience (*PSG* 306, 337, 511; *PPS* 90; *NT* 77; OD 23, 62, 70; *LP* 5, 11, 15, 100, 109, 119, 130, 159, 276).

We experience as givens realities that are themselves experiences. Localized pleasures and pains are the most obvious examples of these relationships. What are often called subject-object relations are actually subject-subject relations. By normalizing such relations the conceptual world is made safer for those who take mystical experiences seriously with their subject-Subject character. Sense experience as understood in mechanistic terms gives us only gross outlines of groups of individuals, rather than pointing us toward the experiencing individuals themselves. What the scholar of mysticism should be concerned with, by contrast, is the idea that God is important to us not simply because God knows us but because we *feel* God with unique adequacy knowing us. In *The Divine Relativity* Hartshorne refers to this realization as the innermost secret of existence. Even if there is something hyperbolic in this judgment, the importance of *aesthesis* in the broadest sense of the term should not escape our notice. Divine presence, it should be emphasized, has throughout the history of mystical theology been described in aesthetic terms: inward light, warmth, radiance, sweetness, fragrance, even beatific vision. Light, in particular, has very often been associated with spiritual exaltation, as Jane Steger ("Some Notes on Light") emphasizes (*AD* 191; *CS* xiv, 59, 75–76, 79–81, 113, 119–20, 126, 132, 145, 284).

It is hard to know how to explore what have historically been seen as the "supersensible" objects of religion if we do not have an adequate concept of the "sensible." The mind is not a machine for delivering information to itself concerning the physical world. Rather, we feel the feelings in our cells that, in turn, feel the feelings of various "objects" in nature, composed of microscopic subjects, on the neoclassical view. The alleged discontinuity between our experience and the objects of experience tends to evaporate in a processual worldview. A nerve cell when stimulated by redness experiences a value or a quality rather than stagnating as an inert lifeless object (*DR* 92, 115, 121, 126; *MVG* 132, 134, 345–46; *PPS* 3, 39, 53, 57, 248, 253).

It is only by descending into the full concreteness of experience that we can have the abstract outlines of our thought filled in with meaning. This concreteness provides the basis for a sort of religious empiricism regarding the divine actuality. To have religious knowledge is not merely to believe in fideistic fashion, nor is it merely to infer from premises; it also involves concrete experience of a sort. Hence, it is dangerous to religion if thought alienates us from the concrete and experiential. Further, the concrete can never be explained by the abstract in any sort of detail, thus the need to be attentive to concrete experience in its particularity. To know *that* there must be an infinity of particular qualities and experiences that characterize God still does not tell us much. The mystic who experiences God helps us to fill in some of the details of the divine life. *That* God has an infinity of contingent features is metaphysical even if what those features are is not. In fact, the highest knowledge is not metaphysical but involves the special *experiences* of gifted individuals.

The concrete actuality of God is "in us" only if we intuit or experience it. Problems arise when we pass from an abstract concept of God (e.g., as unmoved mover) to concrete reality and vice versa without noticing the transitions. Abstract or inferential knowledge is virtual in a way that concrete knowledge is not. Further, abstract knowledge always concerns an "it," whereas concrete knowledge can also concern a "Thou," to use Buber's language. It will be remembered from what was said in an earlier chapter regarding the ontological argument, however, that unalloyed rationalism and unmitigated empiricism are both problematic; the abstract and the concrete are correlative terms in dipolar relationship with each other, as Franklin Gamwell (*On Metaphysical Necessity*) insightfully argues.

There is no inconsistency in seeing God as both the supreme, concrete, contingent actuality and the supreme, abstract, necessary existence. Our intellect is at home in the abstract, and our ability to feel is at home with the concrete. But even God (especially God!) is concrete in one aspect of the divine nature, and it is this aspect of God that is mysterious, just as any concrete particular is, in its uniqueness, somewhat mysterious. Life is fortunately much more than theory. Even if our knowledge of God's concrete actuality is rather small, such mystical knowing at least points us in the right direction regarding *how* God as omnibenevolent can be actualized. One of the difficulties here is that divine actuality is not unified at any particular moment in that in the next moment there is a new concretely actual state of the divine life.

There are two primary responsibilities of philosophers who try to clarify mystical experience: to clarify the nonempirical principles at work in the human effort to understand God, and to use these principles, along with the testimonies from mystics, to illuminate the concreteness of the religious quest. Of course, theorizing itself is a type of experiencing, as is aesthetic experience. The world is felt first and only later known theoretically. We have seen that experience cannot magically create its own content, even in the negative case. To fail to observe a presence is one thing (we do this all the time), but to observe its absence is another. Another complicating factor is that our experience is mediated, indeed there are chains of mediation though which we come into contact with divine reality, as we have seen. This is what we would expect if concrete reality is richer than abstract reality; the chains of mediation help us in various ways, as when God is experienced via a religious painting with various symbols and allusive suggestions. Abstractions themselves rest on concrete reality, as Aristotle correctly argued. God as the supremely concrete reality includes all previous concrete reality by way of omniscience and omnibenevolence; God infinitely combines finites. In God's abstract and necessary aspect God does not feel; divine *aesthesis* occurs in the contingent character of divine actuality.

I have thus far for the most part avoided the word "prayer," not because there is something wrong with this word per se, but rather due to its associations with petitionary prayer in particular and with a supernaturalist view wherein God, once supplicated, magically inserts divine agency into the world from the outside. Something analogous can be said regarding the word "revelation," which has long associations with fundamentalism and other simplistic versions of theism. *If* what is meant by revelation is reference to the biblical God of love, then the term is not nearly as objectionable as the language used to describe the God of classical theism. In fact, the present book is really an extended exploration of revelation if what is meant by this is the idea that some people are capable of uncommon (but not supernatural) insight. Perhaps the most important revelation in the Hebrew scriptures is the famous tetragrammaton event at Exodus 3:14, where a processual reading is possible: I live as I live or I breathe as I breathe. Even the God discussed in Anselm's equally famous ontological argument is not unconnected with revelation, with religious experience, as we have seen. Hartshorne is intent, however, on having religious experience or revelation understood outside the bounds of any particular religion or Abrahamic tradition in that revelatory events occur in the history of ancient Egyptian religion (as in the first monotheist, Ikhnaton), Buddhism, Hinduism, Daoism, etcetera, as well as in Christian thinkers like Teilhard de Chardin (*PCH* 72; *CS* xv). It is the narrow-minded assumption that Christianity is the locus of *the* revelation that gives me pause, as does the notion that the meaning of life is to be found in belief in or experience of supernaturalistic miracles. That is, we are better served trying to understand mysticism as *aesthesis*, both quotidian and extraordinary (*BH* 8; *LP* 8; *MVG* xiii–xiv; *NT* 102–3; *OO* 119; *RSP* 130; *CS* xv).

A final comment regarding prayer is needed. One of the reasons why some people refuse to take religious experience seriously is that they assume that the religious believer is really doing something other than what is claimed (e.g., by prolonging a childlike desire for a parent to care for the one who prays). But it is a mistake to think that all those who pray mean the same things by prayer, even if they are, from a behavioral perspective, doing the same things, as Stephen R. L. Clark (*Mysteries of Religion*) argues. For example, imagine two different tribes that regularly perform rain dances and pronounce rain prayers, one of which assumes that the rain dance and prayer are necessary conditions for the subsequent rain, and the other of which assumes not that it will not rain if the dance and prayer are not performed but that they will not receive the rain in the proper (thankful) frame of mind if the dance and prayer are not performed. That is, perhaps prayer is more plausible when it is realized that there is quite a difference between childlike literalists (the rain makers), who think that petitionary prayer exhausts the prayer options, on the one hand, and more mature symbolists (the rain blessers), on the other. The latter are very much compatible with process mysticism.

Chapter 10

Consequences for Ethics

Thus far I have very briefly touched on what some of the practical ramifications of mystical experience might be. The purpose of the present chapter is to explore these ideas in greater detail so as to rescue the book from what might seem to be its overly abstract character. I will locate the mystical tradition within a kindred tradition in ethics: the virtue ethics approach, with the theological virtue of love occupying a prominent place in my exploration of the consequences of mystical experience for ethics. We will see that the virtue of love has controversial implications for the issue of death; in this regard I will be defending a view called "contributionism." I will also explore a danger in the agent-centered character of virtue ethics that is especially noteworthy from the perspective of mystical experience. Finally, I will examine the virtue or vice of anger, which seems in our especially angry world to provide an impediment to the life of virtue that is a precondition of the contemplative life.

Richard Jones (*Mysticism and Morality*) is surely correct in noting that the spectrum of views on the relationship between mysticism and ethics is broad. On the one hand, some (e.g., Arthur Danto) are skeptical on principle as to whether mystics could ever be ethical. If all reality is alleged to be one, then love is impossible. (My hope is that the sort of divine inclusiveness described above works against the thesis that there are no significant differences among individuals and hence renders love impossible. That is, the "cells" in the divine life can have distinct identities.) Further, there might be a tendency toward selfishness in mystics if they are assumed to have a total disregard for all "worldly" affairs. On the other hand, others (e.g., Walter Stace) might argue that mysticism is actually *necessary* for our concern for others or might even be the source of such concern. On this view, only mystics are truly compassionate and hence moral because only they have escaped from self-centeredness and only they have detected a "presence" in others that is sacred. My hope is to mediate between these two extremes, although admittedly my view leans in the direction of the latter alternative.

Clearly *some* sort of rapprochement between the active life and the contemplative life is possible. Thomas Merton (*Seven Storey Mountain*), for example, has shown how even a cloistered monk can be politically engaged. And the Jesuits, Methodists, and Quakers have historically provided many examples of how to be a contemplative-in-action. Perhaps a good place to start is with the famous four marks of mystical experience developed in William James's *The Varieties of Religious Experience*. Previously I have treated three of these marks. Mystical experiences are: (1) ineffable (as I have qualified this criterion above in my treatment of apophaticism); (2) characterized by a certain passivity or receptivity (as I have qualified passivity in its correlative, dipolar relationship with activity, hence this characteristic should not be equated with hesychasm or quietism, where one need not act in the world in order to be a good person); and (3) noetic (as I have argued above in terms of the knowledge of divine actuality that is made possible in mystical experience, albeit as mediated by the feelings through which the mystical experience occurs). The fourth characteristic of mystical experience is its transiency, which, although accurate as a description of the experience itself, needs interpretation in that those who have had mystical experiences tend to have their lives radically affected by them such that, although their efficacious action in the world *starts* with a transient mystical experience (or at least is *enhanced* by a transient mystical experience), it certainly does not end there, as Bergson noted in *The Two Sources of Morality and Religion*.

In various traditions from around the world, mystical experience seems to require that one discard egoistic accoutrements. Sometimes this takes the look of the Buddhist notion of *anatta* or no self; in other traditions it involves the belief that the self is not a substantial, fixed entity but a process of readjustment and integration. This latter process characterizes the neoclassical view. However, in most of its manifestations mystical experience has been connected with the ethical project of containing what the Greeks called *pleonexia*, which can be very loosely translated as a compulsively consuming, commodity fetishist style of life. The goal in life is not *hedone* (pleasure) but *eudaimonia* (happiness), even if some pleasure is a necessary condition for happiness, to put the point in Aristotelian terms. This goal, from the perspective of mystical experience, involves something like union with God;

or re-union with God, as in the Hindu *samadhi*; or loving intimacy with God, as in Jewish *devekuth*. Frequently the effort to hold the ego in check involves suffering or malaise or Buddhist *dukkha*, although the above chapter on asceticism indicates that care that must be taken in critically accepting this part of mystic tradition. Whatever the terms are that are appropriate in the particular tradition in question, and in the particular historical epoch in which the tradition is instantiated, it seems that egoistic desire has to be slowed down in order to attain "*nirvana*," very broadly construed. Otherwise we should expect the suffering or malaise to continue. In different terms, asceticism is not an end in itself but a means to something very positive. In Wordsworth's terms, the sad, still music of humanity ought not myopically to lead us to premature pessimism but rather to lead us on to something more harmonious at a cosmic level (*MVG* 159; *PSG* 298–99).

We have seen that it is understandable, if not justifiable, that classical theists hold before us the view of God as changeless and stable as a remedy for our troubled lives and troubled times. But this changeless God is also a lifeless one and hence is a false idol. It is crucial that the asceticism that is required for mystical union to occur with a *living* God not be pathological; but it should be conducive to a vaster self, albeit not one that involves a "big ego," to speak colloquially. Merton's way of putting the point, common to both Christianity and Buddhism, is that we need to avoid the "birds of appetite" that circle around a desired good so that we may gain something *for ourselves*. Contemplative experience, like virtue, is its own reward such that the birds of appetite tend to pass it by. Rather than dissolution of the self, however, it might be more accurate to speak of the transformation of the self, or participation or inclusion of the self in God. The mystic's concern, especially emphasized in the concept of God as World Soul, is cosmic rather than anthropocentric, as Teilhard de Chardin in particular emphasizes, although I think the point is found in all of the great theistic mystics. Process spirituality is not merely accidentally connected to diachronic transformation of the self in a way that is conducive to an appreciation of the sacred dimension of life, of wholeness, and of the interconnectedness and relational character of existence.

Albert Schweitzer (see Henry Clark, *Ethical Mysticism*) is one famous mystic who sees experience of God as supremely ethical in the sense that what is experienced in God is preeminently *good*. This makes mysticism and ethics related branches of a single whole. We have seen that it is more important when thinking through the logic of perfection to see God as omnibenevolent than to see God as omnipotent. The hope is that we can dispel the sense that mysticism is a sort of otherworldly luxury in the face of the pressing problems that face humanity. Neoclassical theism itself, and the mysticism it helps us to explicate, is not unconnected to the dipolar drive to achieve a proper synthesis of freedom and order. By contrast, classical theism fosters order at the expense of freedom and encourages obedience as a key virtue, a view that is at odds with democratic politics, as many classical theists themselves have admitted. To encourage *complete* or unmitigated dependence on God is to work against the view of human beings as being made in the divine image (or its equivalent in Islam, with its prohibition of images). Further, by making God immune to human influence, classical theists unwittingly encourage human beings to egoistically strive to benefit only themselves in the ethical life (*PSG* 322).

The only mysticism worth defending is one that works hand in glove with a profound ethical tradition. (This is one reason among others to be skittish about Heideggerian mysticism, considering Heidegger's own life and the subordinated ethics at work in his view, if there is an ethics at all in his view.) The ethical view that seems most congenial with the lives of the great mystics seems to be the virtue ethics tradition, although the importance of duty in the ethical life and the tendency on the part of mystics to enhance the lives of those around them rather than diminish them means that deontological and utilitarian considerations also tell part of the story that needs to be told in this regard. There is also a pragmatic element that is needed in that we ought not to reject (or defend) theoretically that which is inevitable (or impossible) from a practical point of view. The virtue ethics that seems dominant among mystics may very well include ascetical elements, but not to the exclusion of spontaneously joyful experiences that are themselves evidence of an omnipresent goodness at the base of things (*DL* 20–21, 140, 265; *DR* 44–45; *RSP* 209; *IO* 239).

We will see that the ethical lives of the great mystics are not unrelated to a life of love and that it is love that drives the pursuit of virtue. This view dovetails with neoclassical theism's attempt to develop a concept of God that is compatible with divine love and that comes to terms with temporal asymmetry. In this regard divine memory or preservation of achieved value is more crucial than divine "preservation" of future value, as alleged in classical theism. Ethical character, like personal identity, is in process thought an abstraction from a sequence of concrete behaviors that are virtuous. In the Bergsonian open religion defended by process thinkers, however, virtue confers no license to scold or think ill of those who do not have experience of God or who simply do not believe. Of course, we should not congratulate them for nonbelief, either. Rather, to the extent possible, we should respect and take delight in each creature in its own unique contribution to the divine life (*CS* 297).

Mystical experience as interpreted by neoclassical theism can make its greatest contribution to ethics via the virtue tradition, specifically in terms of its understanding of love, the greatest of the theological virtues (along with faith and hope). A genuine acceptance of the thesis that God is love is not easy in classical theism in that few thinkers have really tried to work out a metaphysics compatible with this thesis. Nothing is conceptually superior to love in neoclassical theism, not even power or justice or knowledge or being or cause. It is characteristic of classical theists to shift the conversation regarding God's love to God's power, causality, or knowledge. And there is very little hope of understanding the loving, mutual give-and-take between human beings and God by way of classical theism, despite the fact that such mutuality is a commonplace in the literature surrounding mystical experience. The intimacy between the mystic and God and the sense on the part of the mystic of being loved by God is harder to erase than mistakes in classical theistic interpretations of such intimacy. Neoclassical theism is, by contrast, a metaphysics of love, of mutual interaction and care and change in light of the sufferings of the beloved. In fact, those who experience love (parental, filial, conjugal, communal, cosmic) can be said to experience God. In love we live and move and have our being in a processual worldview wherein a personal God is active and omnipresent in the world of actualized reality (*BH* 208–9, 299; *CE* 7; *DR* 17, 25, 55; *HB* 18, 24; *IO* 231; *LP* 102; *MVG* 3, 70, 111, 116, 127, 165, 173).

This emphasis on the virtue of love helps to rescue a metaphysics of mystical experience from the charge of being overly abstract in that love is a concrete relation between the relata and a partial escape from our abstractions. As with other passions, love is *felt*. Further, it is felt with a degree of intensity that led certain early Christians to insightfully suggest that God *is* love (*Deus est caritas*). In dipolar fashion, love is both an activity and requires passive receptivity with respect to the beloved; it also involves a certain cognitive element as well as a more pronounced aesthetic element. A lover tries to both understand the beloved and willingly receives the joys and sorrows of the beloved. Divine love involves an invariable factor of always caring for the beloved as well as concrete variation with respect to responses to the ever-changing conditions of the beloved. If love involves joy in the joy of others and sorrow in the sorrow of others, supreme love involves these qualities to the highest degree. It is odd that historically

Christian ethics extolled the virtues of love and dependency on others, while Christian theology, influenced by classical theistic ideas, rejected such (partial) dependency when characterizing God. However, our direct (albeit mediated) sense of God's love should be consistent with our ethical views. Complete adequacy to the subject loved is the mark of perfect love, not an impenetrable or unmoved indifference to the subject loved. Because we *are* affected by those we love, we at times are called to be heroic in the exercise of love as a virtue (*BH* 317; *HB* 14, 88; *MVG* xiv; *WP* 134, 168).

The point regarding the nonabstract character of love can be put in stronger terms: Love is the supreme example of individuation in that it involves care for the unique as such and not merely as a member of a class. The value of the beloved is located in the beloved *as an individual*, albeit as a temporally indexed individual. Various mystics have claimed awareness not only of divine love but also of divine love directed toward themselves in their idiosyncrasies and failings. (For example, Saint Therese of Lisieux was very much aware of herself as a neurotic, as Monica Furlong [*Therese of Lisieux*] argues.) On their testimony we are led to think of the world as the increasing specification of a loving feeling of feeling. The idea of divine love is not understood very well apart from the analogical concept of the divine mind animating the cosmic body. This is because it is only in the mind-body relation that divine power (although not omnipotence) can be linked with sensitiveness or sympathetic awareness of the bodily members. In this regard it is perhaps more accurate to say that divine love is sympathy or feeling with the suffering members, rather than mere benevolence, which might convey the idea of external well-wishing. One wonders what one might want in life more than the realization that one is both lovable and loved. This realization provides a spark, however dim, of the idea that there is something good in every concrete singular and in the relations among these (*NT* 12, 16; OD 57, 197–98, 298; *OO* x, 4, 29, 60–61, 112; *PCH* 634; *PPS* 208; *PSG* 110–11, 148, 155, 264, 286, 381, 460; *RSP* 108, 147; *WM* 49, 119; *WP* 36).

Merely being known or loved is not a big thing, but knowing that one is known or loved can be quite significant. Either God really does love all individuals and is loved by at least some of them or theistic belief seems fraudulent. Because the classical theistic God is strictly unchanging and totally nonreceptive, it is not surprising that some thinkers see religion as a big fraud. Further, the authenticity of love does not so much consist in the search for beauty, as indicated in Plato's *Symposium*, but rather *is itself* beautiful. It involves a sharing in the reality of other individuals, with hate consisting in a refusal to engage in such sharing. The term "worship" can be defined in terms of love and consists in loving someone with one's whole being. Strictly speaking only God could be worshipped, although in yet another instance of negative anthropology we can speak analogously of worshipping some particular human being who is especially admirable (for a human being). Once again, analogy fails us, however, when we try to combine love with immutability; it is all-inclusiveness, not completeness, that characterizes deity. Love is the force at work whereby all things are bound together, but bound together in their own uniqueness. Charles Sanders Peirce (*Collected Papers*) referred to this force as "agapism."

It is comparatively easy to *say* that God is love, but it is not as easy to develop the technical (dipolar) metaphysical language that is capable of consistently formulating the content of this claim. I have argued that there are severe limitations in classical theistic language in this regard. These limitations are especially odd when it is considered that love, seen as the interest of experience in other experience, and which involves essentially the notion of sympathy, is something of an ultimate principle of principles, humble aspects of which pervade nature. Feeling of feeling or feeling love is ultimate because it characterizes prehension itself, the way that momentary experiences grasp their immediate predecessors creatively in their thrust into the future. To believe in God (as love) is to believe that love is, in a way, the key to the really basic features of the universe, including prehension. Like Plato's sun or the form of the good, it illumines everything. Classical theism, by contrast, stripped love of any meaning when it was seen as devoid of sympathy or receptivity to the feelings of others. Such sympathy enables us to fruitfully define love in various terms: concern of life for life, experience for experience, feeling for feeling, consciousness for consciousness, freedom for freedom, etcetera.

There is a certain wisdom in lovingly delighting in the lives of others. There is also wisdom in privileging love over even knowledge in the effort to understand mystical experience. Because of the dynamism of the neoclassical view, I am hesitant to refer to neoclassical theism as a system. But if the word "system" is used in a loose sense, love is at the core of the process system and, as a result, enables us to understand mysticism better than in alternatives systems, including classical theism. Love is not primarily intellectual, even if it is compatible with intellectual systematizing. Once again, it involves mutuality or feeling. God is not only love but *pure* love in the sense of absence of distorting bias or egoistic desire. The contrast with classical theism is most readily apparent when it is asserted that it is love that explains divine power, not the other way around. As the process motto has it, the power of God consists in the worship or love that God inspires (*BH* 238).

The mystics *really* believe that serving God is their purpose in life and that the best way to serve God is to promote love in themselves and others. As before, if virtue (including love) is its own reward, as the important cliché has it, then there is nothing beyond love (like immortality of the soul) that matters as much. Further, the mystics' belief in divine omniscience means that the fragility of our achievements has been overcome in that these will be preserved everlastingly in the divine life. It must be admitted that in skepticism regarding personal immortality we find one of the two biggest bones of contention among process theists themselves (the other being the tension between the Whiteheadian tendency to view God as a single actual entity and the Hartshornian tendency to view God as a temporal—albeit everlasting—series of actual occasions of experience). But the reasons to be persuaded by contributionism rather than by personal immortality are numerous and profound. The mystics' experiences haunt our imaginations with the realization that our present experiences do *not* fade but pass (via divine omniscience) into permanent significance for the cosmos. That is, our lives are *not* passing whiffs of insignificance (*AW* 43; *CA* 42; *CS* 16, 118, 121, 230, 321; *DL* 43, 379; *DR* 58, 132–34).

It is surprisingly a hard lesson to learn that God is more important than us. Each of us is a contribution to the experience of God, which experience is indestructible. It is this indestructibility that gives our present experiences abiding significance. Although we help to determine each new stage of the divine life, this does not mean that *we* will live forever in that the series of experiences that constitutes our lives will come to a halt. Each moment of our lives is an addition to the universe, but these additions will come to an end when we die. Contributionism is not the view that we are mere means to some end beyond ourselves in that what we are contributing to God, among other things, is our present happiness. In different terms, in addition to contributing to a divine *telos* there is also something autotelic about our lives. Classical theistic supernaturalism obviously fosters a quite different view wherein, at death, we can be pole-vaulted into a disembodied life. This would be a completely new reality, however, rather than the indestructibility of the old. *If* what is meant by myths concerning heaven and hell is that death does not involve utter destruction of what we have accomplished in life, then there is agreement between classical theists (including a large number of famous mystics) and neoclassical theists. But if what is meant by these myths is that we personally will live forever, then Hartshornian theists part ways with many other theists, both classical and neoclassical. What all theists can agree on is the idea that death does not involve the destruction, or even the fading, of achieved value (*EA* 75; *HB* 97; *IO* 308; *LP* 242, 251–54, 260, 322; *NT* 111).

It would be a mistake to equate contributionism with being "absorbed into deity," although admittedly some mystics (more in some traditions than others) speak in these terms. The problem with this equation is that one remains the same individual, and not some other individual, who contributes present experiences to God. The series of experiences that makes up one mystic's life is not to be confused with some other person's series. Death is not so much sheer destruction as it is the setting of a definite limit to a series of experiences that are personally ordered (through memory, primarily). Death cannot destroy what we, as individuals, have contributed to the everlasting deity. Although it may initially sound oxymoronic, careful consideration of the following will not result in inconsistency: We are ephemeral, but immortally so. This is because all of our ephemeral experiences are woven into the everlasting divine fabric of the cosmos (*PCH* 589; *PD* 81, 84–85; *PSG* vi, 285; *RSP* 143–44, 151, 212; *WM* 62; *WP* 108, 123, 165, 170; *WVR* 20).

Although our subjective experiences in the present may *appear* to perish, this is due to the partial hiddenness of deity, a hiddenness that is less of a problem for the mystics than for the rest of us. In effect, every event in our lives is everlasting by proxy. As before, classical theism fails miserably in this regard in that there seems to be no possibility to serve a God who is completely unmoved by our strivings. Although, in one sense, we will not live forever, hence there is no chance of personal immortality in neoclassical theism, in another paradoxical sense the sort of immortality found in contributionism, sometimes referred to as objective immortality, is even more personal than the conventional form of immortality found in some religious thinkers, especially Christians. This is because God is able to perfectly preserve our actual life on earth as it took place. For practical purposes, however, it is best to refrain from language regarding personal immortality, given the way that this language raises unrealistic hopes in people and gives rise to a dangerous sort of escapism. The self of my childhood experiences has already largely perished, humanly speaking, so we can soften the blow that might be felt when learning of the inappropriateness of insisting on personal immortality. Our real permanence depends on God, who ensures that our lives have and always will have importance.

My hope is that the connection between contributionism and a virtue ethics centered on love can be readily seen. Death can be accepted if we transcend self-interest as our final concern and if we regard our lives as contributions to the good of those who survive us, especially the omnibenevolent divine life. I have also noted that one of our chief contributions is (somewhat autotelic) present happiness in that, by contrast, miserable people donate to posterity their misery. Contentment with mortality is in effect contentment with the fragmentariness and finitude of our contribution to the everlasting whole of things. Further, if there is a strong analogy, often noted, between a human life and a work of art, we should emphasize that even the greatest novels and symphonies have a last chapter, a coda. It might be asked, without personal immortality what do we "get out of" it all? Well, we get the satisfaction of the autotelic experience of living itself, of loving itself, as well as the satisfaction of finding meaning in our lives as parts of an all-loving divine whole. Self-knowledge requires that we come to terms with our fragmentariness. Just as we are spatially fragments of the immensity of space (everyone agrees here), so also we are temporally fragments of the immensity of time's flow (here defenders of personal immortality object). Because of our fragmentariness and our finitude, in a way death thankfully protects us from hopeless monotony as our faculties fade. Of course, premature or intensely painful death are very bad things, but death simply as such does not have to be viewed negatively, as many mystics have attested, although their half-hearted adherence to classical theism may have distorted their best insights in this regard (*PSG* 302).

The view I am defending is different from the stance taken by classical theists who defend belief in divine omnipotence that (even premature or painful) death is sent by God for a reason. Given this implausible belief, it is no wonder that there are religious skeptics who react negatively by saying that life is meaningless. The autotelicity of our experiences militates against such alleged meaninglessness, as do the facts that we acquire meaning by enriching the life of a divine being who really *cares* for us and that death need not be viewed as cancelling out any actual achievement of concrete value. Life has value despite mortality because death does not cancel out our having lived and experienced much of value, including the immense mystical value of having experienced divine actuality. The ideas that we give ourselves to God and that God also seeks us out make sense on the basis of dipolar theism, even if these ideas are difficult to understand on the basis of classical, monopolar theism. Although all actuality (including divine actuality) is contingent, this does not mean that all that exists is contingent.

In writing the books of our lives, so to speak, we should try to make the reading of these "books" as valuable as possible so as to ensure that our lives have abiding significance. But this significance does not entail the hubris found in the desire for personal immortality. Here Judaism avoids a danger found in Christianity and Islam due to the fact that in the latter two religions there is a tendency to challenge the distinctiveness of divine necessary existence. Here again we can see the ethical import of contributionism in its ability to hold in check the egoistic quality found in those who think that they deserve to live forever! We are better served to consult ancient Greek religion, where the defining characteristic of the gods (not humans) was immortality. That is, only the gods were in reality *athanatos* (deathless), although it must be admitted that in contributionism we are such vicariously. In this vicariousness lies our peculiar "salvation." The past, including our own past, is immortal*ized* in God (*CS* 321; *RSP* 212).

Contributionism aids not only in curbing egocentrism but also in holding in check anthropocentrism. If we imagine a poem being read aloud, there is quite a difference between the ability to appreciate the poem if in the audience are found: a water molecule, a bit of moss, a plant, an insect, a turtle or a dog, and two human beings—one who does not know the language of the poem and one who does. Each succeeding being is commendably more receptive to the poem than the previous being. Indeed, the water molecule (as a composite) is impassive, an attribute that the classical theist problematically sees in God. But even some of the "lower" beings contribute their own feelings, however humble, to the divine whole. The dog, for example, will not only hear the sounds of the poem but also perhaps have a sense of the emotional tone of the voice reading the poem, just as we have seen birds exhibiting talent not only as aesthetic objects but also as aesthetic subjects as well with a sense of beauty and an avoidance of monotony. Insects have primitive sensations even if they do not have linguistic symbols to convey their sensations and feelings. Previously I have noted that we should not be surprised to learn that many of the great mystics were very attentive to natural beauty and animal suffering. That is, the extent of the contributions to God is much wider than anthropocentrists assume (*PSG* 361–62; *DR* 49, 77, 91).

I would now like to be a bit more specific about the ways in which mystical experience can inform virtue ethics and the ways in which virtue ethics can help us to better understand mystical experience. The renaissance in virtue ethics in recent decades has supplemented searches for objective decision-making procedures in philosophical ethics, whether utilitarian or deontological, as well as the search for a defensible concept of rights. But this rebirth has not dealt sufficiently with the great mystics, who, in addition to almost all of the great philosophers and theologians in the premodern period, are also in the virtue tradition. One prominent example here is, once again, Saint John of the Cross, who will be seen as a token of a type: a great mystic and a significant figure in the virtue ethics tradition (see *Ascent of Mount Carmel*, 3:27–29). John of the Cross distinguishes among many sorts of goods: normal goods that we experience in everyday life, both sensory and intellectual, as well as moral goods (*bienes morales*) and spiritual goods, including mystic union with God. It is the relationship between moral goods and spiritual goods that interests me (RSW 51).

By "moral goods" is meant virtues and their habits, the practice of works of mercy, urbanity, and mannerly consideration of others. It is a commonplace in mystical literature that the practice of virtue produces joy that is greater than that which attends sensory goods. This is for two reasons: The practice of virtue is valuable in itself and is more conducive to other benefits than are sensory goods. This is consistent with the contributionism defended above in that one of the things that is contributed to God is autotelic happiness. Mystics, in general, have a tendency to think that the virtuous life produces peace and tranquility and a sense of nobility that cannot be gained through sensory goods. We have seen that the cliché that virtue is its own reward became a commonplace for good reason. The task for the virtue ethician under the influence of the mystics is to indicate the superiority of moral and spiritual goods to sensory goods like riches and honor without playing into the hands of classical theistic supernaturalism and dualism. In short, virtue is its own reward because it is both noble and serves to glorify or contribute to God. There is no need to trash sensory goods, however.

One of the distinctive features of virtue ethics as encouraged by the mystical tradition is the caution displayed toward one's assessment of one's own moral character. The trope that virtue is its own reward can ironically be an occasion for vanity and self-interest. The etymological root in Latin of the word "vanity," it should be noted, is related to the concept of emptiness. The mystic's fear is that once we appreciate the consummatory or intrinsic good of the practice of virtue, rather than its instrumentality, we will be tempted by vainglory and presumption. Further, once we are pharisaically puffed up with our own supposed superior moral status, we are likely to see others as inferior. The insight here is that (excessive) self-esteem breeds a morally empty contempt for others or envy regarding others.

It is paradoxically because ennobling virtue is so valuable that we may develop the desire to have others notice our virtue, hence we might be tempted to practice virtue *ut videantur ab hominibus*: in order to be seen by other human beings (see Matthew 23:5). (I do not know how idiosyncratic my supply of emails is, but on a daily basis I receive "virtue signaling" emails that in effect threaten me with "vice shaming" if I do not agree with the sender.) This perversion of the intrinsic goodness of the practice of virtue also has a causal effect on its instrumental goodness. By insufficiently detaching ourselves from the practicing of virtue we are likely to divert the effects of virtuous acts away from the greater glory of God and toward some lesser *telos*. By contrast, John of the Cross, educated by the Jesuits at Medina del Campo, would presumably subscribe to the aforementioned Jesuit motto, *ad majorem Dei gloriam*: all for the greater glory of God. This saying might serve well as a motto for all Abrahamic theists. The biblical injunction not to let the left hand know what the right hand does (see Matthew 6:3) is meant to encourage the requisite detachment.

A well-known philosophical article by Susan Wolf ("Moral Saints") is not unrelated to John of the Cross's point here. She desires that neither she, nor anyone she cares for, be a "moral saint." Her concern is that the perfectionism of a moral saint (she misleadingly cites as examples Saint Francis of Assisi and Mother Teresa, both of whom were more "well-rounded" than Wolf admits) gets in the way of nonmoral goods, presumably the numerous nonmoral goods mentioned by John of the Cross himself. The "driven" character of moral saints makes them susceptible to a certain boorishness and condescension toward others, such that, although a moral saint might well enjoy a good episode of *Father Knows Best*, he or she may not in good conscience be able to laugh at a Marx Brothers movie. Admittedly, Wolf's skepticism regarding moral sainthood is based on aesthetic, rather than religious, reasons connected to her ideal of well-roundedness. But the boorishness and especially the condescension that is possible in (Wolf would say, is likely in) the virtuous life of the moral saint is exactly what concerns John of the Cross as well, albeit for religious reasons. There are dangers involved when we imperiously convince ourselves that we *are* moral saints.

Mystics in general point out the advantages of detachment, rather than attachment to satisfaction, the latter of which may make one impervious to the counsel of others. This emphasis on detachment (John of the Cross's *nada*) has thus far not had as big an impact as one might expect on contemporary discourse regarding virtue ethics, despite its similarity to Stoic *adiaphoria*, Buddhist indifference, etcetera. However, Aristotelian moderation between thinking too much of oneself, at one extreme, and self-abnegation, at the other, is a commonplace in contemporary virtue ethics. But the point I am trying to make is somewhat different. Consider the fact that virtue ethics is usually characterized as agent-centered because the concept of a virtue concerns something that makes *its possessor* good. This is in contrast to the more outward-looking decision-making procedures that are emphasized in utilitarian and deontological ethics. Rather than asking, "What ought I *to do?*" or "How ought I *to act?*," the contemporary virtue ethicist is likely to ask, "What sort of person ought I *to be?*" The contrast between virtue ethics as agent-centered and the action-centered decision-making procedures found in utilitarianism and deontology is complicated, however, by the fact that each virtue generates an instruction: Do what is honest, do what is charitable. And each vice generates a prohibition: Do not do what is dishonest, do not be uncharitable, as Rosalind Hursthouse (*On Virtue Ethics*) argues.

That is, if an agent is said to possess the virtues of honesty and charity, we expect certain actions to follow. To be precise, we should say that virtue ethics is "agent-centered" or "agent-focused" rather than "agent-based" so as to avoid the (perhaps dogmatic) foundationalism implied in the latter phrase. Despite the ancient and medieval roots of virtue ethics, it does not have to be seen as requiring any specific metaphysical foundations; persons from various philosophical perspectives can be attracted to a virtuous life. But an agent-centered or agent-focused ethics is at least compatible with, indeed it requires, right action. John of the Cross and other mystics are virtue ethicists who are nonetheless attentive to the dangers in agent-centered ethics, and herein lies their important insight. Agent-centered ethics is not necessarily narcissistic, but it does run the risk of becoming a form of self-absorption.

To be virtuous paradoxically requires of us *both* that we concern ourselves with moral improvement *and* that we detach ourselves from questions concerning our level of character development and achievement. Regarding the latter, the virtuous life involves performing acts that are virtuous in day-to-day living and patiently allowing those acts to become habit (as in Aristotle). The ancient Greek word *ethos* meant nothing other than "habit," hence the suggestion that we not overly attach ourselves to concerns regarding stages of character development, but rather that we detach ourselves from these so as to go about the daily business of doing what we ought to do. This means that the mystic view of virtue is to be seen quite literally as an *ethics* of detachment.

As a person advances in the spiritual life toward the goal of union with God, envy is one of the vices that is either eliminated altogether or is transformed into a healthy desire to emulate those who have already reached such union. Spiritual advance is not necessarily facilitated by uninterrupted joy, although joy itself is obviously a good thing. Such advance also involves aforementioned detachment and, at times, suffering, which is not good in itself even if it can be instrumentally good. As we have seen, we ought not to assume that virtue ethics is *exclusively* agent-centered in that the whole point to ethics is to provide guidance, a specification of "right" action in terms of what any virtuous agent would typically do in similar circumstances. The ideal Kantian agent (a person who acts from a sense of duty) and the ideal virtuous agent (a person who acts from a character habituated to virtue) are not as different as they might initially seem (*PCH* 622–25; *DR* xvii).

The check on agent-centeredness in virtue ethics provided by insights from the great mystics is due to the fact that a virtuous life requires a certain degree of ascetical discipline; and a carefully circumscribed ascetical discipline requires a significant amount of detachment. Further, for virtue ethicists who are theocentrists (rather than egocentrists or anthropocentrists), the agent in "agent-centered ethics" is not overly inflated. The mystics help us to understand why this is the case.

Those who are interested in the contemplative life should notice that a virtuous character is a necessary condition for such a life. In effect, the exercise of the *meditative* life that is conducive to *contemplation* (as these semitechnical terms were explicated earlier in the book) does not transcend virtuous activity (in contrast, say, to Kierkegaard's defense of Abraham's faith *beyond* the ethical). Rather, a flourishing contemplative life presupposes virtuous habituation such that one need not constantly think about what to do. When virtuous living becomes almost second nature, one is at least partially liberated from egocentric or anthropocentric desire and is, as a result, freed up to actively engage in meditative reading and prayer in the hope of receiving the divine influence that just *is* contemplation or mystical experience.

It is very common to find in the tradition of mystical experience the idea that in order to develop the virtuous life that is a necessary condition for the contemplative life, one needs to bridle the irascible power of anger. I would like to conclude the book with a treatment of anger on the assumption that, in the very angry world that we live in, failure to understand and/or come to terms with anger is a major impediment to both the life of virtue and the contemplative life. In this regard I will be relying not only on John of the Cross but also on *The Philokalia* from the Eastern Orthodox tradition, although other traditions could be tapped in this regard (including the Buddhist one with its notions of the "no self" or at least the "no angry self"), given the fact that anger is seen as a stumbling block in most wisdom traditions. Once anger is better understood, love can more easily flourish. To be exact, there is something liberating about a perfected human being in that love, when habitual, enables a human being to escape the fetters that accompany someone who is driven to and fro by the objects of physical and/or psychic desire.

Anger is a complicated phenomenon, however. Its moral status is ambiguous because it can be either a virtue or a vice, depending on circumstance. What exactly is its place in the contemplative life? A response to this question is facilitated by the relatively recent translations into English of a group of mystical writings by magisterial Eastern Orthodox thinkers under the title *The Philokalia* (literally, love of the beautiful). These writers lived between the fourth and fifteenth centuries, and their writings were compiled in the eighteenth century. The fact that so many authors in *The Philokalia* were interested in anger for over a thousand years indicates the importance of the concept in play; the fact that Plato and Aristotle also were very interested in anger pushes the history of the concept back almost two and a half millennia. However, we have seen that the concept of God I am defending is not like Aristotle's gods or the God of classical theism: God is not primarily the "beginning" of things (although something can be said positively in this regard), not in the past as pusher, not an omnipotent tyrant who crushes, but the great attractor or lure, the aim, the goal toward which we aspire in the very practical creation of a beautiful/ethical life, both individually and collectively.

In *The Philokalia* and in many other cases of mystical literature it is easy to find a very negative attitude toward anger. Sometimes it is asserted that one's practical affairs can be organized so as to avoid anger altogether and that therefore we should do all that we can to avoid it. This view is connected with traditional versions of asceticism in that desire provides fuel for anger, which, in turn, disturbs spiritual concentration. Anger, it is often alleged, ravages, darkens, and confuses us; indeed, it makes us bestial. In poetic language, anger blossoms on the tree of bitterness when its roots are kept moist by the foul water of pride; the fruit here can be quite rotten. Given this view, it seems that the best advice is to dry up the passion of anger and to cast it into the fire.

Although anger seems to be directed at something external, it is often our internal powers of imagination that are held in fetters by anger. Hence freedom from anger involves not losing one's temper in that this vice is the source of many others. The things that provoke us to anger constitute a species of a wider genus that includes things that distress us. There are some things that distress us, as in the death of a friend, that do not provoke us to anger. Opposition to anger suggests that distress, in general, and anger, in particular, should be treated in the same (Stoic) manner: by eliminating the desire to change them. This release from the turbulence of anger involves (sometimes extreme) ascetical practice. Anger, on this interpretation, is contrary to the good life for a human being and particularly for a mystic. When anger is habitual, even the slightest provocation can trigger an explosion, hence this habit should be resisted.

Plato and Aristotle, however, indicate that the matter is not so simple. Their influence on philosophical anthropology in the Abrahamic religions is noteworthy. For example, the famous Platonic view (*Republic*, 435–42) is that the self is tripartite. Human beings are capable of rationality, but they also have an appetitive aspect that is sometimes in tension with rationality. The third part—*thymos*—consists in a "spirited" tendency through which we feel anger. The fact that sometimes anger fights against desire indicates that it is different from the appetitive part. Plato admits that the nobler individual is less likely to be angry than a base individual, but if one has been genuinely wronged (or if others have been genuinely wronged) in a nontrivial way, then one rightfully experiences anger. That is, when anger is subservient to rationality, rather than to appetite, it is a good thing. A just individual who is capable of refined religious experiences is one who has established some sort of harmony among these three parts, including the spirited part that is the repository for anger. A virtuous individual is one who can balance the gentleness of rationality with the legitimate harshness of high-spirited anger.

Aristotle makes explicit what is implicit in Plato: that anger is a virtue when it is present in moderation (e.g., *Nicomachean Ethics*, 2:7). The most admirable feature of high-spiritedness is courage (*andreia*) in the display of anger. Unqualified Homeric praise of anger is indeed problematic, but hylomorphs like us cannot do away with anger altogether. Because our rationality is always integrally connected to our animal bodies, we cannot lightly dismiss our animal-like courage in the face of danger. The task is to see legitimate anger (*orge*) as a virtue without giving in to vengeful anger as a vice. Anger as a virtue is difficult to achieve because of all the variables that have to be weighed: feeling anger on the right grounds, and against the right persons, at the right moment, for the right amount of time, and in the right manner. This is no easy task! The problem is not so much with anger per se as with an irascible anger at the wrong things, at the wrong time, etcetera. Bitterness occurs when there is no end to the anger, when anger festers like a dirty wound, and hence is not at all easy to cure.

The two theses defended thus far regarding anger—that it can be a vice that gets in the way of the virtuous life, but also that it is nonetheless required for both the virtuous life and the contemplative life—are not necessarily opposed. The power of anger can be used negatively in self-indulgent vendettas as well as positively to repel complacency in the face of evil. The link to mystical experience is clear in that every deiform soul has its appetitive part harmonized with the rational and "spirited" parts, but not necessarily by "taming" the body or engaging in body hatred. If anger is to achieve something positive, it has to be conjoined to that which is rational and loving; it has to be guided by an ethical use of reason and directed toward a fruitful contemplative silence. Oddly enough, by releasing justified anger an inward calm can come to the fore. In a case like this, we can achieve contemplative repose not despite of, but rather because of, our anger. In fact, it is doubtful if one can "make progress" in the contemplative life if one does not, at times, get angry with one's own mistakes and with those made by others. To put the point in the strongest terms, it might be an ethical failing to never get angry. One *should* get angry when one reads about the horrors of Nazism or gang violence. Or less dramatically, one *should* be angry at academic infighting or someone lying to receive a promotion over an honest competitor. And at times we *should* be angry with ourselves, say if we detect a malicious motive behind our action.

Once again, the virtue of anger is essential in the contemplative life if only because we are hylomorphs, rather than disembodied cogitos. Throughout the book I have tried to distance neoclassical theism from classical theism, often because of the latter's dualism of the human person as well as its cosmological dualism. But there are different meanings of the word "flesh" (*sarx*) in *The Philokalia* that deserve attention from a neoclassical context: (1) flesh could signify a contrast with the divine; (2) flesh could signify the fact that we human beings are fallible; or (3) flesh could refer to a substantial body (*soma*) in contrast to a substantial mind or soul. Sense (1) is not problematic, given the obvious differences between what it means to be a human being and what it would mean to be God—although these differences do not include the idea that the greatest conceivable being would utterly transcend embodiment, as we have seen regarding the dipolar relationship between mind/soul and body. A defensible asceticism involves a contest with flesh in sense (2), but not against the body as such. And

(3) seems to involve the dualism to which neoclassical theists are opposed, whether it be a dualism of the individual or cosmological dualism. As hylomorphic, embodied beings it makes sense that at times we get angry, perhaps even very angry.

Anger can be a helpful weapon against evil. However, it can also be a weapon against good, just as a spirited dog can sometimes attack predators and sometimes attack the sheep themselves. Proper incensiveness is propaedeutic to precisely the sort of fervor that often is at work at the start of the contemplative life. However, in no way should the virtuous person actually get pleasure from anger. Its value is strictly instrumental, rather than consummatory. One of the authors anthologized in *The Philokalia*, Saint John Cassian, functions commendably as a casuist when he encourages us, when we are angry, *not* to always escape from the source of anger, but rather to undertake the more difficult task of developing the wisdom to understand when to engage with, and when to disengage from, the world that sometimes gives us joy and sometimes is an occasion for anger. (The monastic way to make the point is to commend the cenobitic rather than the eremitic life.) This sort of complicated engagement with anger is part and parcel of living in the world, in contrast to escaping from it in a cowardly way (*BH* 295).

To always run away from the irritant that causes us to be angry might actually be a sort of self-indulgent pride, rather than authentic solitude. Angry passions carried with us into "solitude" might not be erased but only temporarily hidden. In order to purge anger, it must first be openly acknowledged. Premature (or misguided) solitude yields only the illusion of humility because no one is there to test us. However, as soon as something occurs that tempts us to be angry, our previous and temporarily hidden angry passions may easily reassert themselves with a vengeance. Only the pejorative type of anger needs to be ameliorated. The experiences of the great mystics can make a valuable contribution to virtue ethics by helping us to calibrate our way to a mean between premature (or unreflective) retreat to the "desert" and an easy acceptance of the garrulousness that characterizes commerce with society. The demons that tempt us most—as Moses and Jesus and Mohammed learned in the desert—are far away from human society. It is not silence per se than enables us to advance toward mystic union, but rather high-quality silence found where anger has been, or is in the process of being, handled properly. Here "properly" includes at least the possibility for loving reconciliation with the one who has made us angry.

In closing I would like to emphasize, along with David Tracy, two main contributions that can be made to understanding the relationship between philosophy and mysticism: (1) The logical rigor of the neoclassical concept of God results in the conclusion that theistic metaphysics deals not with contingent facts (Anselm's discovery) but with meanings. The key question is not so much whether God exists but whether we can reach a coherent concept of God. If we can, then (via the ontological argument) God exists necessarily; if not, then God is impossible (*AD* 84–87). (2) A coherent concept of God, however, demands a critique of monopolar classical theism. Dipolar neoclassical theism rests on the distinction between existence and actuality (Hartshorne's discovery), a distinction that not only enables us to better understand mystical experience, but also enables us to better understand the practical ramifications of theistic metaphysics, given the crucial difference between the necessary and the contingent. The latter is the region of both the virtuous life and the contemplative life. It is up to *us* to get the ball rolling in a virtuous life that is propaedeutic to something far greater.

Bibliography

Albright, Carol Raush. "Neuroscience in Pursuit of the Holy: Mysticism, the Brain, and Ultimate Reality." *Zygon: Journal of Religion and Science* 36 (2001): 485–92.
Alston, William. "Hartshorne and Aquinas: A Via Media." In *Existence and Actuality*, edited by John Cobb and Franklin Gamwell, 78–98. Chicago, IL: University of Chicago Press, 1984.
———. *Perceiving God: The Epistemology of Religious Experience*. Ithaca, NY: Cornell University Press, 1991.
Anselm, Saint. *Basic Writings*. 1075–1078. Translated by S. N. Deane. LaSalle, IL: Open Court, 1982.
Aristotle. *The Complete Works of Aristotle*. 2 vols. Translated by Jonathan Barnes. Princeton, NJ: Princeton University Press, 1984.
Arnison, Nancy. "A Tragic Vision for Christianity: Aeschylus and Whitehead." PhD diss., University of Chicago, 2012.
Artson, Bradley. *God of Becoming and Relationship*. Woodstock, VT: Jewish Lights, 2013.
Augustine, Saint. *Confessions*. 396–400. Translated by Henry Chadwick. New York: Oxford University Press, 1998.
Barrett, Nathaniel, and Wesley Wildman. "Seeing Is Believing? How Reinterpreting Perception as Dynamic Engagement Alters the Justificatory Force of Religious Experience." *International Journal for Philosophy of Religion* 66 (2009): 71–86.
Berdyaev, Nicolas. *The Beginning and the End*. 1947. Translated by R. M. French. London: University Press of Glasgow, 1952.
Bergson, Henri. *Creative Evolution*. Translated by Arthur Mitchell. New York: Henry Holt, 1911.
———. *The Creative Mind*. 1934. Translated by Mabelle Andison. New York: Philosophical Library, 1946.
———. *Les deux sources de la morale et de la religion*. Paris: Presses Universitaires de France, 1932.

———. *The Two Sources of Morality and Religion*. 1932. Translated by R. Ashley Audra and Cloudesley Brereton. Notre Dame, IN: University of Notre Dame Press, 1977.

Boehme, Jacob. *Jacob Boehme's "The Way to Christ."* 1624. Translated by Rufus Jones. New York: Harper, 1947.

Boethius. *The Consolation of Philosophy*. Translated by P. G. Walsh. Oxford: Clarendon Press, 1999.

Brenan, Gerald. *St. John of the Cross*. Cambridge: Cambridge University Press, 1973.

Brunner, Emil. *Revelation and Reason*. Translated by Olive Wyon. Philadelphia, PA: Westminster, 1946.

Buber, Martin. *I and Thou*. Translated by R. G. Smith. Edinburgh: T. and T. Clark, 1937.

Carter, Robert. "Plato and Mysticism." *Idealistic Studies* 5 (1975): 255–68.

Case-Winters, Anna. *God's Power: Traditional Understandings and Contemporary Challenges*. Louisville, KY: Westminster John Knox Press, 1990.

Chalmers, David. "Idealism and the Mind-Body Problem." In *The Routledge Handbook of Panpsychism*, edited by William Seager, 353–73. London: Routledge, 2020.

Chandrasekhar, S. *Newton's "Principia" for the Common Reader*. New York: Oxford University Press, 2003.

Chicka, Benjamin. *God the Created: Pragmatic Constructive Realism in Philosophy and Theology*. Albany: State University of New York Press, 2022.

Christ, Carol. *She Who Changes: Re-Imagining the Divine in the World*. New York: Palgrave Macmillan, 2003.

Clark, Henry. *The Ethical Mysticism of Albert Schweitzer*. Boston, MA: Beacon, 1962.

Clark, Stephen R. L. *The Mysteries of Religion*. Oxford: Basil Blackwell, 1986.

Coakley, Sarah. *The New Asceticism: Sexuality, Gender, and the Quest for God*. New York: Bloomsbury, 2015.

Cobb, John. *A Christian Natural Theology Based on the Thought of Alfred North Whitehead*. 2nd ed. Louisville, KY: Westminster John Knox Press, 2007.

———. *Christ in a Pluralistic Age*. Philadelphia, PA: Westminster Press, 1975.

Cross, Richard. *Duns Scotus on God*. Burlington, VT: Ashgate, 2005.

Danto, Arthur. *The Abuse of Beauty*. LaSalle, IL: Open Court, 2003.

———. "Ethical Theory and Mystical Experience." *Journal of Religious Ethics* 4 (1976): 37–46.

d'Aquili, Eugene. "The Neurobiological Bases of Myth and Concepts of Deity." *Zygon: Journal of Religion and Science* 13 (1978): 257–75.

'Aquili, Eugene, and Andrew Newberg. *The Mystical Mind: Probing the Biology of Religious Experience*. Minneapolis, MN: Fortress Press, 1999.

———. *Why God Won't Go Away: Brain Science and the Biology of Belief*. New York: Ballantine, 2001.

Davaney, Sheila Greeve, ed. *Feminism and Process Thought*. Lewiston, NY: Edwin Mellen Press, 1981.

Davis, Andrew. "Sparks before a Theopoetic Wildfire." In *Depths as Yet Unspoken: Whiteheadian Excursions in Mysticism, Multiplicity, and Divinity*. Eugene, OR: Pickwick Publications, 2020.

Descartes, René. *Discourse on Method and Meditations on First Philosophy*. Translated by Donald Cress. Indianapolis, IN: Hackett, 1998.

Dombrowski, Daniel. "Alston and Hartshorne on the Concept of God." *International Journal for Philosophy of Religion* 36 (1994): 129–46.

———. *Analytic Theism, Hartshorne, and the Concept of God*. Albany: State University of New York Press, 1996.

———. "Anger in *The Philokalia*." *Mystics Quarterly* 24 (1998): 101–18.

———. "Asceticism as Athletic Training in Plotinus." *Aufstieg und Niedergang der Romischen Welt* 36, no. 1 (1987): 701–12.

———. *Contemporary Athletics and Ancient Greek Ideals*. Chicago, IL: University of Chicago Press, 2009.

———. *Divine Beauty: The Aesthetics of Charles Hartshorne*. Nashville, TN: Vanderbilt University Press, 2004.

———. "Eating and Spiritual Exercises: Food for thought from Saint Ignatius and Nikos Kazantzakis." *Christianity & Literature* 34 (1983): 25–32.

———. *A History of the Concept of God: A Process Approach*. Albany: State University of New York Press, 2016.

———. "Kazantzakis and Mysticism." In *God's Struggler: Religion in the Writings of Nikos Kazantzakis*, edited by Darren Middleton and Peter Bien, 71–91. Macon, GA: Mercer University Press, 1996.

———. "Mysticism and Divine Mutability." *Process Studies* 23 (1994): 149–54.

———. "Neoclassical Theism and Spiritual Exercises: Pierre Hadot and Nikos Kazantzakis on *Askesis*." *Process Studies* 38 (2009): 93–107.

———. *Not Even a Sparrow Falls: The Philosophy of Stephen R. L. Clark*. East Lansing: Michigan State University Press, 2000.

———. "Plato and Panpsychism." In *The Routledge Handbook of Panpsychism*, edited by William Seager, 15–24. London: Routledge, 2020.

———. *A Platonic Philosophy of Religion: A Process Perspective*. Albany: State University of New York Press, 2005.

———. *Process Philosophy and Political Liberalism: Rawls, Whitehead, Hartshorne*. Edinburgh: Edinburgh University Press, 2019.

———. *Rethinking the Ontological Argument: A Neoclassical Theistic Response*. New York: Cambridge University Press, 2006.

———. "Rival Concepts of God and Rival Versions of Mysticism." *International Journal for Philosophy of Religion* 68 (2010): 153–65.

———. *Saint John of the Cross: An Appreciation*. Albany: State University of New York Press, 1992.

———. "Saint John of the Cross and Virtue Ethics." *Mystics Quarterly* 30 (2004): 7–14.

———. "Visions and Voices vs. Mystic Union." *Sophia* 40, no. 1 (2001): 33–43.
———. *Whitehead's Religious Thought: From Mechanism to Organism, from Force to Persuasion*. Albany: State University of New York Press, 2017.
Enxing, Julia, ed. *Perfect Changes*. Regensburg, Bavaria: Verlag Friedrich Pustet, 2012.
Faber, Roland. *Depths as Yet Unspoken: Whiteheadian Excursions in Mysticism, Multiplicity, and Diversity*. Edited by Andrew Davis. Eugene, OR: Pickwick Publications, 2020.
———. "The Mystical Whitehead." In *Seeking Common Ground: Evaluation and Critique of Joseph Bracken's Comprehensive Worldview*, edited by Marc Pugliese and Gloria Schaab, 213–34. Milwaukee, WI: Marquette University Press, 2012.
Fechner, Gustav. *Zend Avesta*. Leipzig, Germany: Leopold Voss, 1922.
Feuerbach, Ludwig. *The Essence of Christianity*. 1842. Translated by George Eliot. New York: Harper Torchbooks, 1957.
Freud, Sigmund. *The Future of an Illusion*. 1927. Translated by James Strachey. New York: W. W. Norton, 1975.
Furlong, Monica. *Therese of Lisieux*. New York: Knopf Doubleday, 1987.
Galik, Slavomir, Sabina Galikova Tolnaiova, and Arkadiusz Modrzejewski. "Mystical Death in the Spirituality of Saint Teresa of Ávila." *Sophia* 59 (2020): 593–612.
Galileo. *The Essential Galileo*. Translated by Maurice Finocchiaro. Indianapolis, IN: Hackett, 2008.
Gamwell, Franklin. *On Metaphysical Necessity*. Albany: State University of New York Press, 2020.
Gilroy, John. "Neuro Wine in Old Vessels: A Critique of D'Aquili and Newberg." *Process Studies Supplements* 8 (2005): 1–42.
Goff, Philip. "Cosmopsychism, Micropsychism, and the Grounding Relation." In *The Routledge Handbook of Panpsychism*, edited by William Seager, 144–56. London: Routledge, 2020.
Green, Deirdre. "St. John of the Cross and Mystical Unknowing." *Religious Studies* 22 (1986): 29–40.
Griffin, David Ray. *Reenchantment without Supernaturalism: A Process Philosophy of Religion*. Ithaca, NY: Cornell University Press, 2001.
Hartshorne, Charles. "The Aesthetic Dimensions of Religious Experience." In *Logic, God, and Metaphysics*, edited by James Franklin Harris, 9–18. Boston, MA: Kluwer, 1992.
———. "An Anglo-American Phenomenology." In *Pragmatism Considers Phenomenology*, edited by Robert Corrington, 59–71. Washington, DC: University Press of America, 1987.
———. "An Outline and Defense of the Argument for the Unity of Being in the Absolute or Divine Good." PhD diss., Harvard University, 1923.
———. *Anselm's Discovery*. LaSalle, IL: Open Court, 1965.
———. *Aquinas to Whitehead*. Milwaukee, WI: Marquette University Press, 1976.
———. "Arthur Berndtson on Mystical Experience." *Personalist* 32 (1951): 191–93.

———. *Beyond Humanism*. Chicago, IL: Willet, Clark, 1937.
———. *Born to Sing*. Bloomington: Indiana University Press, 1973.
———. *Creative Experiencing*. Edited by Donald Viney and Jincheol O. Albany: State University of New York Press, 2011.
———. *Creative Synthesis and Philosophic Method*. LaSalle, IL: Open Court, 1970.
———. *Creativity in American Philosophy*. Albany: State University of New York Press, 1984.
———. *The Darkness and the Light*. Albany: State University of New York Press, 1990.
———. *The Divine Relativity*. New Haven, CT: Yale University Press, 1948.
———. "The Divine Relativity and Absoluteness." *Review of Metaphysics* 4 (1950): 31–59.
———. "The Environmental Results of Technology." In *Philosophy and Environmental Crisis*, edited by William Blackstone, 69–78. Athens: University of Georgia Press, 1974.
———. *Existence and Actuality*. Edited by John Cobb and Franklin Gamwell. Chicago, IL: University of Chicago Press, 1984.
———. "The Formal Validity and Real Significance of the Ontological Argument." *Philosophical Review* 53 (1944): 225–45.
———. "The God of Religion and the God of Philosophy." In *Talk of God* (Royal Institute of Philosophy Lectures), 152–67. New York: St. Martin's, 1969.
———. *Hartshorne and Brightman on God, Process, and Persons*. Edited by Randall Auxier and Mark Davies. Nashville, TN: Vanderbilt University Press, 2001.
———. "In Defense of Wordsworth's View of Nature." *Philosophy and Literature* 4 (1980): 80–91.
———. *Insights and Oversights of Great Thinkers*. Albany: State University of New York Press, 1983.
———. "The Intelligibility of Sensations." *Monist* 44 (1934): 161–85.
———. *The Logic of Perfection*. LaSalle, IL: Open Court, 1962.
———. *Man's Vision of God*. New York: Harper, 1941.
———. "Metaphysical and Empirical Aspects of the Idea of God." In *Witness and Existence: Essays in Honor of Schubert M. Ogden*, edited by Philip Devenish and George Goodwin, 177–89. Chicago, IL: University of Chicago Press, 1989.
———. "Metaphysics and the Modality of Existential Judgments." In *The Relevance of Whitehead*, edited by Ivor Leclerc, 107–21. New York: Macmillan, 1961.
———. "Mysticism and Rationalistic Metaphysics." *Monist* 59, no. 4 (1976): 463–69.
———. *A Natural Theology for Our Time*. LaSalle, IL: Open Court, 1967.
———. *Omnipotence and Other Theological Mistakes*. Albany: State University of New York Press, 1984.
———. "Peirce's Philosophy on Religion." In *Peirce and Contemporary Thought*, edited by Kenneth Ketner, 339–55. New York: Fordham University Press, 1995.
———. *Philosophers Speak of God*. Chicago, IL: University of Chicago Press, 1953.

———. *Philosophy and Psychology of Sensation*. Chicago, IL: University of Chicago Press, 1934.
———. *The Philosophy of Charles Hartshorne*. Edited by Lewis Hahn. LaSalle, IL: Open Court, 1991.
———. "A Philosophy of Death." In *Philosophical Aspects of Thanatology*, vol. 2., edited by Florence Hetzler and Austin Kutscher, 81–89. New York: Arno, 1978.
———. "Psychology and the Unity of Knowledge." *Southern Journal of Philosophy* 5 (1967): 81–90.
———. *Reality as Social Process*. Boston, MA: Beacon Press, 1953.
———. "Review of Gerda Walter, *Phanomenologie der Mystik*." *Philosophy and Phenomenological Research* 18 (1957): 140–41.
———. "The Rights of the Subhuman World." *Environmental Ethics* 1 (1979): 49–60.
———. "Science as the Search for the Hidden Beauty of the World." In *The Aesthetic Dimension of Science*, edited by Deane Curtin, 85–106. New York: Philosophical Library, 1980.
———. "Sense Quality and Feeling Tone." In *Proceedings of the Seventh International Congress of Philosophy*, edited by Gilbert Ryle, 168–72. London: Oxford University Press, 1931.
———. "The Social Theory of Feelings." *Southern Journal of Philosophy* 3 (1965): 87–93.
———. "Some Theological Mistakes and Their Effects on Modern Literature." *Journal of Speculative Philosophy* 1 (1987): 55–72.
———. "Three Important Scientists on Mind, Matter, and the Metaphysics of Religion." *Journal of Speculative Philosophy* 3 (1994): 211–27.
———. "Whitehead's Idea of God." In *The Philosophy of Alfred North Whitehead*, edited by Paul Schilpp, 515–59. LaSalle, IL: Open Court, 1941.
———. *Whitehead's Philosophy*. Lincoln: University of Nebraska Press, 1972.
———. *Whitehead's View of Reality*. New York: Pilgrim Press, 1981.
———. *Wisdom as Moderation*. Albany: State University of New York Press, 1987.
———. *The Zero Fallacy and Other Essays in Neoclassical Philosophy*. Edited by Mohammed Valady. LaSalle, IL: Open Court, 1997.
Heschel, Abraham. *The Prophets*. New York: Harper and Row, 1962.
Hume, David. *Dialogues Concerning Natural Religion*. 1776. Indianapolis, IN: Hackett, 1980.
Hursthouse, Rosalind. *On Virtue Ethics*. Oxford: Oxford University Press, 1999.
Ibn Abbad of Ronda. *Letters on the Sufi Path*. Translated by John Renard. New York: Paulist Press, 1986.
Ignatius of Loyola, Saint. *The Spiritual Exercises*. 1535. New York: Doubleday, 1964.
Inati, S. C. *Ibn Sina and Mysticism*. London: Kegan Paul, 1996.
Iqbal, Mohammed. *The Reconstruction of Religious Thought in Islam*. 1930. Translated by M. Saeed Sheikh. Stanford, CA: Stanford University Press, 2013.

James, William. *The Varieties of Religious Experience*. 1902. Cambridge, MA: Harvard University Press, 1985.
John of the Cross, Saint. *The Collected Works of St. John of the Cross*. Translated by Kieran Kavanaugh and Otilio Rodriguez. Washington, DC: Institute of Carmelite Studies, 1973.
Jones, Richard. *Mysticism and Morality*. New York: Lexington Books, 2004.
———. *Mysticism Examined: Philosophical Inquiries into Mysticism*. Albany: State University of New York Press, 1993.
Kant, Immanuel. *Dreams of a Spirit-Seer*. 1766. Translated by E. Goerwitz and F. Sewall. New York: Macmillan, 1900.
———. *Religion within the Limits of Reason Alone*. 1793. Translated by Theodore Greene. New York: Harper, 1960.
Katz, Steven, ed. *Mysticism and Philosophical Analysis*. London: Sheldon Press, 1978.
———. *Mysticism and Religious Traditions*. New York: Oxford University Press, 1983.
Keller, Helen. *The World I Live In*. New York: Century, 1910.
Kelly, Edward, ed. *Beyond Physicalism: Toward Reconciliation of Science and Spirituality*. Lanham, MD: Rowman and Littlefield, 2015.
Kling, Sheri. *A Process Spirituality: Christian and Transreligious Resources for Transformation*. Lanham, MD: Lexington Books, 2020.
Lawrence, Nathaniel. *Whitehead's Philosophical Development*. Berkeley: University of California Press, 1956.
Levenson, Jon. *Creation and the Persistence of Evil: The Jewish Drama of Divine Omnipotence*. San Francisco, CA: Harper and Row, 1988.
Levi, Albert William. *Philosophy and the Modern World*. Bloomington: Indiana University Press, 1959.
Loomer, Bernard. "The Size of the Everlasting God." 1975. *Process Studies Supplements* 18 (2013): 1–45.
Maritain, Jacques. *The Degrees of Knowledge*. Translated by G. B. Phelan. New York: Scribner's, 1959.
Marshall, Paul. *Mystical Encounters with the Natural World*. New York: Oxford University Press, 2005.
Marx, Karl, and Friedrich Engels. *The German Ideology*. 1845–1846. Translated by C. J. Arthur. London: Lawrence and Wishart, 1970.
Mathews, Freya. "Living Cosmos Panpsychism." In *The Routledge Handbook of Panpsychism*, edited by William Seager, 131–43. London: Routledge, 2020.
May, Gerhard. *Creatio ex Nihilo: The Doctrine of "Creation Out of Nothing" in Early Christian Thought*. Translated by A. S. Worrall. Edinburgh: T. and T. Clark, 1994.
Merleau-Ponty, Maurice. *The Phenomenology of Perception*. Translated by Colin Smith. New York: Humanities Press, 1962.

Merton, Thomas. *The Seven Storey Mountain.* 1948. New York: Harcourt Brace Jovanovich, 1978.

Molière. *Tartuffe and the Would-Be Gentleman.* 1664. Translated by Henri Peyre. New York: Heritage Press, 1963.

Murphy, John. "St. John of the Cross and Philosophy of Religion." *Mystics Quarterly* 22 (1996): 163–86.

Nagasawa, Yujin. "Panpsychism versus Pantheism, Polytheism, and Cosmopsychism." In *The Routledge Handbook of Panpsychism*, edited by William Seager, 259–68. London: Routledge, 2020.

Neville, Robert. "John E. Smith and Metaphysics." In *Reason, Experience, and God: John E. Smith in Dialogue*, edited by Vincent Colapietro, 71–82. New York: Fordham University Press, 1997.

Newberg, Andrew. "Putting the Mystical Mind Together." *Zygon: Journal of Religion and Science* 36 (2001): 501–7.

Nietzsche, Friedrich. *The Will to Power.* 1901. Translated by Walter Kauffman. New York: Random House, 1968.

Nussbaum, Martha. *The Therapy of Desire.* Princeton, NJ: Princeton University Press, 1994.

Oppy, Graham. *Ontological Arguments and Belief in God.* Cambridge: Cambridge University Press 1995.

Origen. *Origen: Selections from the Commentaries and Homilies.* Translated by R. B. Tollinton. New York: Macmillan, 1929.

Otto, Rudolph. *Mysticism East and West.* 1926. New York: Macmillan, 1975.

Pascal, Blaise. *Pensées.* 1670. Translated by Roger Ariew. Indianapolis, IN: Hackett, 2005.

Payne, Steven. *St. John of the Cross.* Boston, MA: Kluwer, 1990.

Peirce, Charles Sanders. *The Collected Papers of Charles Sanders Peirce.* 6 vols. Edited by Charles Hartshorne and Paul Weiss. Cambridge, MA: Harvard University Press, 1935.

Pfleiderer, Otto. *The Philosophy of Religion on the Basis of Its History.* 2 vols. Translated by A. Menzies. London: Williams and Norgate, 1886.

Philo. *Philo.* 10 vols. Translated by F. H. Colson, et al. Cambridge, MA: Harvard University Press, 1929–1962.

Philokalia. 4 vols. Translated by G. Palmer, et al. London: Faber and Faber, 1979–1995.

Pike, Nelson. *God and Timelessness.* New York: Schocken, 1970.

———. "John of the Cross on the Epistemic Value of Mystic Visions." In *Rationality, Religious Belief, and Moral Commitment*, edited by Robert Audi and William Wainwright, 15–37. Ithaca, NY: Cornell University Press, 1986.

———. *Mystic Union: An Essay in the Phenomenology of Mysticism.* Ithaca, NY: Cornell University Press, 1992.

Plato. *The Collected Dialogues of Plato.* Edited by Edith Hamilton and Huntington Cairns. Princeton, NJ: Princeton University Press, 1999.

Plotinus. *The Enneads*. 6 vols. Translated by A. H. Armstrong. Cambridge, MA: Harvard University Press, 1966.
Plutarch. *Plutarch's Morals*. 5 vols. Edited by William Goodwin. Boston, MA: Little, Brown, 1870.
Popper, Karl. *Objective Knowledge*. Oxford: Clarendon Press, 1979.
Rachels, James. *Created from Animals*. New York: Oxford University Press, 1990.
Raeder, Linda. *John Stuart Mill and the Religion of Humanity*. Columbia: University of Missouri Press, 2002.
Raposa, Michael. *Peirce's Philosophy of Religion*. Bloomington: Indiana University Press, 1989.
Ruzgar, Mustafa. "Islam and Process Theology." In *Handbook of Whiteheadian Process Thought*, edited by Michel Weber and Will Desmond, 601–12. Frankfurt, Germany: Ontos Verlag, 2008.
Schelling, Friedrich von. *The Ages of the World*. 1811–1815. Translated by F. de Wolfe Bolman. New York: Columbia University Press, 1942.
Sedley, David. "'Becoming Like God' in the *Timaeus* and Aristotle." In *Interpreting the "Timaeus-Critias,"* edited by Thomas Calvo and Luc Brisson, 327–39. Sankt Augustin, Germany: Academia Verlag, 1997.
———. "The Ideal of Godlikeness." In *Plato*, vol. 2, edited by Gail Fine, 309–28. Oxford: Oxford University Press, 1999.
Sherry, Patrick. *Spirit and Beauty: An Introduction to Theological Aesthetics*. Oxford: Clarendon Press, 1982.
Shields, George, and Donald Viney. *The Mind of Charles Hartshorne*. Anoka, MN: Process Century Press, 2020.
Smart, Ninian. "Interpretation and Mystical Experience." *Religious Studies* 1 (1965): 75–87.
Smith, John. *Experience and God*. New York: Oxford University Press, 1968.
———. *Purpose and Thought: The Meaning of Pragmatism*. New Haven, CT: Yale University Press, 1978.
———. *Reason and God: Encounters of Philosophy with Religion*. New Haven, CT: Yale University Press, 1961.
———. *Religion and Empiricism*. Milwaukee, WI: Marquette University Press, 1967.
———. "Some Aspects of Hartshorne's Treatment of Anselm." In *Existence and Actuality*, edited by John Cobb and Franklin Gamwell, 103–9. Chicago, IL: University of Chicago Press, 1984.
Spezio, Michael. "Understanding Biology in Religious Experience: The Biogenetic Structuralist Approach of Eugene D'Aquili and Andrew Newberg." *Zygon: Journal of Religion and Science* 36 (2001): 477–84.
Stace, Walter. *Mysticism and Philosophy*. Philadelphia, PA: Lippincott, 1960.
———. *The Teachings of the Mystics*. New York: New American Library, 1960.
Steger, Jane. "Some Notes on Light." *Atlantic*, 1926, 315–25.

Suchocki, Marjorie. "Charles Hartshorne and Subjective Immortality." *Process Studies* 21 (1992): 118–22.

Swinburne, Richard. *Was Jesus God?* Oxford: Oxford University Press, 2008.

Teilhard de Chardin, Pierre. *The Divine Milieu*. 1957. Translated by Sion Cowell. Brighton, UK: Sussex Academic Press, 2004.

———. *Science and Christ*. 1918–1955. Translated by Rene Hague. New York: Harper and Row, 1968.

Tennyson, Alfred. *The Poems of Tennyson*. Vol. 2, 2nd ed. Edited by Christopher Ricks. New York: Atheneum, 1969.

Teresa of Ávila, Saint. *The Collected Works of St. Teresa of Ávila*. Translated by E. A. Peers. Washington, DC: Institute of Carmelite Studies, 1976.

Thomas Aquinas, Saint. *Summa Theologiae*. 1265–1274. New York: McGraw-Hill, 1972.

Thoreau, Henry David. *Walden*. 1854. Princeton, NJ: Princeton University Press, 1989.

Tracy, David. "Analogy, Metaphor, and God-Language: Charles Hartshorne." *Modern Schoolman* 62 (1985): 249–64.

———. *Blessed Rage for Order*. New York: Seabury, 1975.

Trianosky, Gregory. "What Is Virtue Ethics All About?" *American Philosophical Quarterly* 27 (1990): 335–44.

Underhill, Evelyn. *The School of Charity*. New York: Longmans, Green, 1934.

Viney, Donald. *Charles Hartshorne and the Existence of God*. Albany: State University of New York Press, 1985.

———. "Hartshorne's Dipolar Theism and the Mystery of God." In *Models of God and Alternative Ultimate Realities*, edited by Jeanine Diller and Asa Kasher, 333–56. New York: Springer, 2013.

———. "Relativizing the Classical Tradition: Hartshorne's History of God." In *Models of God and Alternative Ultimate Realities*, edited by Jeanine Diller and Asa Kasher, 63–80. New York: Springer, 2013.

Whitehead, Alfred North. *Adventures of Ideas*. 1933. New York: Free Press, 1967.

———. *The Aims of Education and Other Essays*. 1929. New York: Free Press, 1967.

———. *The Concept of Nature*. Cambridge: Cambridge University Press, 1920.

———. *Dialogues of Alfred North Whitehead*. Edited by Lucien Price. Boston, MA: Little, Brown, 1954.

———. *An Enquiry Concerning the Principles of Natural Knowledge*. Cambridge: Cambridge University Press, 1919.

———. "Freedom and Order." Whitehead Research Library online. Accessed January 15, 2020. https://whiteheadresearch.org/occasions/whitehead-reading-group/freedom-and-order/.

———. *An Introduction to Mathematics*. Oxford: Oxford University Press, 1911.

———. *Modes of Thought*. 1938. New York: Free Press, 1968.

———. *The Philosophy of Alfred North Whitehead*. 2nd ed. Edited by P. A. Schilpp. LaSalle, IL: Open Court, 1951.

———. *Process and Reality: An Essay in Cosmology*. 1929. Edited by David Ray Griffin and Donald Sherburne. New York: Free Press, 1978.
———. *Religion in the Making*. 1926. New York: Fordham University Press, 1996.
———. "Religious Psychology of the Western Peoples." 1939. Whitehead Research Library online. Accessed January 15, 2020. https://whiteheadresearch.org/occasions/whitehead-reading-group/religious-psychology/.
———. *Science and the Modern World*. 1925. New York: Free Press, 1967.
———. *Symbolism*. 1927. New York: Fordham University Press, 1985.
Wilamowitz-Moellendorff, Ulrich von. *Platon*. Vol. 1. Berlin: Weidmann, 1920.
Wolf, Susan. "Moral Saints." *Journal of Philosophy* 79 (1982): 419–39.
Wolterstorff, Nicholas. *Divine Discourse*. New York: Cambridge University Press, 1995.
Wordsworth, William. *Poetical Works*. New York: Oxford University Press, 1981.

Index of Names

Abraham, 5, 7–8, 17–18, 22, 31, 35, 42, 66, 75, 91, 107, 122, 129–130, 132–133, 138–140, 149, 154, 167, 184, 199, 201, 203
Aeschylus, 152
Al-Ghazzali, 17
Alston, William, 6, 80–82
Anselm, St., 4, 12, 16–17, 22, 27, 67, 69–70, 85, 120, 184, 206
Aristotle, 13, 16, 20, 30–31, 35, 60–61, 89, 99, 108, 123–124, 140, 153–155, 167, 183, 188, 199–200, 202–203
Aquinas, St. Thomas, 13, 17, 19, 24, 29, 73, 79, 135–136, 150
Arnison, Nancy, 151–152
Augustine, St., 17, 163
Averroes, 17
Avicenna, 17

Barrett, Nathaniel, 82
Berdyaev, Nicholas, 23, 56
Bergson, Henri, 1, 8–9, 23, 64, 147–165, 188, 190
Bernini, Gian Lorenzo, 77, 80
Boehme, Jacob, 23
Boethius, 79, 83
Bradley, F. H., 47
Brahman, 116
Breugel, Pieter, 173

Bruner, Emile, 132
Buber, Martin, 140, 182
Buddha, 5, 39, 89, 94, 138, 142, 180, 184, 188–189, 199, 202

Caesar, 61
Calvin, John, 17
Case-Winters, Anna, 62
Cather, Willa, 168
Chalmers, David, 47
Chicka, Benjamin, 82
Chopin, Frederic, 168
Christ, Carol, 62
Clark, Henry, 189
Clark, Stephen R. L., 184
Cobb, John, 98
Coltrane, John, 172–173
Confucius, 180

Danto, Arthur, 172, 187
D'Aquili, Eugene, 141–145
Davaney, Sheila Greeve, 62
David, 130
Day, Doris, 64
Day, Dorothy, 76, 180
Descartes, Rene, 25, 45, 156
Dionysus, 152
Duns Scotus, 71

Eddy, Mary Baker, 180

Faber, Roland, 98–101
Fa Tsang, 47
Fechner, Gustav, 31
Feuerbach, Ludwig, 18, 84, 115, 122
Fox, George, 76
Francis of Assisi, St., 142, 178–179, 199
Freud, Sigmund, 18
Furlong, Monica, 192

Galileo, 25
Gamwell, Franklin, 183
Gersonides, 163
Gilroy, John, 7, 141–145
Goff, Philip, 47
Gorecki, Henryk, 172
Goswami, Sri Jiva, 5
Griffin, David Ray, 75

Handel, George Frederick, 172
Heidegger, Martin, 106, 190
Heschel, Abraham, 56, 60, 79
Homer, 203
Hume, David, 31, 61, 102–103, 110
Hursthouse, Rosalind, 200

Ikhnaton, 184
Iqbal, Mohammed, 5, 55
Isaiah, 77
Ishvara, 140

Jacob, 130
James, William, 2, 4, 79, 94, 155, 188
Jeremiah, 130
Jesus, 22, 76, 89, 94, 100, 116, 119, 149–150, 154, 180, 205
John, St., 129
John Cassian, St., 205
John of the Cross, St., 5, 56, 73, 75–77, 118–119, 123, 125, 129, 131, 135–138, 153, 178–179, 198–201

Jones, Jim, 180
Jones, Richard, 84–85, 187
Jones, Rufus, 3–4

Kant, Immanuel, 18, 31, 45, 61, 80, 117, 163, 201
Katz, Steven, 116–119
Keller, Helen, 122
Kepler, Johannes, 8
Kierkegaard, Soren, 140, 201

Lao Tse, 180
Lawrence, Nathaniel, 94
Leibniz, Gottfried, 45, 47, 99, 103, 156
Levenson, Jon, 50
Levi, Albert William, 149
Loomer, Bernard, 28
Luther, Martin, 17

Maimonides, Moses ben, 17
Marx, Karl, 18
Mary, 63
Mathews, Freya, 47
May, Gerhard, 50
Meister Eckhart, 62
Merleau-Ponty, Maurice, 42
Merton, Thomas, 55, 78–79, 188–189
Mill, John Stuart, 117
Mohammed, 76, 89, 154, 180, 205
Moliere, 45
Mona Lisa, 173
Moses, 76, 147, 154, 180, 205

Nagasawa, Yujin, 47
Neville, Robert, 74
Newberg, Andrew, 141–145
Newton, Isaac, 37, 59
Nicholas of Cusa, 62, 99–100
Nietzsche, Friedrich, 7, 107, 109

Oppy, Graham, 85
Origen, 22, 31, 130

Otto, Rudolph, 62

Pascal, Blaise, 75
Paul, St., 33, 42, 108, 131
Peirce, Charles Sanders, 80, 169, 193
Pfleiderer, Otto, 31
Philo, 17, 31, 150
Pike, Nelson, 116–119, 130
Plato, 6, 30, 34, 36, 42, 49, 59–60, 91, 93, 100, 123–125, 151, 153–154, 160, 162, 192–193, 202–203
Plotinus, 64–65, 123, 153
Plutarch, 31
Poe, Edgar Allen, 170
Popper, Karl, 3, 42
Prometheus, 89

Ravel, Maurice, 173
Rawls, John, 94
Revere, Paul, 130
Russell, Bertrand, 38, 81

Sankara, 64, 180
Sartre, Jean-Paul, 61
Schelling, Friedrich, 23
Schweitzer, Albert, 189
Shakespeare, William, 57, 173
Sherry, Patrick, 173
Shields, George, 101, 111
Smart, Ninian, 117
Smith, John, 6, 72, 74, 76–77
Socinus, Faustus, 163
Socrates, 124, 149–150
Spinoza, Baruch, 16, 65–66

Stace, Walter, 117–119, 187
Suchocki, Marjorie, 79
Swinburne, Richard, 79

Teilhard de Chardin, Pierre, 98, 101, 184, 189
Tennyson, Alfred, 87
Teresa, Mother, 199
Teresa of Avila, St., 76–77, 80, 109, 119, 131, 137, 150
Tertullian, 85
Therese of Lisieux, St., 192
Thoreau, Henry David, 46, 121
Tracy, David, 205

Underhill, Evelyn, 96

Verdi, Giuseppi, 173
Viney, Donald, 2, 101, 111, 176

Whitehead, Alfred North, 1, 6–7, 9, 23, 35–36, 42, 55–56, 61, 69, 82–83, 87–106, 147, 158, 160–161, 179, 194
Wilamowitz-Moellendorf, Ulrich von, 125
Wildman, Wesley, 82
Wittgenstein, Ludwig, 71
Wolf, Susan, 199
Wordsworth, William, 42, 46, 74–75, 87–88, 180, 189

Zeus, 152
Zoroaster, 180